MOONSHOT
THE INDIGENOUS COMICS COLLECTION
VOLUME 2

PUBLISHER'S NOTE

Inhabit Education Books is pleased to distribute this important collection of Indigenous comic stories, developed and originally published by Alternate History Comics (AH Comics). We have changed very little from the original printing, as we wanted to respect the editorial decisions made by AH Comics.

As an Inuit-owned publishing company, we recognize the importance of sharing and preserving the work of Indigenous storytellers. We hope this new printing will help these stories reach a wider audience and continue to promote the work of Indigenous authors and artists.

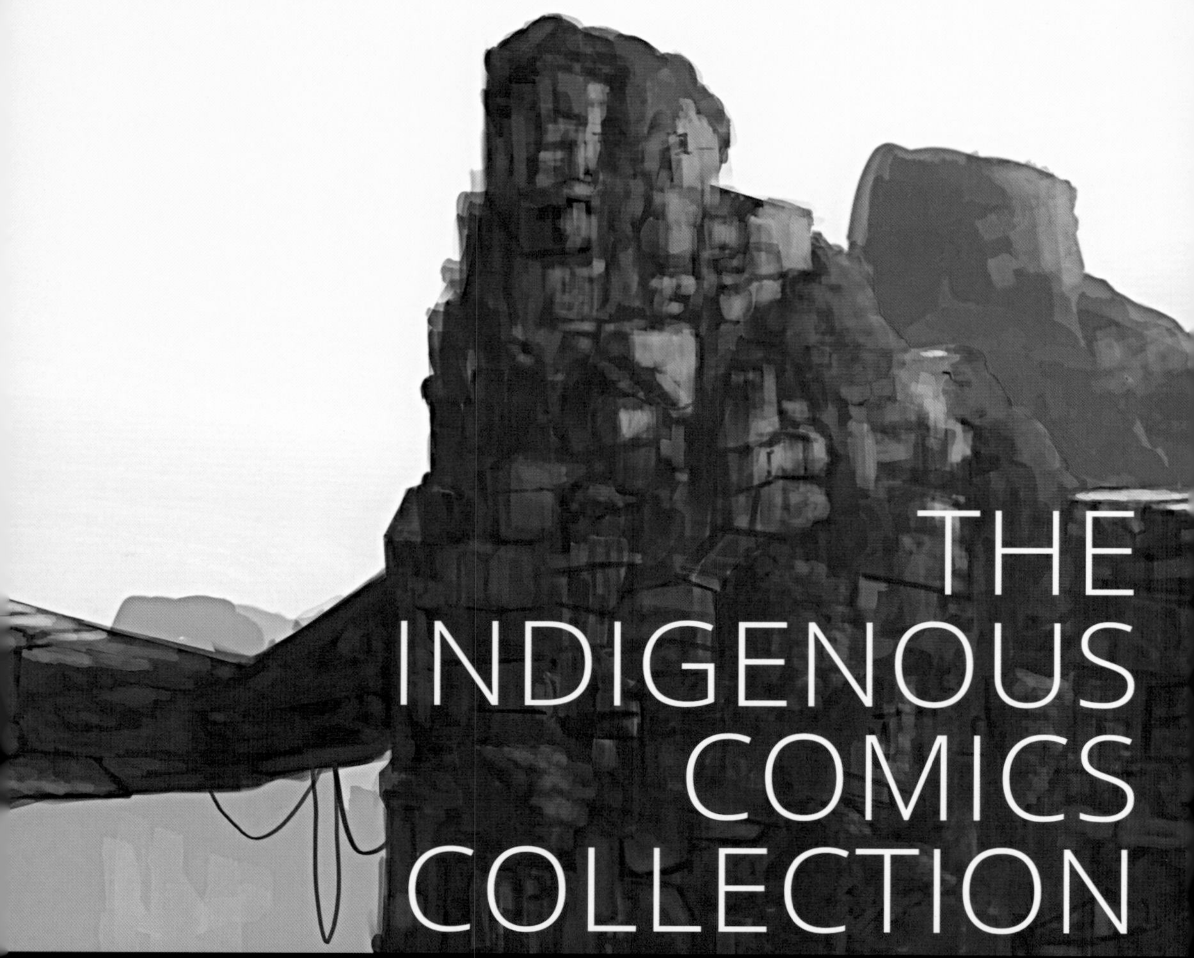

THE INDIGENOUS COMICS COLLECTION

This edition published in 2020 by Avani, an imprint of Inhabit Education Books Inc.
www.inhabiteducation.com

INHABIT EDUCATION BOOKS INC.
(Iqaluit) P.O. Box 2129, Iqaluit, Nunavut, X0A 1H0
(Toronto) 191 Eglinton Avenue East, Suite 301, Toronto, Ontario, M4P 1K1

Edited by Hope Nicholson
Book layout and design by Andy Stanleigh

Printed in Canada.

Softcover ISBN: 978-0-2287-0621-2
Hardcover ISBN: 978-0-2287-0680-9

AVANI
AN IMPRINT OF INHABIT EDUCATION BOOKS INC.

▲ "Indian Planet" **by Stephen Gladue**

MOONSHOT
VOLUME 2

This piece is representative of a world with resources untouched. What would a planet look like without industry, with the landscape unsullied by construction and commerce? Growing up in Alberta, Canada, the artist was not able to envision a landscape such as this. This piece was created as a fantasy world from a time and place that appears timeless. This conforms to the overall theme of **Volume 2** of ***MOONSHOT: The Indigenous Comics Collection*** – stories that take place in worlds that are familiar or fantasy, sci-fi, or spiritual, while being told in a timeless way. Every work in this volume is meant to be in the present, highlighting that Indigenous culture is not from the historical record. It is here, now.

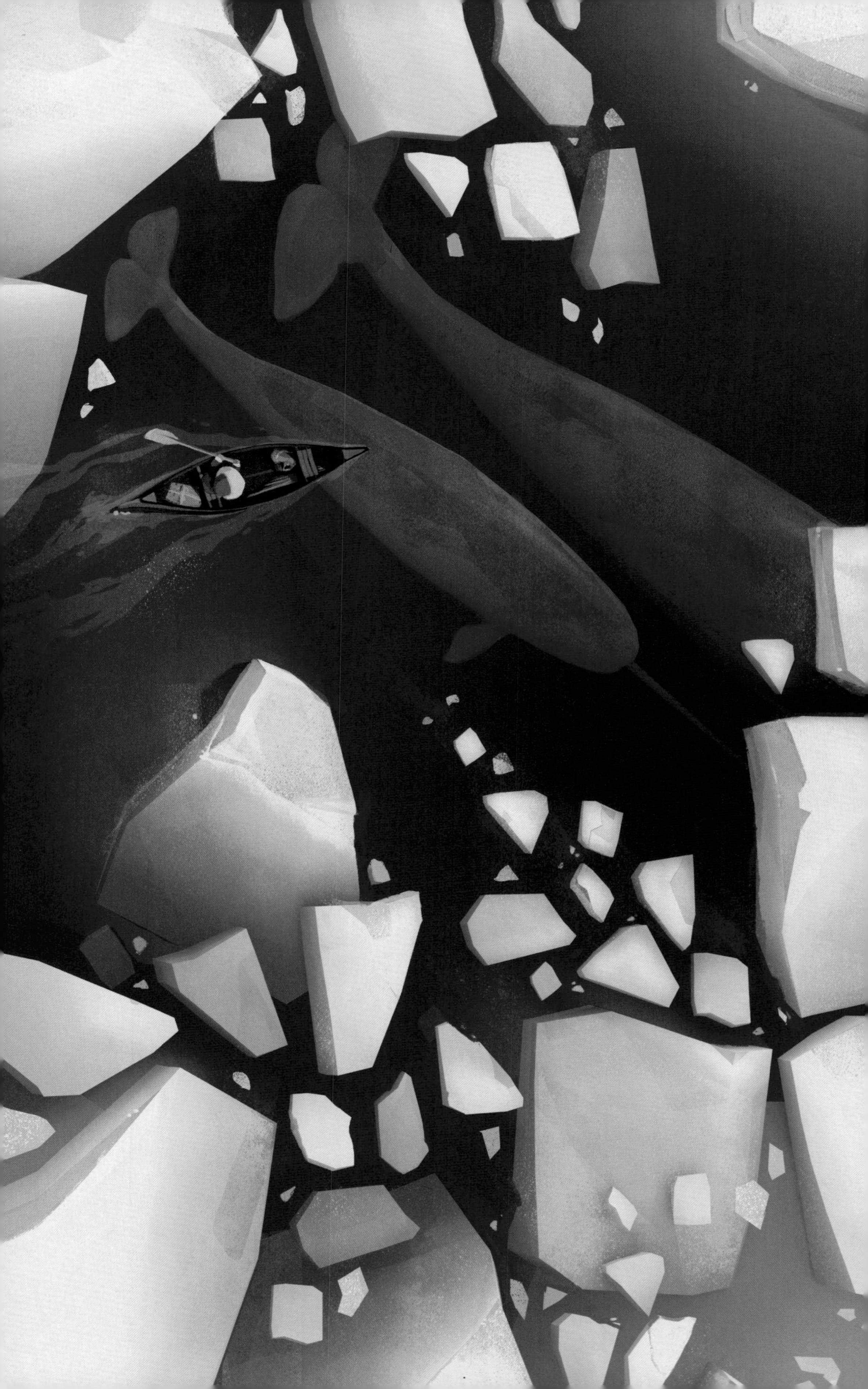

TABLE OF CONTENTS

FOREWORD   6
by James Leask

INTRODUCTION   8
by Michael Sheyahshe

THEY WHO WALK AS LIGHTNING   10
by Elizabeth LaPensée, Ph.D, illustrated by Richard Pace

WINTER'S SHELL   19
by Sean and Rachel Qitsualik-Tinsley, illustrated by Alexandria Neonakis

WORST BARGAIN IN TOWN   33
by Darcie Little Badger, illustrated by Rossi Gifford

KA'TEPWA: WHO CALLS?   44
by Alina Pete, illustrated by Trudi Castle

BOOKMARK   55
by David Alexander Robertson, illustrated by Natasha Alterici

THE AWAKENING   66
by Armand Garnet Ruffo, illustrated by David Cutler

THE MAGIC OF WOLVERINES   78
by Richard Van Camp, illustrated by Scott Henderson

9 MILE LAKE   82
by Tanya Tagaq, illustrated by Stephen Gladue

THE BOYS WHO BECAME THE HUMMINGBIRDS   84
by Daniel Heath Justice, illustrated by Weshoyot Alvitre

WATER SPIRITS   95
by Richard Van Camp, illustrated by Haiwei Hou

THE CREATOR TAMOSI   104
by Gerard and Peta-Gay Roberts, illustrated by Nicholas Burns

WHERE WE LEFT OFF   115
by Steve Keewatin Sanderson

DO WILD TURKEYS DREAM OF ELECTRIC DRUMS   124
by Michael Sheyahshe, illustrated by Kim Hunter

JOURNEYS   130
by Jeffrey Veregge

AFTERWORD   144
by Elizabeth LaPensée, Ph.D

BIOGRAPHIES   147

SKETCHBOOK   158

END CREDITS   164

◀ *"Iluk" by Alexandria Neonakis*

FOREWORD

The first volume of *MOONSHOT* is one of the most important books I've ever read.

Those are lofty words, I know, but it's almost impossible to overstate *MOONSHOT*'s importance because it's hard to overstate how starved for it I had been for my entire life. Books like this just weren't available, much to my chagrin and, I think, that of my parents, who always encouraged my reading no matter where it led me.

Where it led me was comics, ever since the first morning I saw one in the newspaper, cut it out, and coloured it in with pencil crayons. From there, it went outwards to superhero comics and European ones like *Tintin*. I was so hungry for comics that I even pulled out my mother's old *Poetry Comics* collection, full of material I wasn't prepared for. But everywhere I went, one thing stuck out to me: I couldn't see any characters like me.

Don't get me wrong, there were sometimes Native people in comics, but they bore no resemblance to the ones I knew, either my family or our friends. For one, they were usually dead, or at least a grotesque parody, a leering death mask, of what people thought we were. They wore buckskin and feathers; I wore jeans and hoodies. They were stoic; I bubbled over with emotion. And my concerns weren't about the ancient treasures or ways of my people; I just wanted to ride my bike and see movies.

It's not like the images I was seeing in comics – or TV, or movies – were totally alien to me. I went to a public school, and we had a unit on the settlement of Alberta. Of course, we were taught that the history started with the pioneers, and the "prehistoric" Natives – who were all too happy to step aside in favour of progress – dressed in buckskin and beads. None of it seemed right, but for once the other kids were interested in my moccasins and stories, and that seemed fine. I let it slide because for once being Indigenous was, in a sad way, acknowledged. But the unit ended and my schooling wouldn't mention Indigenous peoples again until six years later, when a classmate stood up and said we were all drunks who'd spend any money we were given on cigarettes.

Publicly, being Métis didn't exist for me, because I didn't look like, sound like, or act like the Native people I saw in textbooks, or in the media I loved. I wasn't an Indian, so I wasn't really Native. At home, of course, it was different; our household was full of discussion of Indigenous history, politics, and, most importantly, stories. Some of them were old stories, about Wīhsakecāhkw, who caused the great flood and helped create the moon, or winking stories about Coyote's mischief. Some were about the rebellions of the previous century. But most were just about our family through the generations and the people in our lives. My mom dedicated her professional life to Indigenous education, and her students played a big role in her stories. My grandpa decided it was time he learn Cree, but he accidentally took a course for medical professionals; he couldn't carry a conversation, but he could ask where it hurt. He passed away a decade ago, but that story won't ever die, at least if I can help it.

As a kid, stories were where I felt happiest, and where my indigeneity felt most alive. They were where my family lived on, and where I learned about the ones I never knew. They kept our history alive, but they were also where we talked about who we were, and who we could be. However, the disparity between that home or community life and a broader public one was often jarring; when nothing that makes you you is visible in mass media, it can be very easy to get some very unhealthy ideas of what it means to be you. And when "diverse" media still leaves you out, it tells you that you're a rung below being even a token. You're just not there.

It's hard to live like that. I know because I did, and it took a lot of hard work to get out of that headspace. I spent a lot of my adolescence and young adulthood struggling to figure out what it meant to be Indigenous in a society that didn't seem particularly interested in what that was. But gradually, and with support, I began to figure out my own path. There isn't one thing that magically did it for me, but a lot of things helped. *MOONSHOT* helped punctuate that phase of my life.

The first *MOONSHOT* volume was a revelation when I read it. Here were stories I knew or could recognize. Some of them I knew from my own childhood, but others were glimpses of other people's stories, families, and lives. In *MOONSHOT*, I saw our pasts, and also indigeno-futurism of the way things could be. But most importantly, I also saw how we exist now. That's what is missing from so many of the things I've read and watched in my life, and there it was, plain as day. *MOONSHOT* was maybe the first comic I read that I saw myself in.

That's why I'm so excited about the second volume that you hold in your hands. This is a volume focused on our peoples as we are now, and how we navigate our worlds. One of the most profoundly insulting ways Indigenous peoples can be treated – and sadly, one of the most

common – is as something dead, a prehistoric curiosity preserved in amber, viewed and distorted from the outside. That's not who we are. We are water, fluid, and ever-changing. Our communities are alive, and we teach our traditions to our new generations. We preserve, but we grow, too. *MOONSHOT* is a catalog of the ways we are most alive, with ourselves and with each other.

We live and breathe in a world that often pretends it got rid of us. In the face of that, *MOONSHOT Volume 2*, which is bursting with stories, is an act of love and also of resistance. We love ourselves and our communities. We're still here, unbroken lines of stories. We not only survive, but thrive. We're not victims. We are protectors. This book is defiant, unabashed love.

I love to read stories and discover not just something familiar to me, but something that another nation treasures. I see myself in this book, but I also cherish being able to see so many other peoples and their lines. For them to share their stories with me and with us is a blessing, and not one I take lightly. We are stronger and more vibrant for all of our Indigenous multiplicities. There is no one Indigenous box or experience, and it's always nice to be reminded of that when reading these stories.

To be a part of it, even in a small way like this, is not something I take lightly. Thank you for reading part of my story, and for all the ones in this book, and helping our lines go on. Thank you to the contributors for sharing your love with me and with all of us. Hiy hiy!

James Leask
Métis Comic Critic and Commentator,
ComicsAlliance

Based on the synergetic creativity of Volume 1, I couldn't wait to get started working on Volume 2 of the *MOONSHOT* collection. I was elated; excited. That feeling of both something familiar and new, co-mingled with the excitement of collaborating with other Indigenous creatives.

From the first volume, you may know my stance on the importance of Indigenous-created storytelling (we need tell our own stories) as well as propagating Indigenous continuance (we are not just relics of the past). *MOONSHOT Volume 2* has the benefit of having the same editorial team from the first volume to help the various Indigenous storytellers and artists create comic stories that celebrate our continuance.

AH Comics and the editor from the first volume were once again back and were instrumental and vital to the success of this volume. They held a common creative vision for Volume 2, asking Indigenous writers to pull from our own backgrounds, traditions, and communities in comic stories that merge this richness into contemporary masterpieces; then continued their vigilance, as they ensured Indigenous artists provided accurate and eloquent visual representations for our stories.

Highlighting present-day beliefs and traditions, each Indigenous author has written their story based on an *existing* ritual and/or belief from their community, as Indigenous culture is not relegated to stories of *"Long ago..."*. It exists here, today. While some stories are based in science fiction, some appear in the past, and some appear in places beyond, they all take place in the "now." I am once again honoured to be a part of a collaboration that showcases Indigenous talent: an impressive list of names of Indigenous creators, industry leaders, and creative powerhouses. Several of the contributors are familiar to me, along with some new names and faces to add to the playlist. Many I know professionally, and some I can even proudly say are friends.

Richard Van Camp (Tlicho) gives us "The Magic of Wolverines," illustrated by Scott Henderson, about the mysterious power and beauty of the wolverine, told from grandfather to grandson. Additionally, Van Camp writes "Water Spirits," illustrated by Haiwei Hou. It is a story of a high school science class on a trip inside the largest gold mining operation in Canada, where they encounter history and reality in a way they never expected.

Elizabeth LaPensée, Ph.D. (Anishinaabe, Métis, and Irish), talks of "They Who Walk As Lightning," illustrated by Richard Pace. A young Anishinaabe girl discovers a legacy of protectors and a connection to Thunderbirds she never knew existed.

Jeffrey Veregge (Port Gamble S'Klallam Tribe) authors and illustrates "Journeys," where an interdimensional ship is bound for the unknown. After the launch, the pilot finds himself in a place both strange and familiar. Jeffrey has created cover work for some of the biggest publishers in the industry, including Marvel, but "Journeys" is his very first full story!

Darcie Little Badger (Lipan Apache Tribe of Texas) writes "Worst Bargain In Town," illustrated by Rossi Gifford. This is a story that follows two young women who find their own strength as they confront an evil being who wants to drain their townspeople's life energy.

Steve Keewatin Sanderson (Plains Cree) – a comic book creator, illustrator, and animator – both writes and illustrates "Where We Left Off," in which small communities form after the world is destroyed by various disasters, while others quickly succumb to more primal behaviour, threatening to destroy what little is left of humanity.

Gerard and Peta-Gay Roberts (Abouyou and Tayaliti, respectively) provide "The Creator Tamosi," an Iroquoian Creation story, about a father looking for answers to his family's struggle who finds help in an unexpected place, beautifully painted by Nicholas Burns.

Armand Ruffo (Anishinaabe) authors "The Awakening," illustrated by David Cutler. After being stranded in the dark, a young gang member must choose between abandoning the survivors of a plane crash in exchange for his freedom, or stay and become their unlikely protector.

Daniel Health Justice (Cherokee) reveals, with art by Weshoyot Alvitre, "The Boys Who Became The Hummingbirds" – a two-spirit story in which a young man dreams of colour, life, and love, while living on the edge of the world.

Michael Sheyahshe (Caddo) writes "Do Wild Turkeys Dream of Electric Drums," illustrated by Kim Hunter. This is a humorous tale that focuses on the Caddo Turkey Dance songs, where natural enemies – a hungry bobcat and a cunning cottontail – work together in an attempt to attract some wild turkeys.

David Alexander Robertston (Swampy Cree) supplies "Bookmark," with artwork by Natasha Alterici. Here, a teenager silently questions what reason there might be to stay in this world, after the loss of his best friend.

Alina Pete (Little Pine First Nation) authors "Ka'tepwa: Who Calls," a story that follows a young Cree man who finds himself on the edge of a lake in the Qu'appelle Valley, drawn by the familiar calling voices, hauntingly illustrated by Trudi Castle.

Sean and Rachel Qitsualik-Tinsley (Scottish and Mohawk and Inuk-Scottish-Cree, respectively) fashion the Arctic fantasy "Winter's Shell," illustrated by Alexandra Neonakis. Set in a world where nature and technology are one, a brilliant scientist embarks on a treacherous journey with his daughter over ice and snow to recover an object that holds the key to saving the land, and life itself.

Tanya Tagaq (Inuk) recounts "Nine Mile Lake," an original story about an older sister taking her younger cousin on an afternoon adventure across the tundra. This piece features original art by *MOONSHOT* Volumes 1 and 2 cover artist Stephen Gladue.

MOONSHOT: The Indigenous Comics Collection, Volume 2 is another important milestone in Indigenous-created comic book stories, featuring a fantastic ensemble of Indigenous creativity coupled with phenomenal artists. As you read these stories and enjoy the marvellous art, remember that we Indigenous people – our cultures, traditions, and communities – exist in the present-time and are here to stay!

Additionally, as you read, you are helping us celebrate this continuance – and for that, we thank you.

Háw-wih. ("Thank you.")

Michael Sheyahshe (Caddo)
Author, *Native Americans in Comics: A Critical Study*

Elizabeth LaPensée, Ph.D's

THEY
WHO
WALK
AS LIGHTNING

Illustrated by Richard Pace

BACKGROUND

Anishinaabeg carry many Thunderbird stories and teachings across
their communities. Known as animikiig, Thunderbirds take many forms
with immense power. In one form, lightning strikes from their eyes. In
Baawaating, which includes Batchewana First Nations in Ontario, when
the water flowed as rapids, people who walked with lightning in their
eyes would cover their faces so as to not harm anyone. Thunderbirds
are respected for their contribution to the balanced wellbeing of
Aki, meaning Earth. They have been called on to help the waters
threatened across the world, taking form in storms, art, and action.
Just as they always were and will always be, Thunderbirds are seen
in glimpses through peripheral vision, and in lightning that brightens
both the skies, and our hearts.

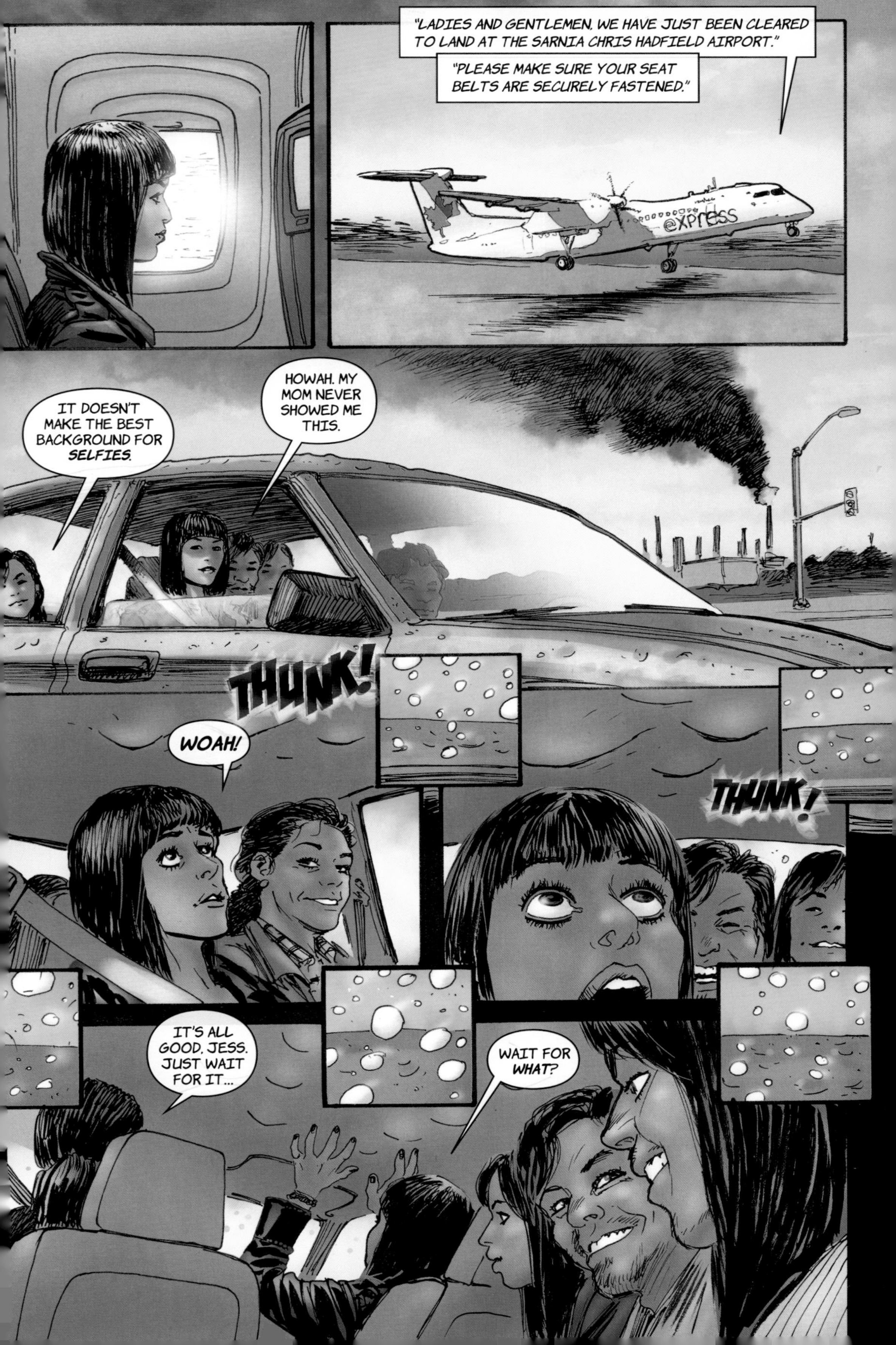
"LADIES AND GENTLEMEN, WE HAVE JUST BEEN CLEARED TO LAND AT THE SARNIA CHRIS HADFIELD AIRPORT."
"PLEASE MAKE SURE YOUR SEAT BELTS ARE SECURELY FASTENED."
express
IT DOESN'T MAKE THE BEST BACKGROUND FOR SELFIES.
HOWAH. MY MOM NEVER SHOWED ME THIS.
THUNK!
WOAH!
THUNK!
IT'S ALL GOOD, JESS. JUST WAIT FOR IT...
WAIT FOR WHAT?

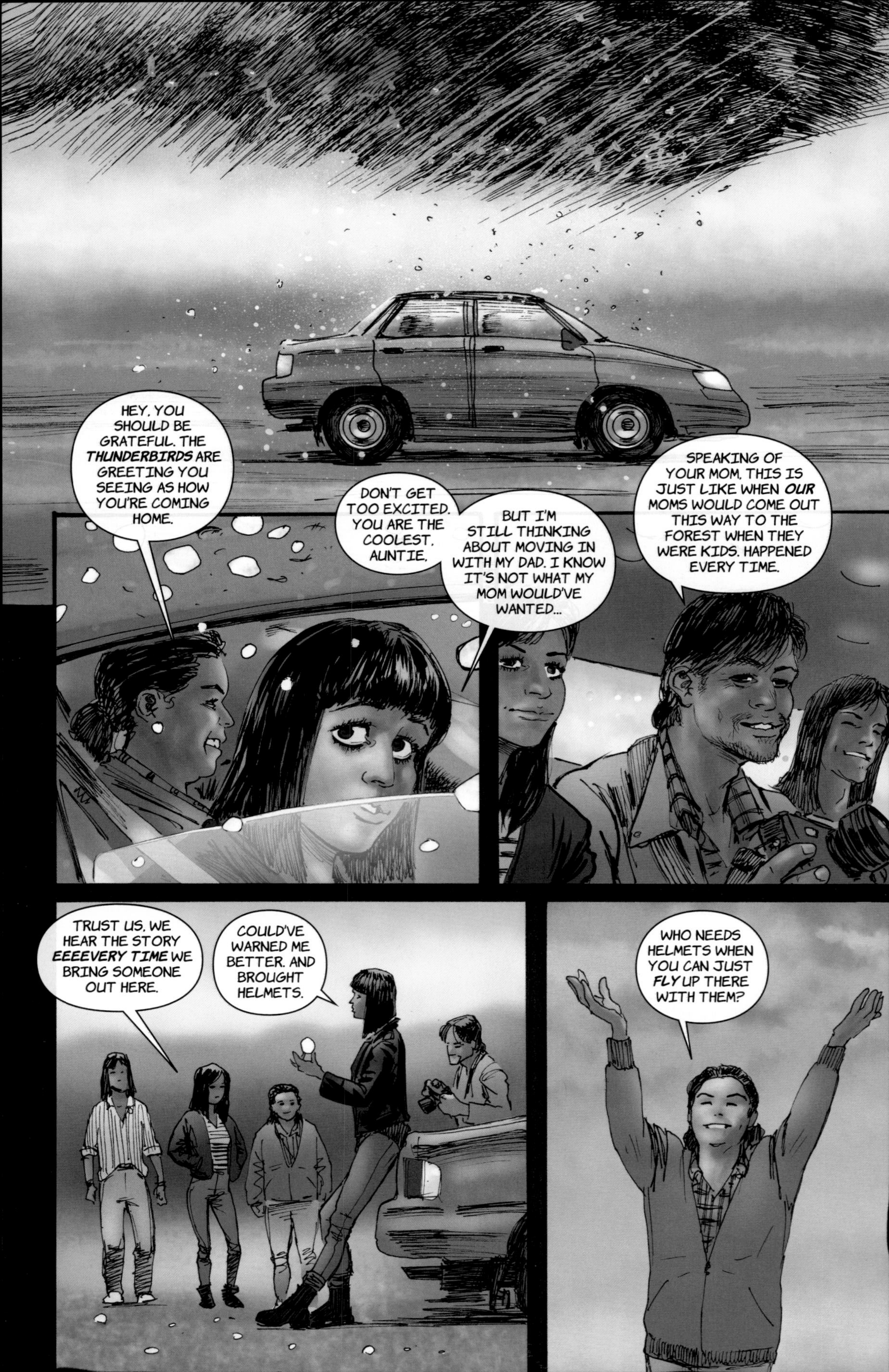
HEY, YOU SHOULD BE GRATEFUL. THE THUNDERBIRDS ARE GREETING YOU SEEING AS HOW YOU'RE COMING HOME.
DON'T GET TOO EXCITED. YOU ARE THE COOLEST, AUNTIE.
BUT I'M STILL THINKING ABOUT MOVING IN WITH MY DAD. I KNOW IT'S NOT WHAT MY MOM WOULD'VE WANTED...
SPEAKING OF YOUR MOM, THIS IS JUST LIKE WHEN OUR MOMS WOULD COME OUT THIS WAY TO THE FOREST WHEN THEY WERE KIDS. HAPPENED EVERY TIME.
TRUST US, WE HEAR THE STORY EEEVERY TIME WE BRING SOMEONE OUT HERE.
COULD'VE WARNED ME BETTER. AND BROUGHT HELMETS.
WHO NEEDS HELMETS WHEN YOU CAN JUST FLY UP THERE WITH THEM?

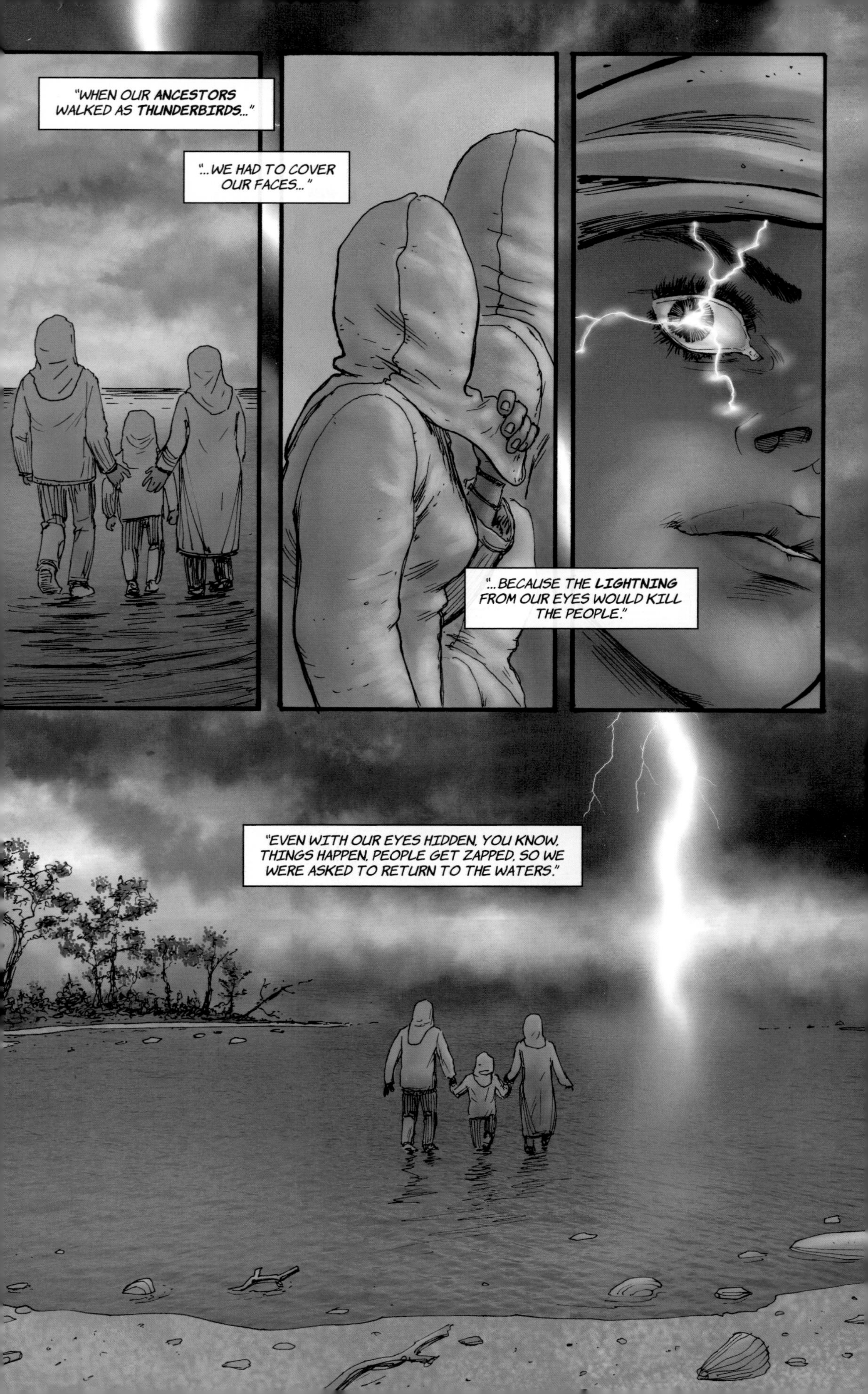
"WHEN OUR ANCESTORS WALKED AS THUNDERBIRDS..."
"...WE HAD TO COVER OUR FACES..."
"...BECAUSE THE LIGHTNING FROM OUR EYES WOULD KILL THE PEOPLE."
"EVEN WITH OUR EYES HIDDEN, YOU KNOW, THINGS HAPPEN. PEOPLE GET ZAPPED, SO WE WERE ASKED TO RETURN TO THE WATERS."

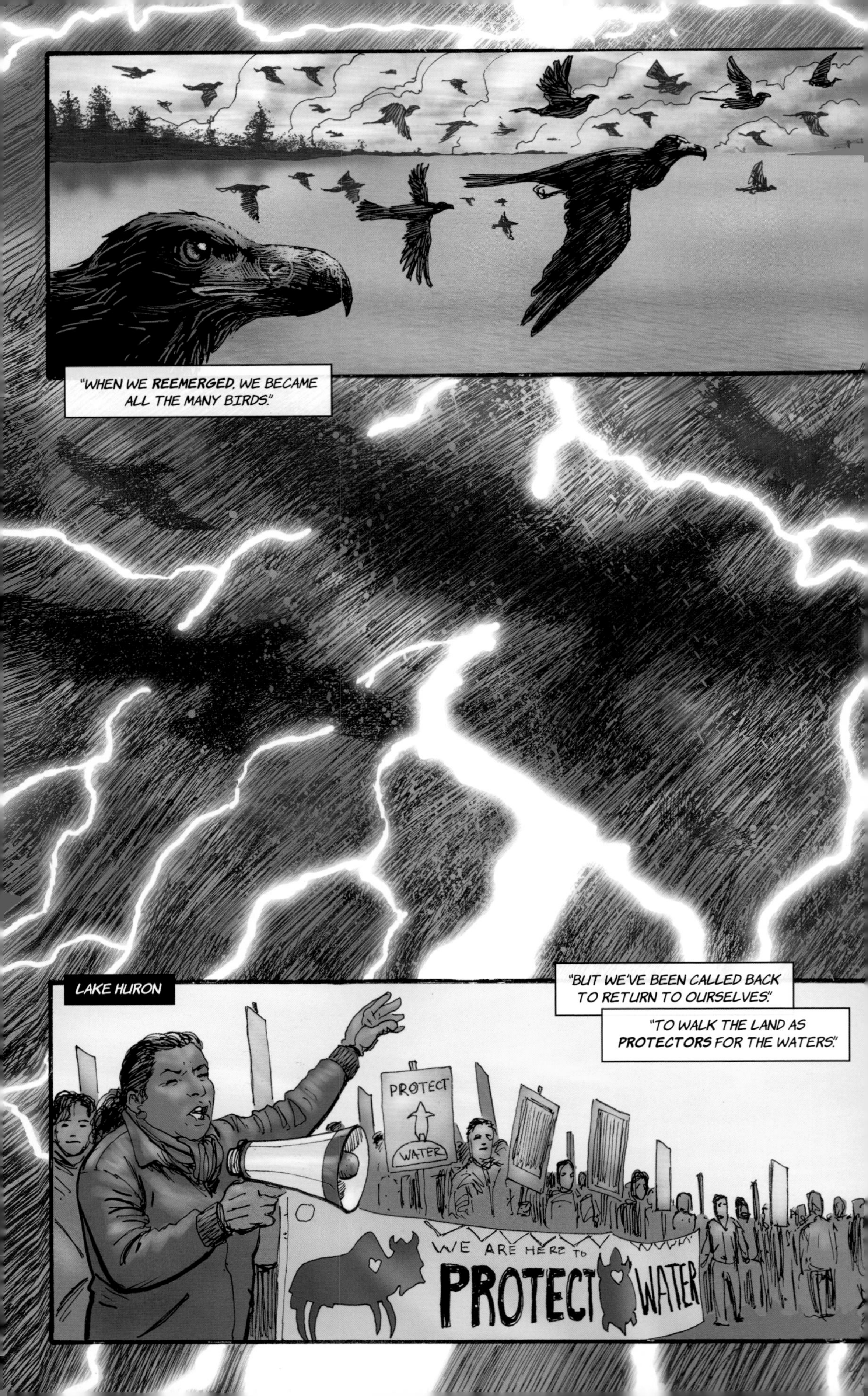
"WHEN WE REEMERGED, WE BECAME ALL THE MANY BIRDS."
LAKE HURON
"BUT WE'VE BEEN CALLED BACK TO RETURN TO OURSELVES."
"TO WALK THE LAND AS PROTECTORS FOR THE WATERS."
PROTECT WATER
WE ARE HERE TO PROTECT WATER

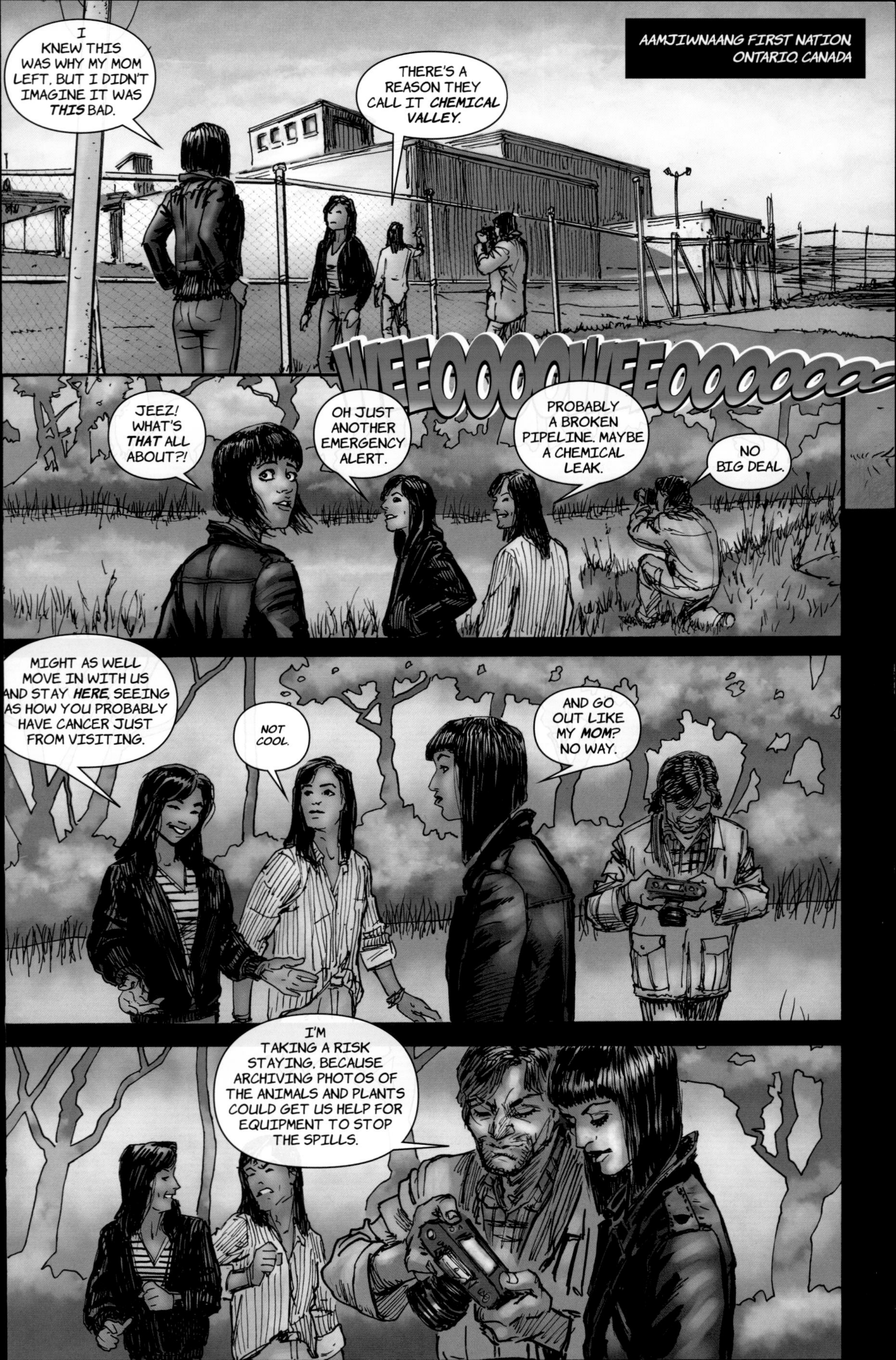
AAMJIWNAANG FIRST NATION, ONTARIO, CANADA
I KNEW THIS WAS WHY MY MOM LEFT. BUT I DIDN'T IMAGINE IT WAS THIS BAD.
THERE'S A REASON THEY CALL IT CHEMICAL VALLEY.
WEEOOOOWEEOOOOOO
JEEZ! WHAT'S THAT ALL ABOUT?!
OH JUST ANOTHER EMERGENCY ALERT.
PROBABLY A BROKEN PIPELINE. MAYBE A CHEMICAL LEAK.
NO BIG DEAL.
MIGHT AS WELL MOVE IN WITH US AND STAY HERE, SEEING AS HOW YOU PROBABLY HAVE CANCER JUST FROM VISITING.
NOT COOL.
AND GO OUT LIKE MY MOM? NO WAY.
I'M TAKING A RISK STAYING, BECAUSE ARCHIVING PHOTOS OF THE ANIMALS AND PLANTS COULD GET US HELP FOR EQUIPMENT TO STOP THE SPILLS.

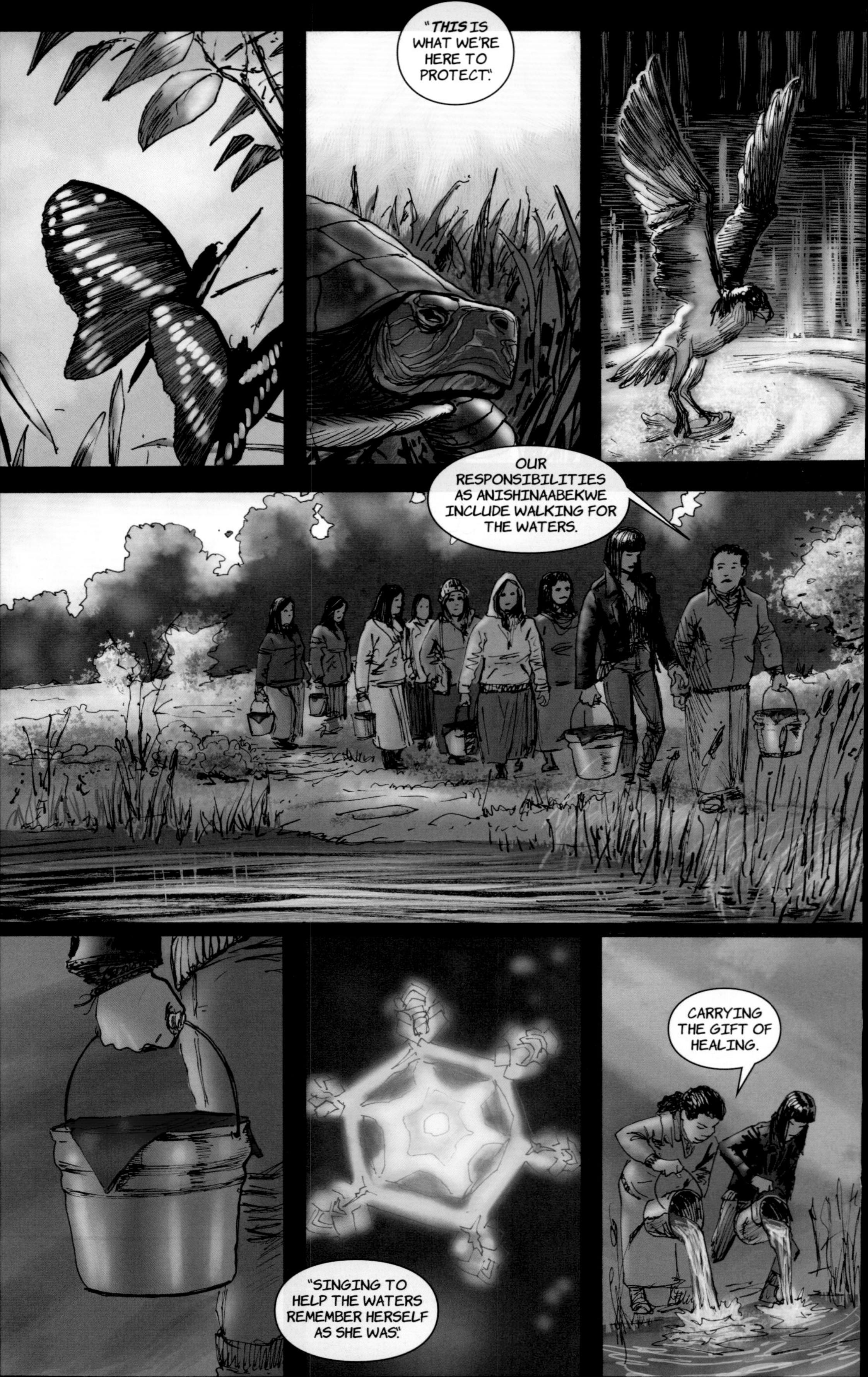
"THIS IS WHAT WE'RE HERE TO PROTECT."
OUR RESPONSIBILITIES AS ANISHINAABEKWE INCLUDE WALKING FOR THE WATERS.
"SINGING TO HELP THE WATERS REMEMBER HERSELF AS SHE WAS."
CARRYING THE GIFT OF HEALING.

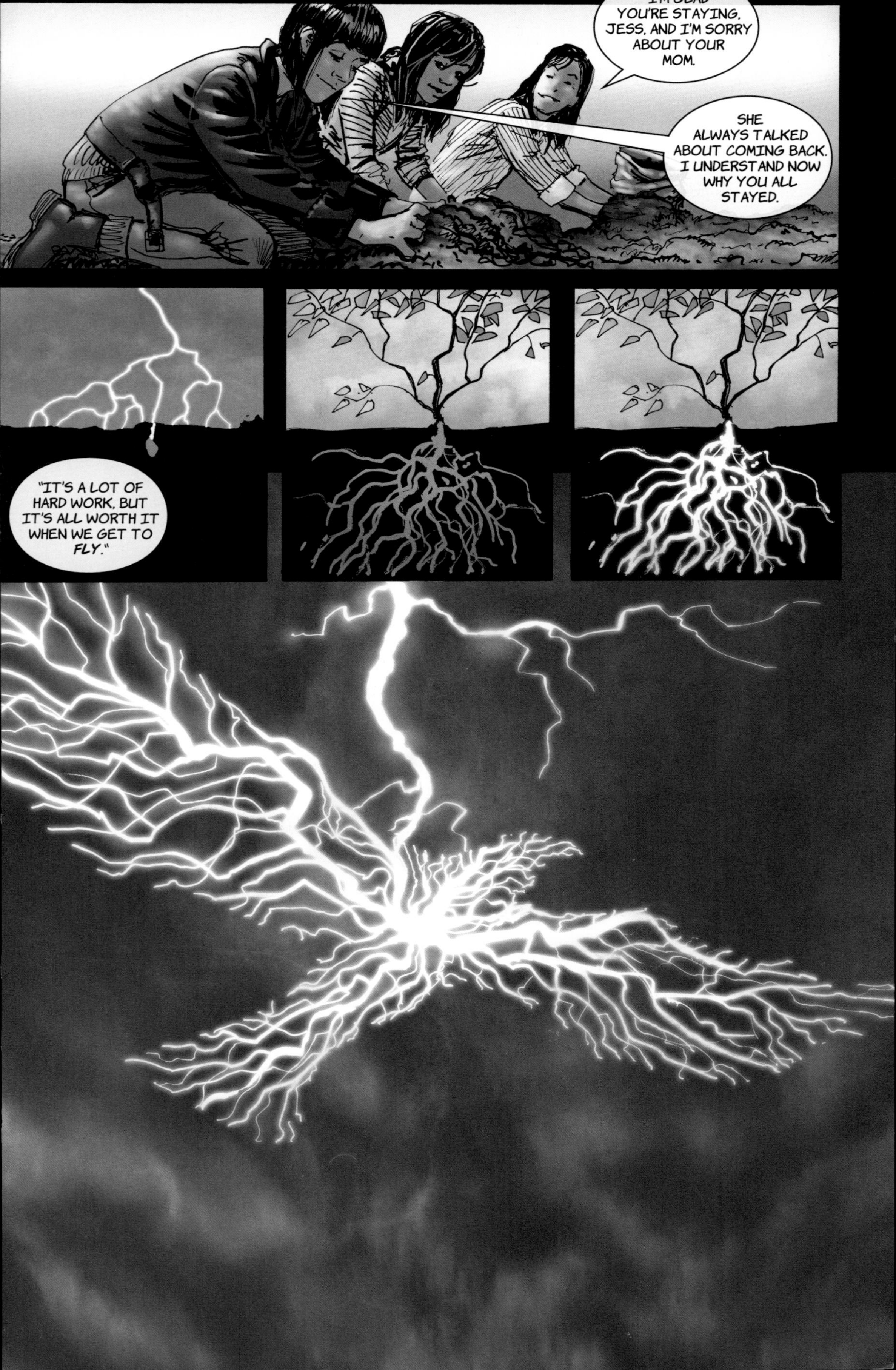
I'M GLAD YOU'RE STAYING, JESS, AND I'M SORRY ABOUT YOUR MOM.
SHE ALWAYS TALKED ABOUT COMING BACK. I UNDERSTAND NOW WHY YOU ALL STAYED.
"IT'S A LOT OF HARD WORK, BUT IT'S ALL WORTH IT WHEN WE GET TO *FLY*."

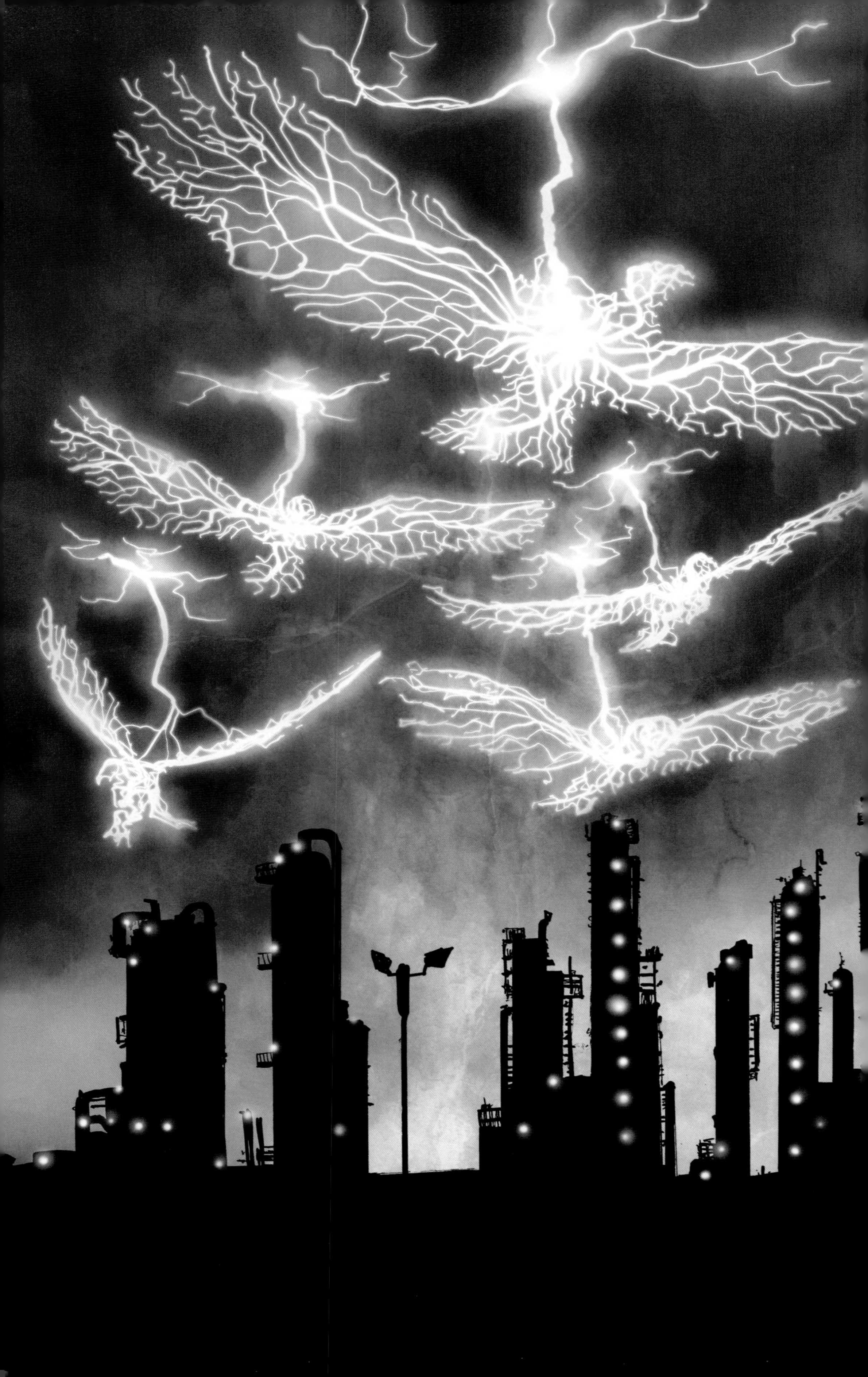

Sean and Rachel Qitsualik-Tinsley's

WINTER'S SHELL

Illustrated by Alexandria Neonakis

BACKGROUND

The Arctic is an extreme place. So extreme that even snow and ice occur differently from Southern climates. In order to understand this extremity, Inuit developed unique systems of thought, based on the interactions of elemental powers. "Winter's Shell" is a nod to this worldview, which is hidden but alive today. In the story, several unique concepts are presented (the "Land's Egg" and "Land's Strength," introduced by the Nuktaq character who opens the story), which are adaptations of Inuit shamanic symbols. Like the Arctic climate, many of the meanings are extremely complex, and Inuit never discussed them openly. This cosmogony ("world-understanding") is instead expressed through art, story, and *aangakkuuniq* ("shamanism"). This story was written by the authors in a way that introduces us to some of these elemental concepts by placing the reader in an Arctic fantasy environment that can be felt, but not fully explained.

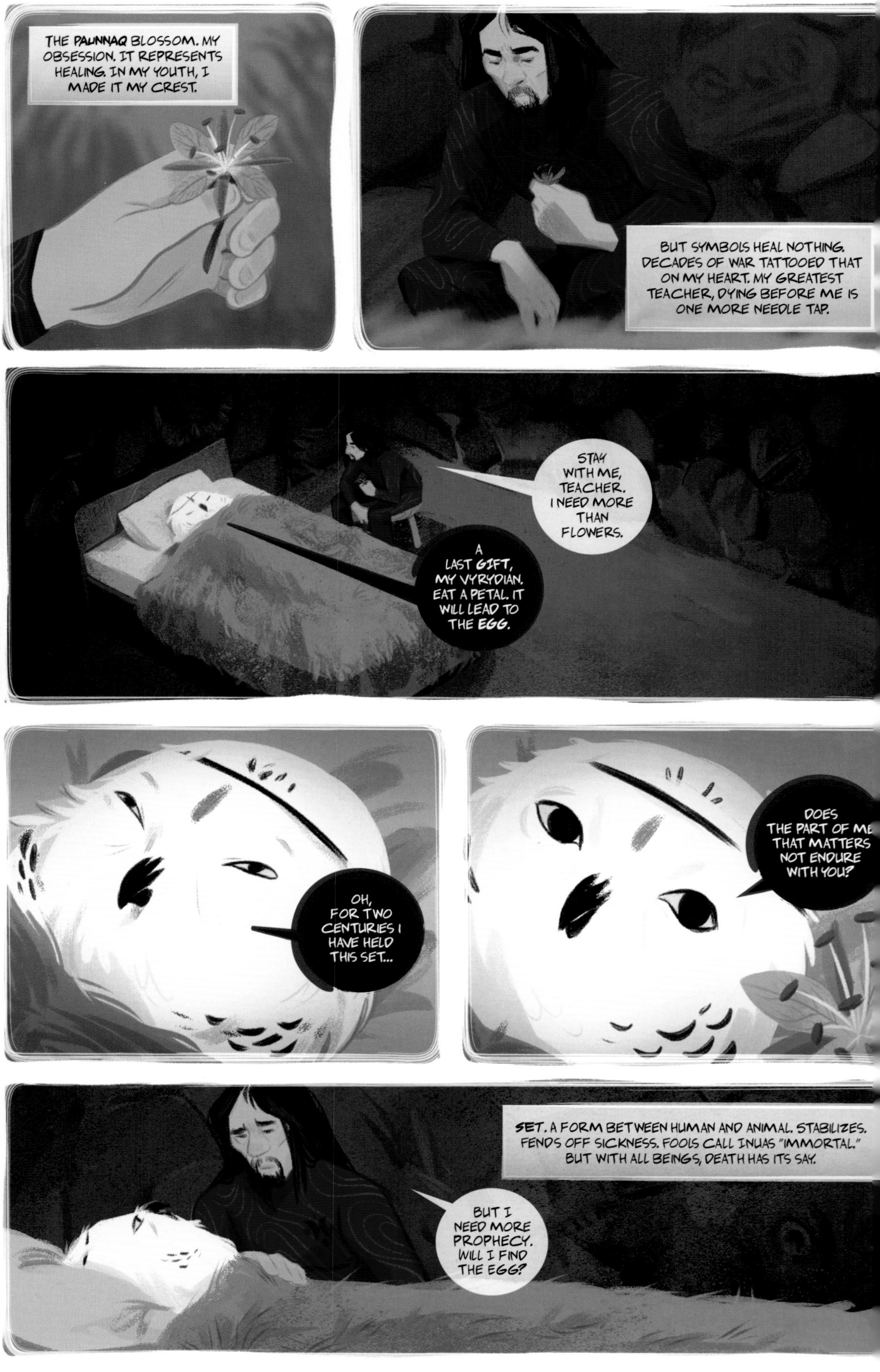
THE PAUNNAQ BLOSSOM. MY OBSESSION. IT REPRESENTS HEALING. IN MY YOUTH, I MADE IT MY CREST.
BUT SYMBOLS HEAL NOTHING. DECADES OF WAR TATTOOED THAT ON MY HEART. MY GREATEST TEACHER, DYING BEFORE ME IS ONE MORE NEEDLE TAP.
STAY WITH ME, TEACHER. I NEED MORE THAN FLOWERS.
A LAST GIFT, MY VYRYDIAN. EAT A PETAL. IT WILL LEAD TO THE EGG.
OH, FOR TWO CENTURIES I HAVE HELD THIS SET...
DOES THE PART OF ME THAT MATTERS NOT ENDURE WITH YOU?
SET. A FORM BETWEEN HUMAN AND ANIMAL. STABILIZES. FENDS OFF SICKNESS. FOOLS CALL INUAS "IMMORTAL." BUT WITH ALL BEINGS, DEATH HAS ITS SAY.
BUT I NEED MORE PROPHECY. WILL I FIND THE EGG?

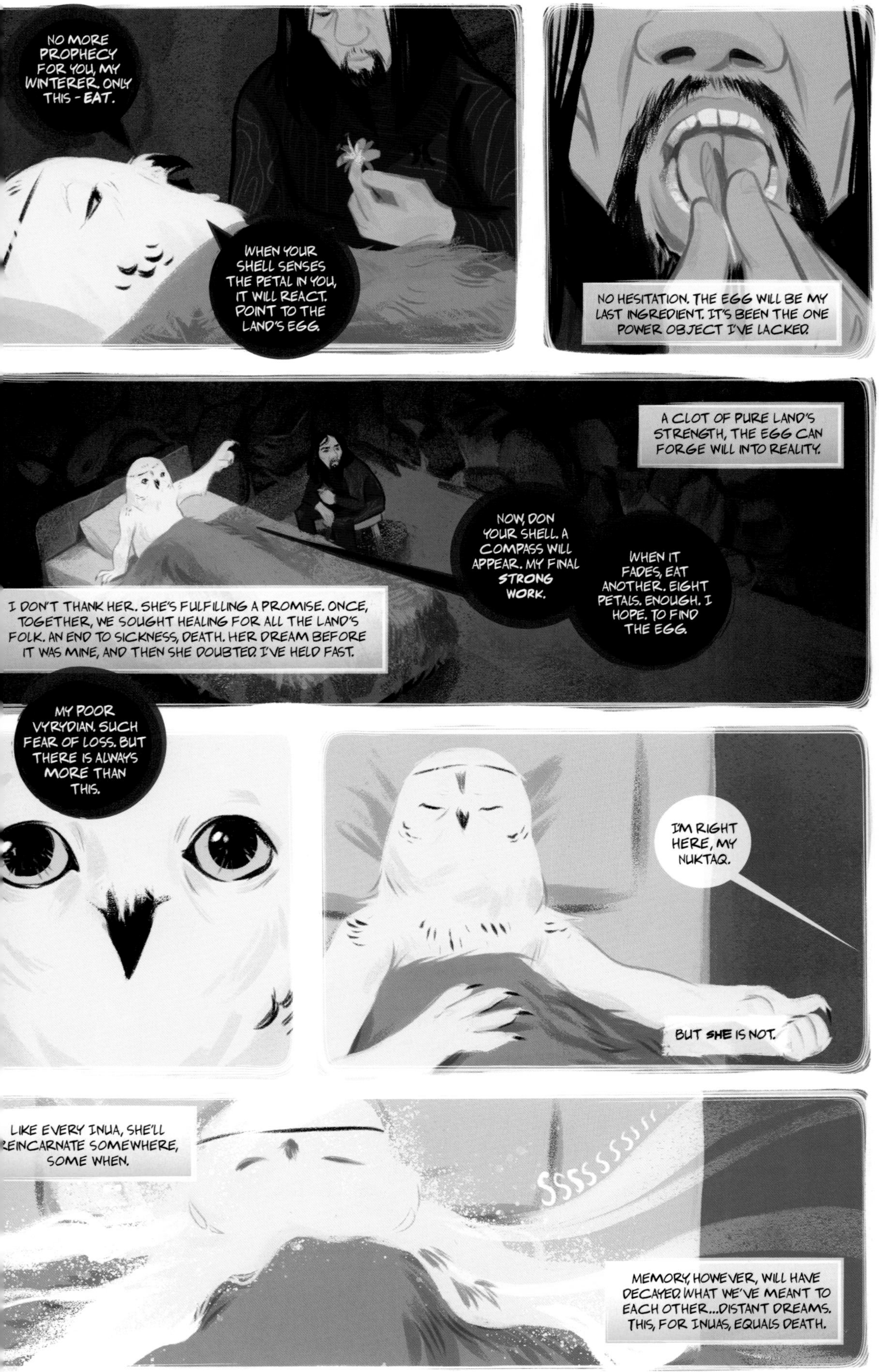
NO MORE PROPHECY FOR YOU, MY WINTERER. ONLY THIS - EAT.
WHEN YOUR SHELL SENSES THE PETAL IN YOU, IT WILL REACT. POINT TO THE LAND'S EGG.
NO HESITATION. THE EGG WILL BE MY LAST INGREDIENT. IT'S BEEN THE ONE POWER OBJECT I'VE LACKED.
A CLOT OF PURE LAND'S STRENGTH, THE EGG CAN FORGE WILL INTO REALITY.
NOW, DON YOUR SHELL. A COMPASS WILL APPEAR. MY FINAL STRONG WORK.
WHEN IT FADES, EAT ANOTHER. EIGHT PETALS. ENOUGH. I HOPE. TO FIND THE EGG.
I DON'T THANK HER. SHE'S FULFILLING A PROMISE. ONCE, TOGETHER, WE SOUGHT HEALING FOR ALL THE LAND'S FOLK. AN END TO SICKNESS, DEATH. HER DREAM BEFORE IT WAS MINE, AND THEN SHE DOUBTED. I'VE HELD FAST.
MY POOR VYRYDIAN. SUCH FEAR OF LOSS. BUT THERE IS ALWAYS MORE THAN THIS.
I'M RIGHT HERE, MY NUKTAQ.
BUT SHE IS NOT.
LIKE EVERY INUA, SHE'LL REINCARNATE SOMEWHERE, SOME WHEN.
SSSSSSSSSS
MEMORY, HOWEVER, WILL HAVE DECAYED. WHAT WE'VE MEANT TO EACH OTHER...DISTANT DREAMS. THIS, FOR INUAS, EQUALS DEATH.

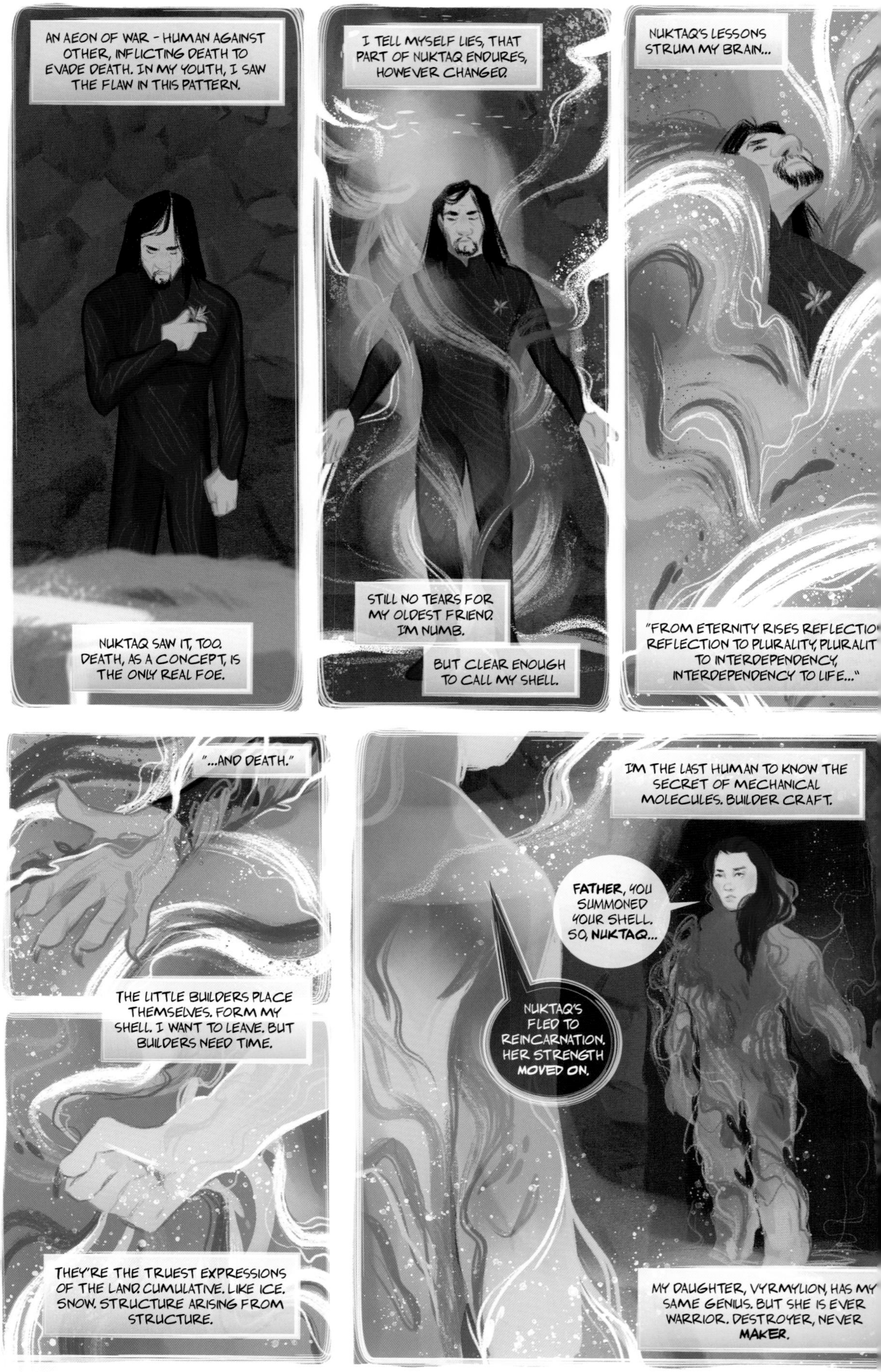
AN AEON OF WAR - HUMAN AGAINST OTHER, INFLICTING DEATH TO EVADE DEATH. IN MY YOUTH, I SAW THE FLAW IN THIS PATTERN.
NUKTAQ SAW IT, TOO. DEATH, AS A CONCEPT, IS THE ONLY REAL FOE.
I TELL MYSELF LIES, THAT PART OF NUKTAQ ENDURES, HOWEVER CHANGED.
STILL NO TEARS FOR MY OLDEST FRIEND. I'M NUMB.
BUT CLEAR ENOUGH TO CALL MY SHELL.
NUKTAQ'S LESSONS STRUM MY BRAIN...
"FROM ETERNITY RISES REFLECTIO REFLECTION TO PLURALITY, PLURALIT TO INTERDEPENDENCY, INTERDEPENDENCY TO LIFE..."
"...AND DEATH."
THE LITTLE BUILDERS PLACE THEMSELVES. FORM MY SHELL. I WANT TO LEAVE. BUT BUILDERS NEED TIME.
THEY'RE THE TRUEST EXPRESSIONS OF THE LAND. CUMULATIVE. LIKE ICE. SNOW. STRUCTURE ARISING FROM STRUCTURE.
I'M THE LAST HUMAN TO KNOW THE SECRET OF MECHANICAL MOLECULES. BUILDER CRAFT.
FATHER, YOU SUMMONED YOUR SHELL. SO, NUKTAQ...
NUKTAQ'S FLED TO REINCARNATION. HER STRENGTH MOVED ON.
MY DAUGHTER, VYRMYLION, HAS MY SAME GENIUS. BUT SHE IS EVER WARRIOR. DESTROYER, NEVER MAKER.

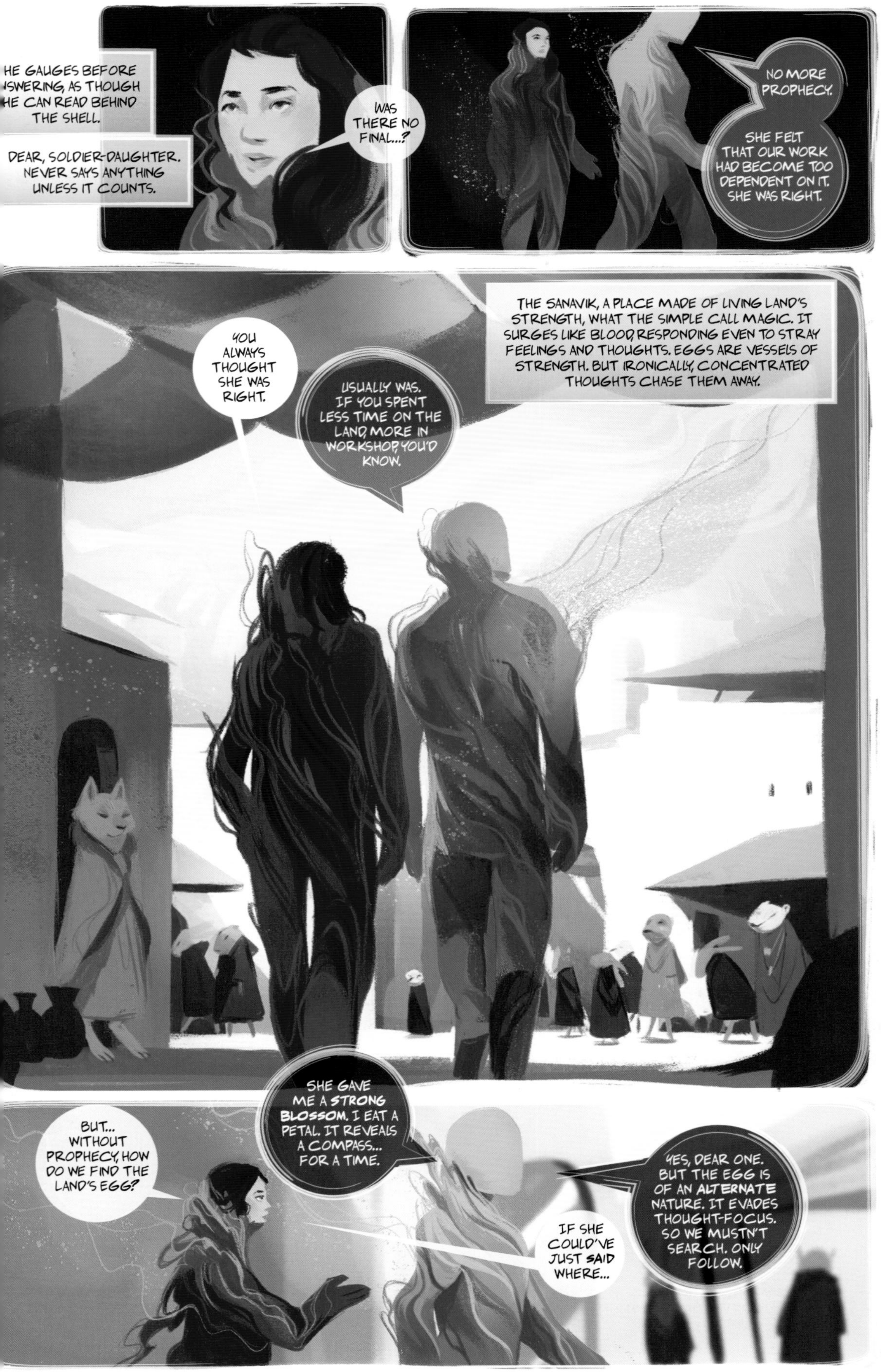
HE GAUGES BEFORE NSWERING, AS THOUGH HE CAN READ BEHIND THE SHELL.
DEAR, SOLDIER-DAUGHTER. NEVER SAYS ANYTHING UNLESS IT COUNTS.
WAS THERE NO FINAL...?
NO MORE PROPHECY.
SHE FELT THAT OUR WORK HAD BECOME TOO DEPENDENT ON IT. SHE WAS RIGHT.
THE SANAVIK, A PLACE MADE OF LIVING LAND'S STRENGTH, WHAT THE SIMPLE CALL MAGIC. IT SURGES LIKE BLOOD, RESPONDING EVEN TO STRAY FEELINGS AND THOUGHTS. EGGS ARE VESSELS OF STRENGTH. BUT IRONICALLY, CONCENTRATED THOUGHTS CHASE THEM AWAY.
YOU ALWAYS THOUGHT SHE WAS RIGHT.
USUALLY WAS. IF YOU SPENT LESS TIME ON THE LAND, MORE IN WORKSHOP, YOU'D KNOW.
BUT... WITHOUT PROPHECY, HOW DO WE FIND THE LAND'S EGG?
SHE GAVE ME A **STRONG BLOSSOM**. I EAT A PETAL. IT REVEALS A COMPASS... FOR A TIME.
IF SHE COULD'VE JUST **SAID** WHERE...
YES, DEAR ONE. BUT THE EGG IS OF AN **ALTERNATE** NATURE. IT EVADES THOUGHT-FOCUS. SO WE MUSTN'T SEARCH. ONLY FOLLOW.

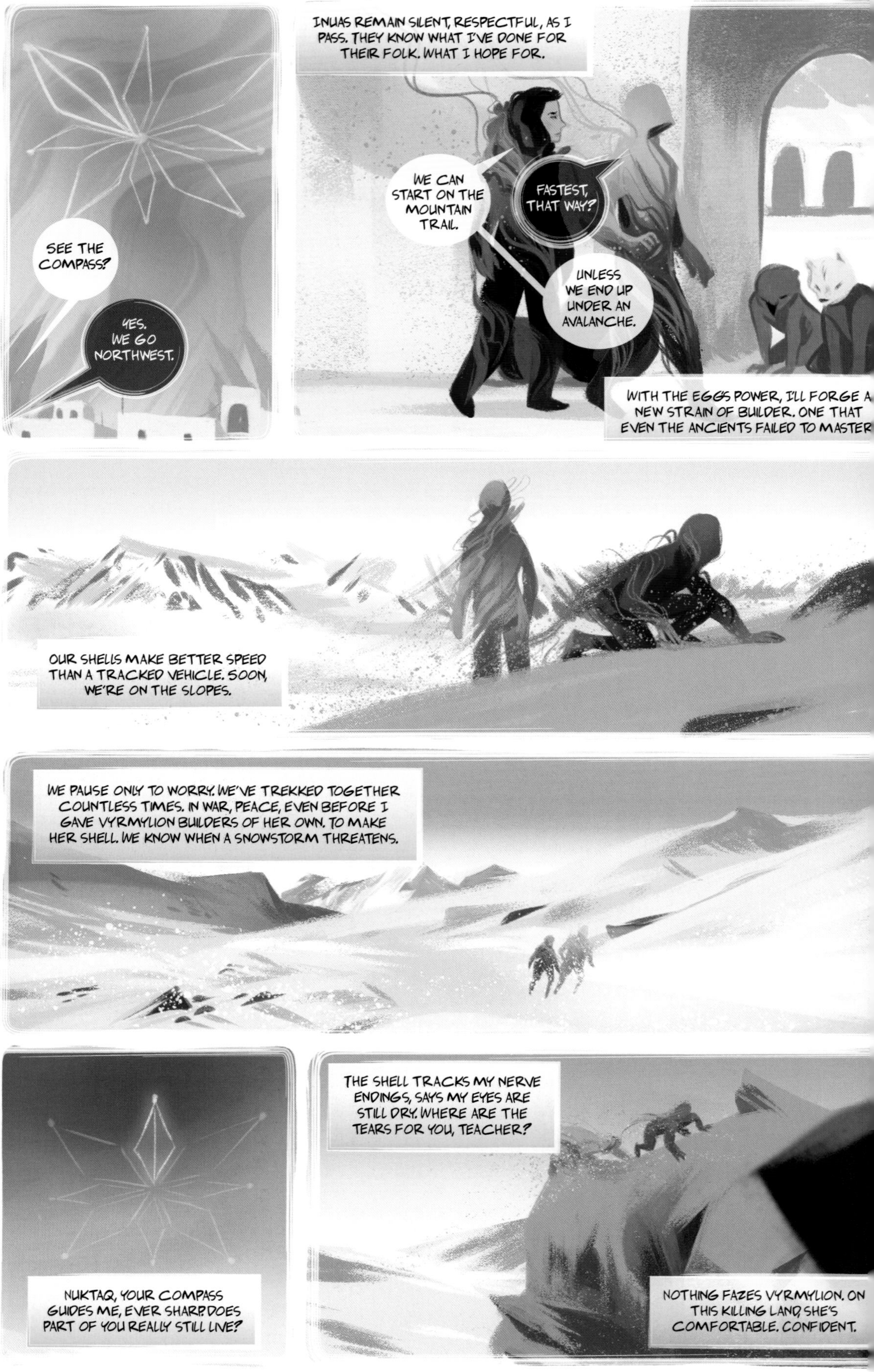
SEE THE COMPASS?
YES. WE GO NORTHWEST.
INUAS REMAIN SILENT, RESPECTFUL, AS I PASS. THEY KNOW WHAT I'VE DONE FOR THEIR FOLK. WHAT I HOPE FOR.
WE CAN START ON THE MOUNTAIN TRAIL.
FASTEST, THAT WAY?
UNLESS WE END UP UNDER AN AVALANCHE.
WITH THE EGG'S POWER, I'LL FORGE A NEW STRAIN OF BUILDER. ONE THAT EVEN THE ANCIENTS FAILED TO MASTER
OUR SHELLS MAKE BETTER SPEED THAN A TRACKED VEHICLE. SOON, WE'RE ON THE SLOPES.
WE PAUSE ONLY TO WORRY. WE'VE TREKKED TOGETHER COUNTLESS TIMES. IN WAR, PEACE, EVEN BEFORE I GAVE VYRMYLION BUILDERS OF HER OWN. TO MAKE HER SHELL. WE KNOW WHEN A SNOWSTORM THREATENS.
NUKTAQ, YOUR COMPASS GUIDES ME, EVER SHARP. DOES PART OF YOU REALLY STILL LIVE?
THE SHELL TRACKS MY NERVE ENDINGS, SAYS MY EYES ARE STILL DRY. WHERE ARE THE TEARS FOR YOU, TEACHER?
NOTHING FAZES VYRMYLION. ON THIS KILLING LAND, SHE'S COMFORTABLE. CONFIDENT.

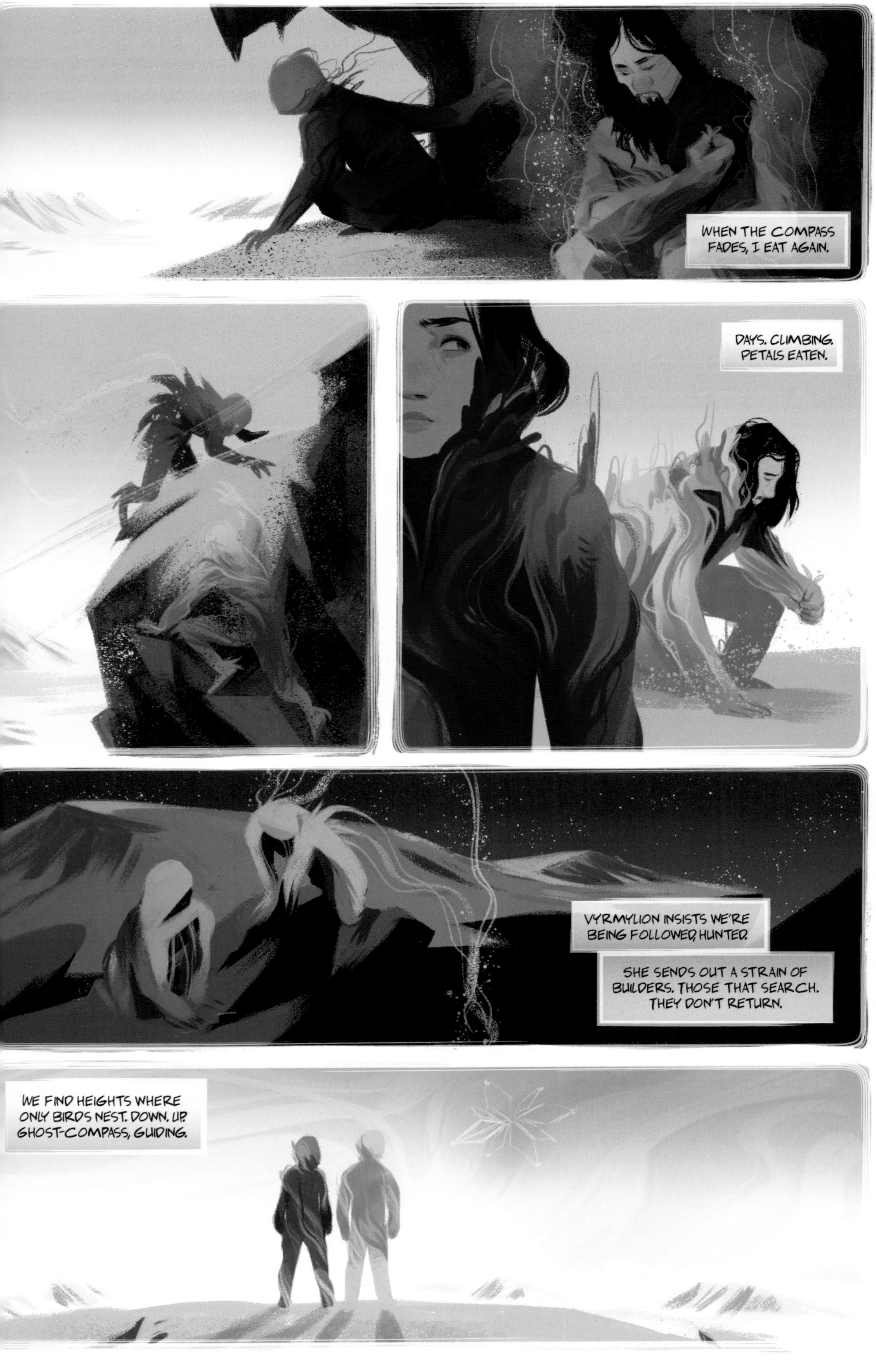
WHEN THE COMPASS FADES, I EAT AGAIN.
DAYS. CLIMBING. PETALS EATEN.
VYRMYLION INSISTS WE'RE BEING FOLLOWED, HUNTED.
SHE SENDS OUT A STRAIN OF BUILDERS. THOSE THAT SEARCH. THEY DON'T RETURN.
WE FIND HEIGHTS WHERE ONLY BIRDS NEST. DOWN. UP. GHOST-COMPASS, GUIDING.

WE'RE **WATCHED** SAYS VYRMYLION. YET NOTHING APPEARS.

FEEL HOLLOW. TIRED. SAD. CAN'T RELY ON SENSES...

ONCE AT THE CLIFF TOP WE'LL REST AND...

NO TALK, NOW. FATIGUE DRAINS FOCUS. THE LAST PETAL JUST SWALLOWED. HOW LONG BEFORE THE COMPASS DIES?

RRRRRUMBLE

BY THE **AGONIES!**

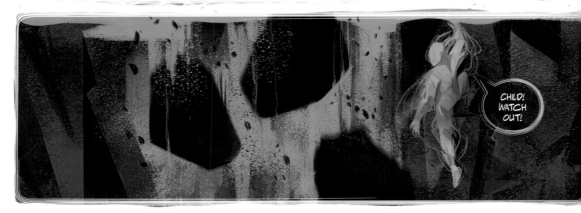

CHILD! WATCH OUT!

BE STILL, FATHER! WE DON'T KNOW WHO IT IS!

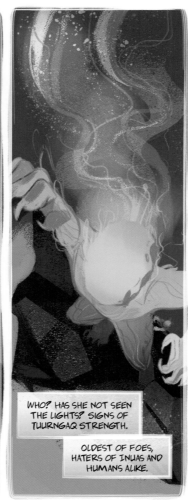

WHO? HAS SHE NOT SEEN THE LIGHTS? SIGNS OF TUURNGAQ STRENGTH.

OLDEST OF FOES, HATERS OF INUAS AND HUMANS ALIKE.

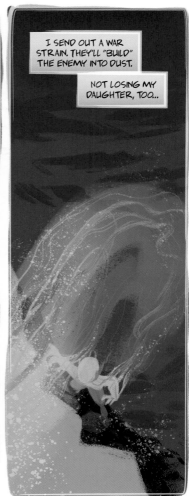

I SEND OUT A WAR STRAIN. THEY'LL "BUILD" THE ENEMY INTO DUST.

NOT LOSING MY DAUGHTER, TOO...

OLD WANHOPE, **MOVE!** ABOVE, I CAN HEAR THE BUILDERS AT WORK.

AA-HI-EEEEE

VYRMYLION ROARS. BUT I CAN'T MOVE. ENEMY ABOVE, ONLY CHILD BELOW, I ALONE AM IN BETWEEN.

RIDICULOUS. FEARING FOR HER. SHE'S ALL FIGHTER, NO CHILD.

WHAT WEAKNESS IS THIS?

MY MIND IS SUDDENLY WINDSWEPT. INERT. A DUSTY HOLLOW. I DON'T KNOW WHY.

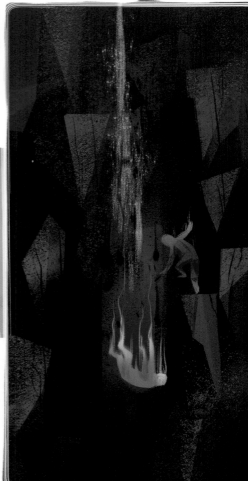

KRRRK

THEN THE ENEMY'S STRENGTH SHATTERS THE CLIFF

"FROM LOSS ARISES GRIEF. GRIEF, SICKNESS. SICKNESS, DOUBT. DOUBT..."

"...DEATH."

NICE HEADSTONE: "VYRYDIAN THE WINTERER. AVOWED VANQUISHER OF SICKNESS, AGE, AND DEATH. KILLED BY A SNOWBANK."

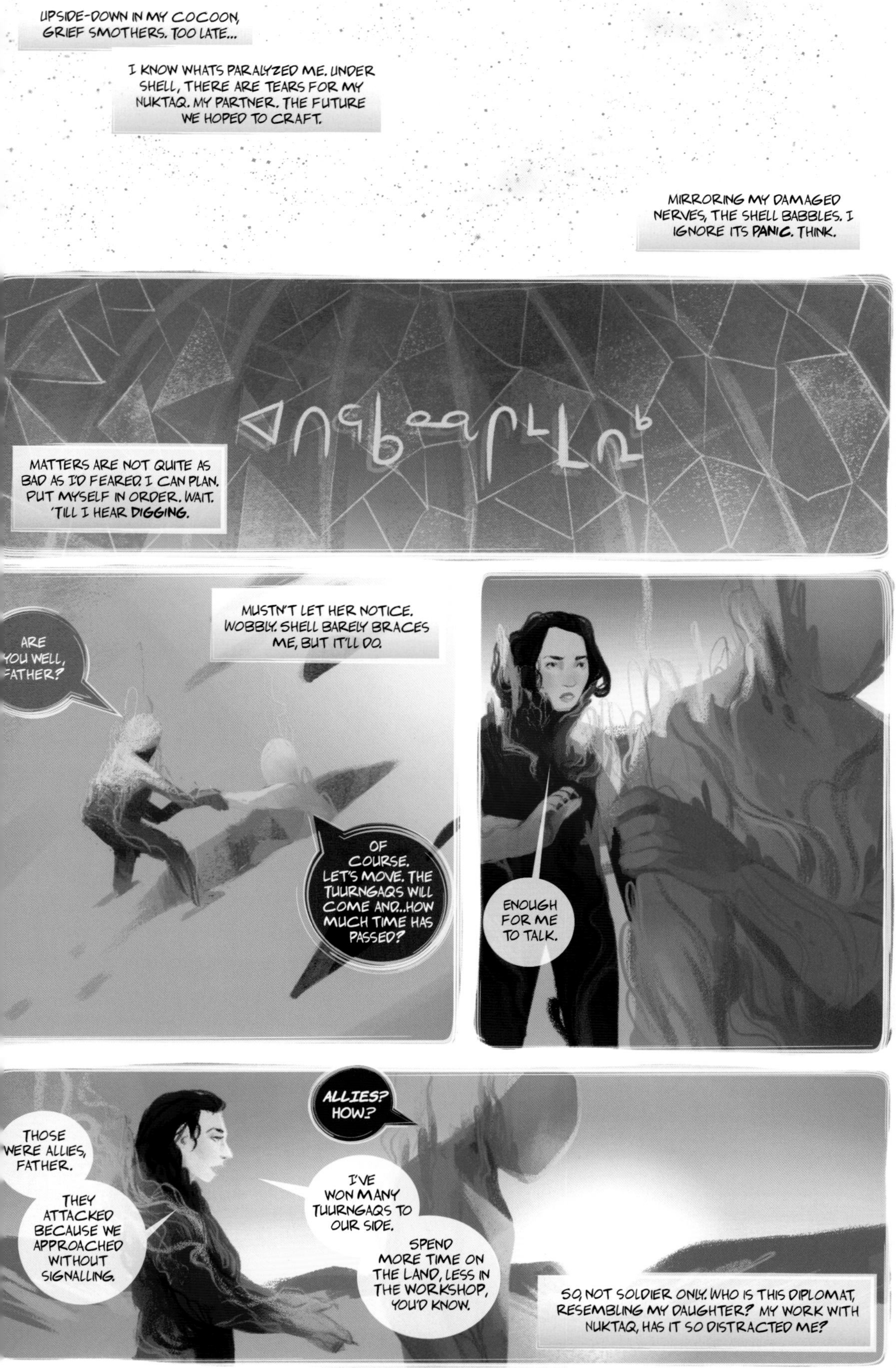
UPSIDE-DOWN IN MY COCOON, GRIEF SMOTHERS. TOO LATE...
I KNOW WHATS PARALYZED ME. UNDER SHELL, THERE ARE TEARS FOR MY NUKTAQ. MY PARTNER. THE FUTURE WE HOPED TO CRAFT.
MIRRORING MY DAMAGED NERVES, THE SHELL BABBLES. I IGNORE ITS PANIC. THINK.
MATTERS ARE NOT QUITE AS BAD AS I'D FEARED. I CAN PLAN. PUT MYSELF IN ORDER. WAIT. 'TILL I HEAR DIGGING.
ARE YOU WELL, FATHER?
MUSTN'T LET HER NOTICE. WOBBLY. SHELL BARELY BRACES ME, BUT IT'LL DO.
OF COURSE. LET'S MOVE. THE TUURNGAQS WILL COME AND...HOW MUCH TIME HAS PASSED?
ENOUGH FOR ME TO TALK.
THOSE WERE ALLIES, FATHER.
THEY ATTACKED BECAUSE WE APPROACHED WITHOUT SIGNALLING.
ALLIES? HOW?
I'VE WON MANY TUURNGAQS TO OUR SIDE.
SPEND MORE TIME ON THE LAND, LESS IN THE WORKSHOP, YOU'D KNOW.
SO, NOT SOLDIER ONLY. WHO IS THIS DIPLOMAT, RESEMBLING MY DAUGHTER? MY WORK WITH NUKTAQ, HAS IT SO DISTRACTED ME?

THE COMPASS HAS NOT YET DIED. LET'S...

WANHOPE, MAKING A SPECTACLE. JUST WALK...

DO YOU THINK I'M A FOOL, FATHER?

CLEVER, BEAUTIFUL VYRMYLION.

WHAT ELSE WOULD YOU DO, IF YOUR NECK WERE BROKEN?

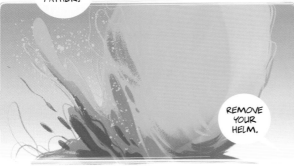

REMOVE YOUR HELM.

YOU'RE USING A BUILDER STRAIN, AREN'T YOU? TO HOLD YOUR BONES TOGETHER.

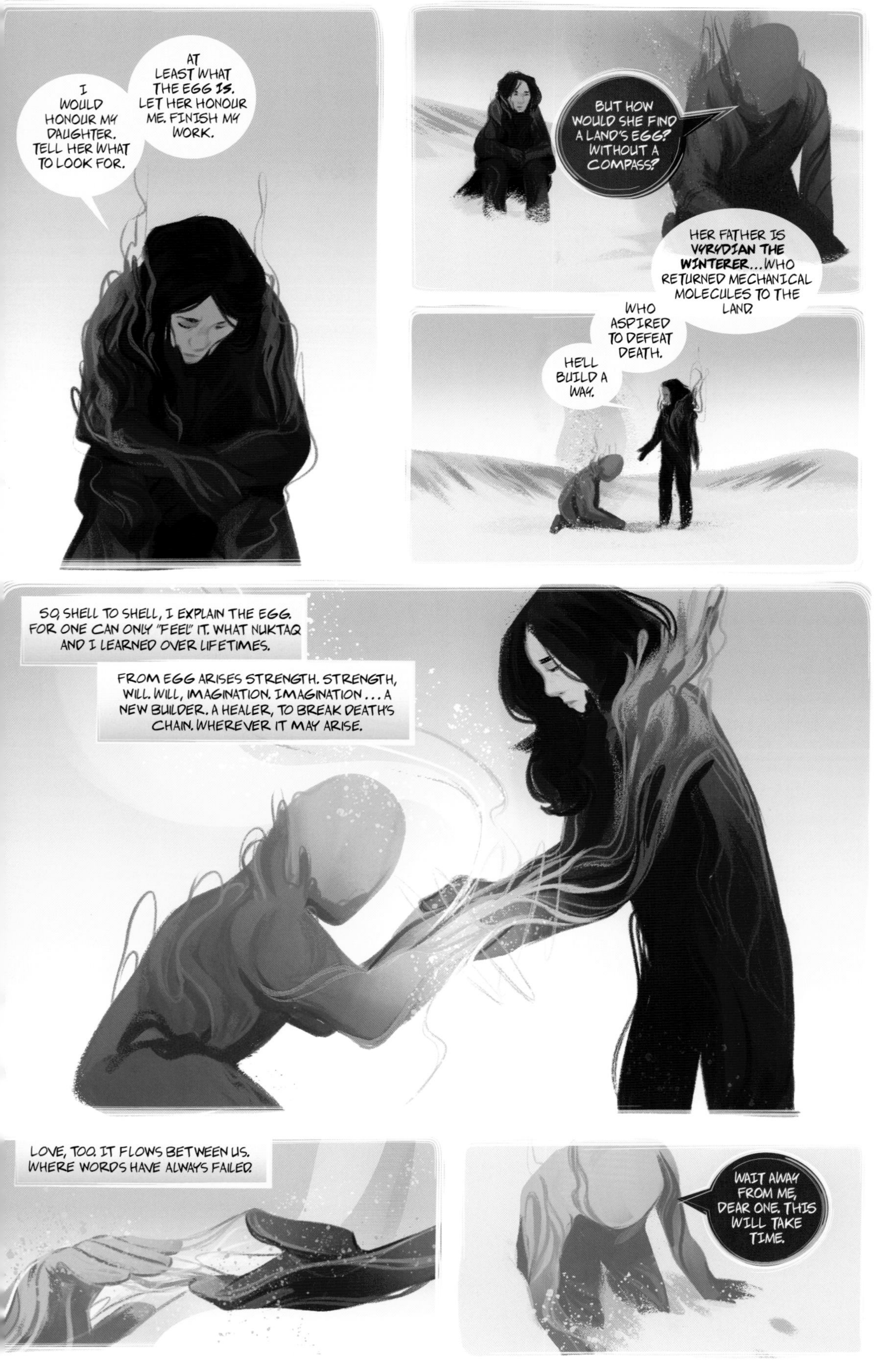
I WOULD HONOUR MY DAUGHTER. TELL HER WHAT TO LOOK FOR.
AT LEAST WHAT THE EGG IS. LET HER HONOUR ME. FINISH MY WORK.
BUT HOW WOULD SHE FIND A LAND'S EGG? WITHOUT A COMPASS?
HER FATHER IS VYRYDIAN THE WINTERER... WHO RETURNED MECHANICAL MOLECULES TO THE LAND.
WHO ASPIRED TO DEFEAT DEATH.
HE'LL BUILD A WAY.
SO, SHELL TO SHELL, I EXPLAIN THE EGG. FOR ONE CAN ONLY "FEEL" IT. WHAT NUKTAQ AND I LEARNED OVER LIFETIMES.
FROM EGG ARISES STRENGTH. STRENGTH, WILL. WILL, IMAGINATION. IMAGINATION . . . A NEW BUILDER. A HEALER, TO BREAK DEATH'S CHAIN. WHEREVER IT MAY ARISE.
LOVE, TOO. IT FLOWS BETWEEN US. WHERE WORDS HAVE ALWAYS FAILED.
WAIT AWAY FROM ME, DEAR ONE. THIS WILL TAKE TIME.

FALL BACK, LISTEN TO HER FOOTFALL IN SNOW.

SHE KNOWS, OF OLD, I MUST **BECOME**.

MY OWN WORKSHOP. MY FACTORY. MY **CRAFT**.

I FORGE. A NEW BUILDER ARISES. BUT NOT MY HEALER. FOR FORGING THAT IS NOW VYRMYLION'S TASK. THIS ONE JUST...FORAGES.

IN MY GUT, IT FINDS THE LAST OF NUKTAQ'S BLOSSOM.

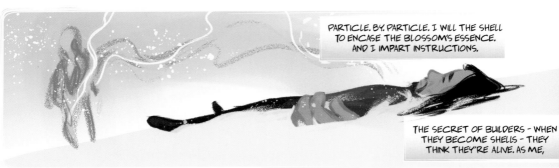

PARTICLE. BY. PARTICLE. I WILL THE SHELL TO ENCASE THE BLOSSOM'S ESSENCE. AND I IMPART INSTRUCTIONS.

THE SECRET OF BUILDERS – WHEN THEY BECOME SHELLS – THEY THINK THEY'RE ALIVE. AS ME,

BLOSSOM INSIDE, MY SHELL WILL LEAD VYRMYLION.

LONG ENOUGH. TO FIND AN EGG. THEN? UP TO HER.

GENIUS-DAUGHTER, NEVER JUST WARRIOR, HER WISDOM WALKS WITH MY SHELL.

NUKTAQ, YOU SAID THERE WAS ALWAYS MORE. I WILL DREAM HERE. OF FIREWEED. AND WAIT.

– END –

Darcie Little Badger's

WORST BARGAIN IN TOWN

Illustrated by Rossi Gifford

BACKGROUND

For many Lipan people, hair is more than a fashion statement; it has spiritual significance and must not be cut without an important reason. (In 2009, a Lipan Apache boy in Texas successfully defended his religious rights and freedom in court after the school claimed his long hair was a dress code violation.) The Lipan recognize hair as a source of personal strength. They also believe partners can support each other by weaving a lock of hair into their own. In some traditional stories, young people were warned about corrupted individuals who are able to drain strength from stolen hair. Members of the Lipan Apache Tribe have always fought to protect themselves from sinister forces, including the colonialism-driven appropriation of cultural beliefs. "Worst Bargain in Town" was written as a metaphor for the ongoing appropriation and erasure of Indigenous cultures, using the traditional belief of hair as a fountain of enduring strength and spirit. In this way, the antagonist in this story represents both new and ancient evil.

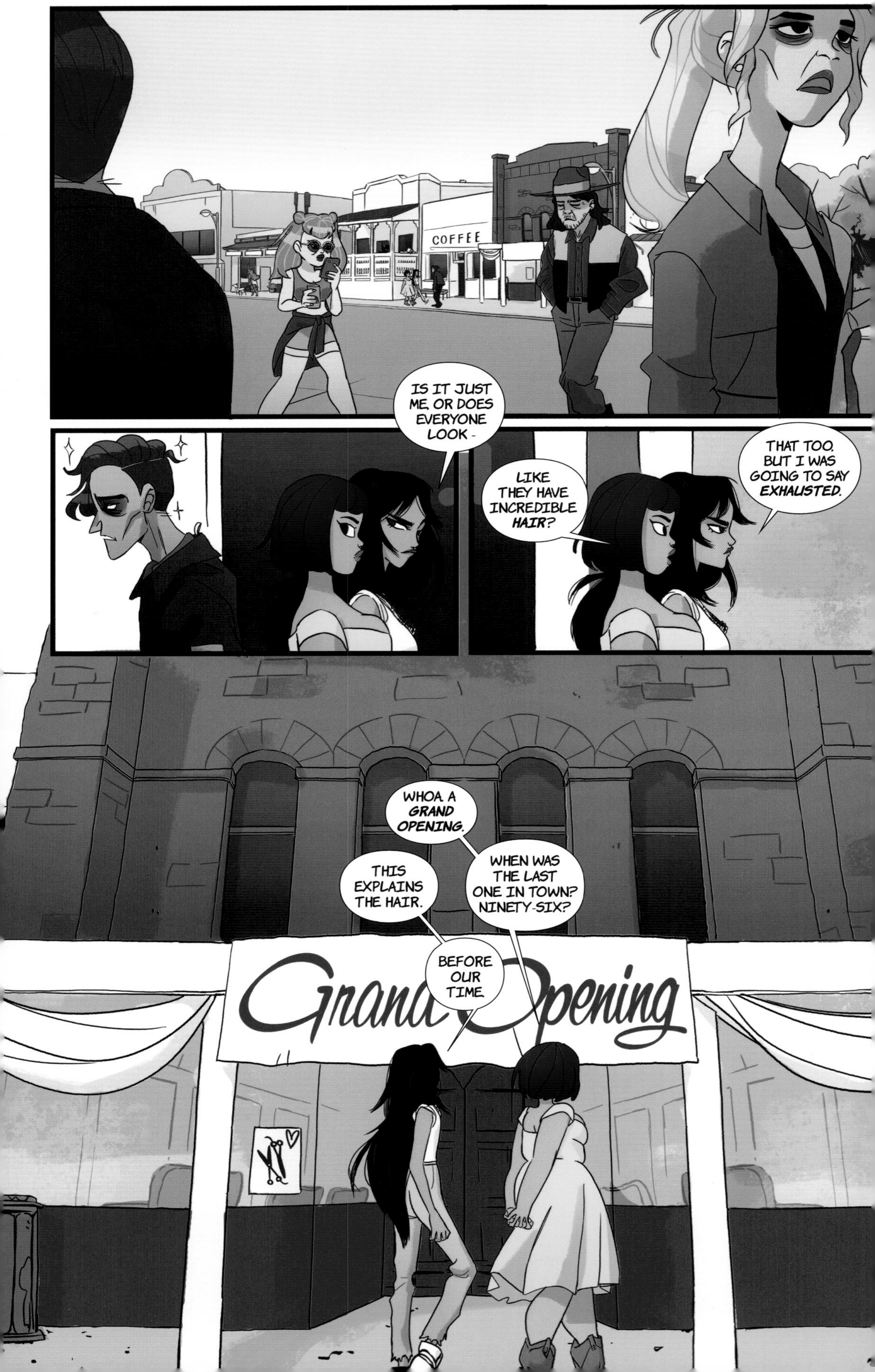
COFFEE
IS IT JUST ME, OR DOES EVERYONE LOOK -
LIKE THEY HAVE INCREDIBLE HAIR?
THAT TOO. BUT I WAS GOING TO SAY EXHAUSTED.
WHOA. A GRAND OPENING.
WHEN WAS THE LAST ONE IN TOWN? NINETY-SIX?
THIS EXPLAINS THE HAIR.
BEFORE OUR TIME.
Grand Opening

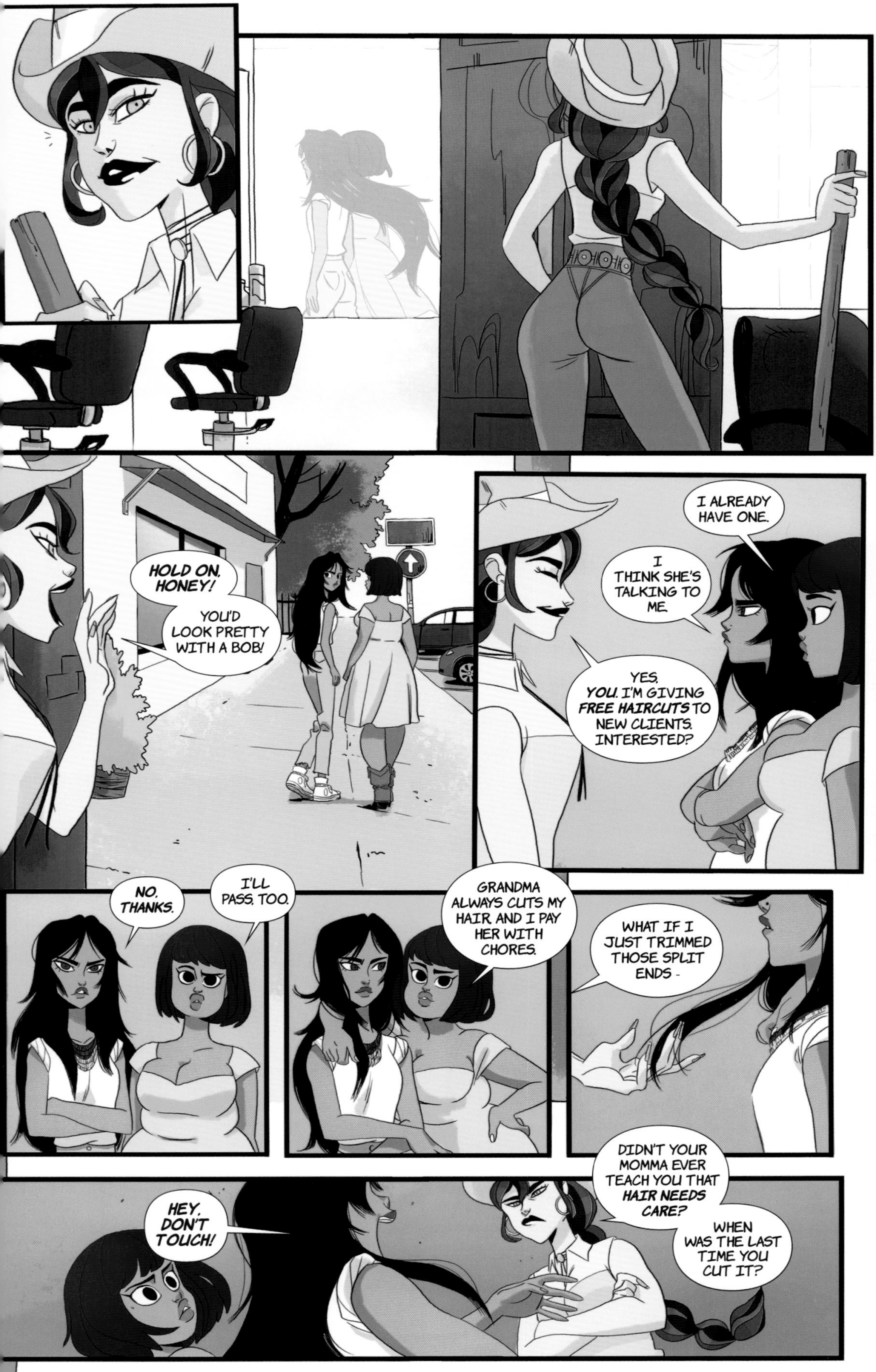
HOLD ON, HONEY!
YOU'D LOOK PRETTY WITH A BOB!
I ALREADY HAVE ONE.
I THINK SHE'S TALKING TO ME.
YES, YOU. I'M GIVING FREE HAIRCUTS TO NEW CLIENTS. INTERESTED?
NO, THANKS.
I'LL PASS, TOO.
GRANDMA ALWAYS CUTS MY HAIR, AND I PAY HER WITH CHORES.
WHAT IF I JUST TRIMMED THOSE SPLIT ENDS -
HEY, DON'T TOUCH!
DIDN'T YOUR MOMMA EVER TEACH YOU THAT HAIR NEEDS CARE?
WHEN WAS THE LAST TIME YOU CUT IT?

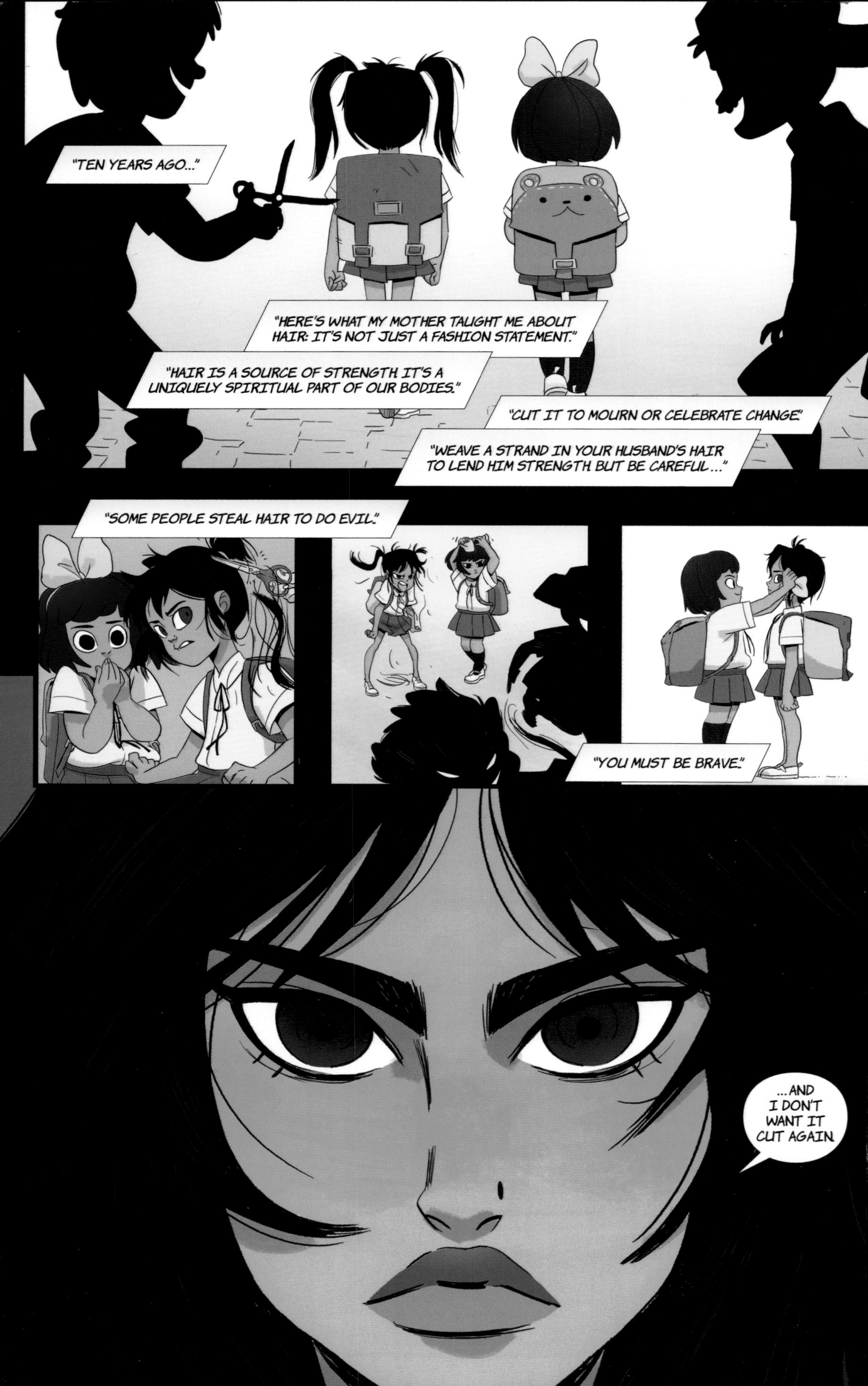
"TEN YEARS AGO..."
"HERE'S WHAT MY MOTHER TAUGHT ME ABOUT HAIR: IT'S NOT JUST A FASHION STATEMENT."
"HAIR IS A SOURCE OF STRENGTH. IT'S A UNIQUELY SPIRITUAL PART OF OUR BODIES."
"CUT IT TO MOURN OR CELEBRATE CHANGE."
"WEAVE A STRAND IN YOUR HUSBAND'S HAIR TO LEND HIM STRENGTH. BUT BE CAREFUL..."
"SOME PEOPLE STEAL HAIR TO DO EVIL."
"YOU MUST BE BRAVE."
...AND I DON'T WANT IT CUT AGAIN.

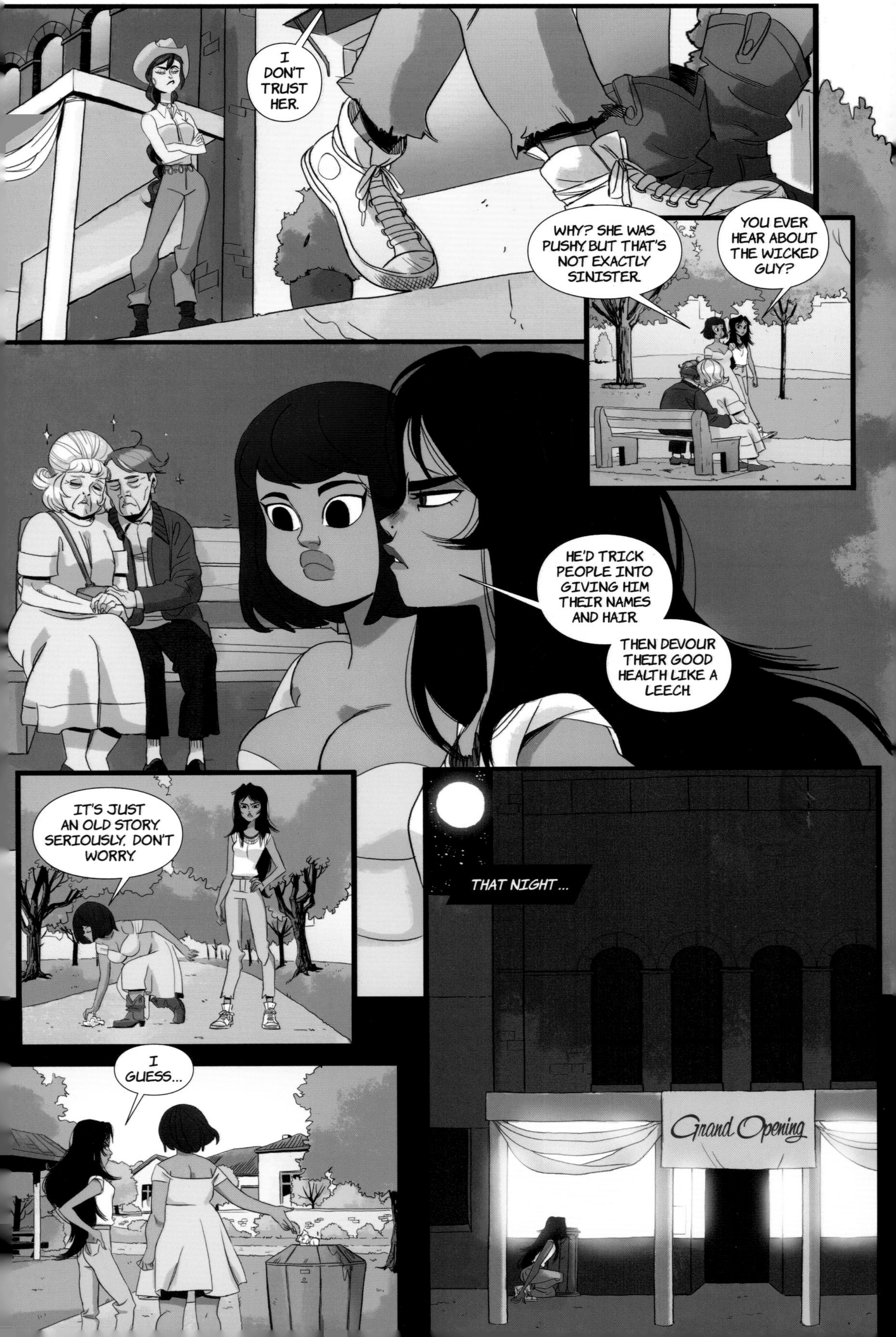

I DON'T TRUST HER.
WHY? SHE WAS PUSHY. BUT THAT'S NOT EXACTLY SINISTER.
YOU EVER HEAR ABOUT THE WICKED GUY?
HE'D TRICK PEOPLE INTO GIVING HIM THEIR NAMES AND HAIR.
THEN DEVOUR THEIR GOOD HEALTH LIKE A LEECH.
IT'S JUST AN OLD STORY. SERIOUSLY, DON'T WORRY.
I GUESS...
THAT NIGHT...
Grand Opening

LEECH.

THIS IS NOT
HOW I PLANNED
TO SPEND MY
LUNCH BREAK
KAI

SORRY.
BUT WE
HAVE TO DO
SOMETHING.

SHE'S
MAKING
EVERYONE
SICK!

LIKE THE
STORY YO
TOLD ME
REALLY?

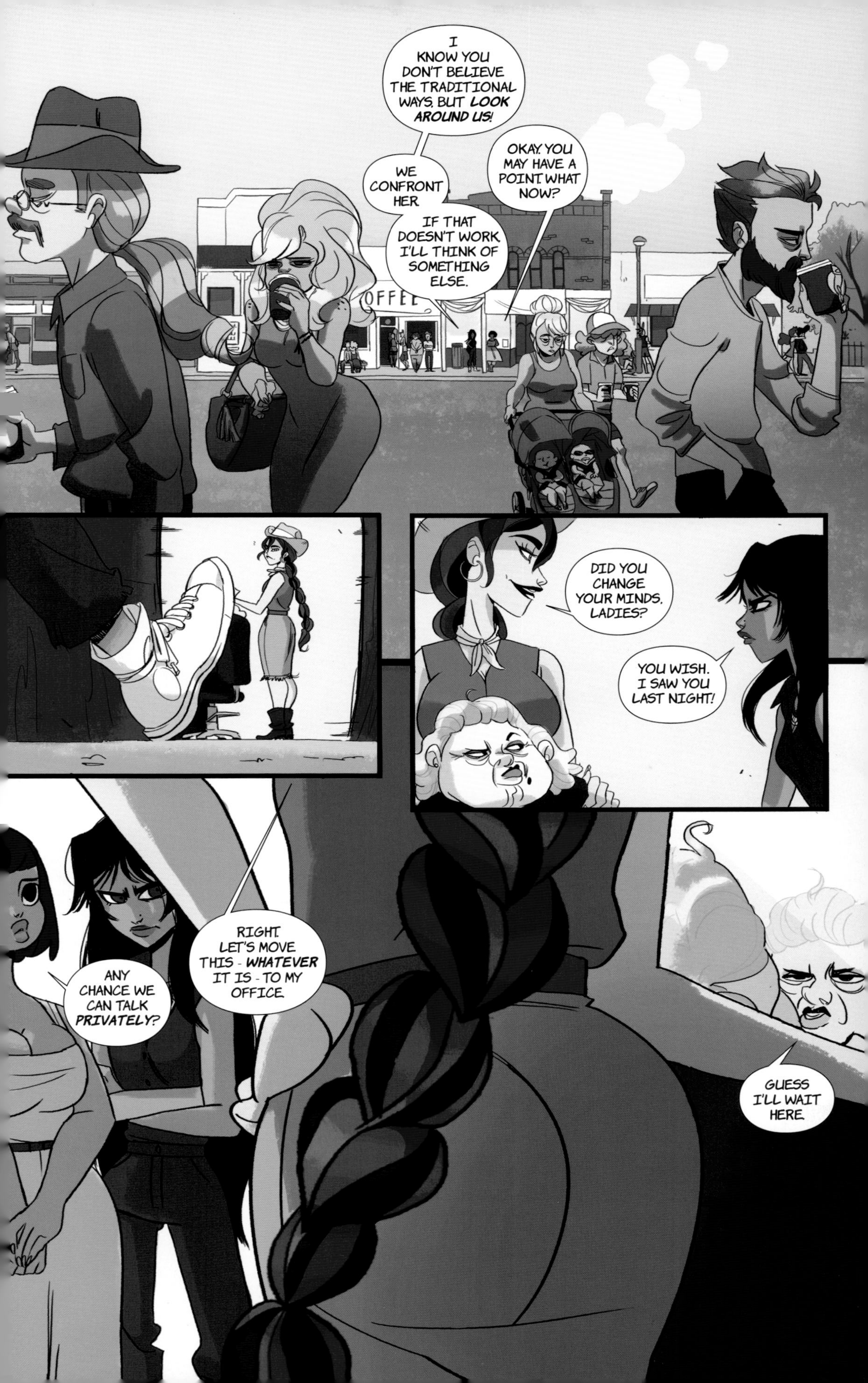
I KNOW YOU DON'T BELIEVE THE TRADITIONAL WAYS, BUT LOOK AROUND US!
WE CONFRONT HER.
IF THAT DOESN'T WORK, I'LL THINK OF SOMETHING ELSE.
OKAY. YOU MAY HAVE A POINT. WHAT NOW?
OFFEE
DID YOU CHANGE YOUR MINDS, LADIES?
YOU WISH. I SAW YOU LAST NIGHT!
ANY CHANCE WE CAN TALK PRIVATELY?
RIGHT. LET'S MOVE THIS - WHATEVER IT IS - TO MY OFFICE.
GUESS I'LL WAIT HERE.

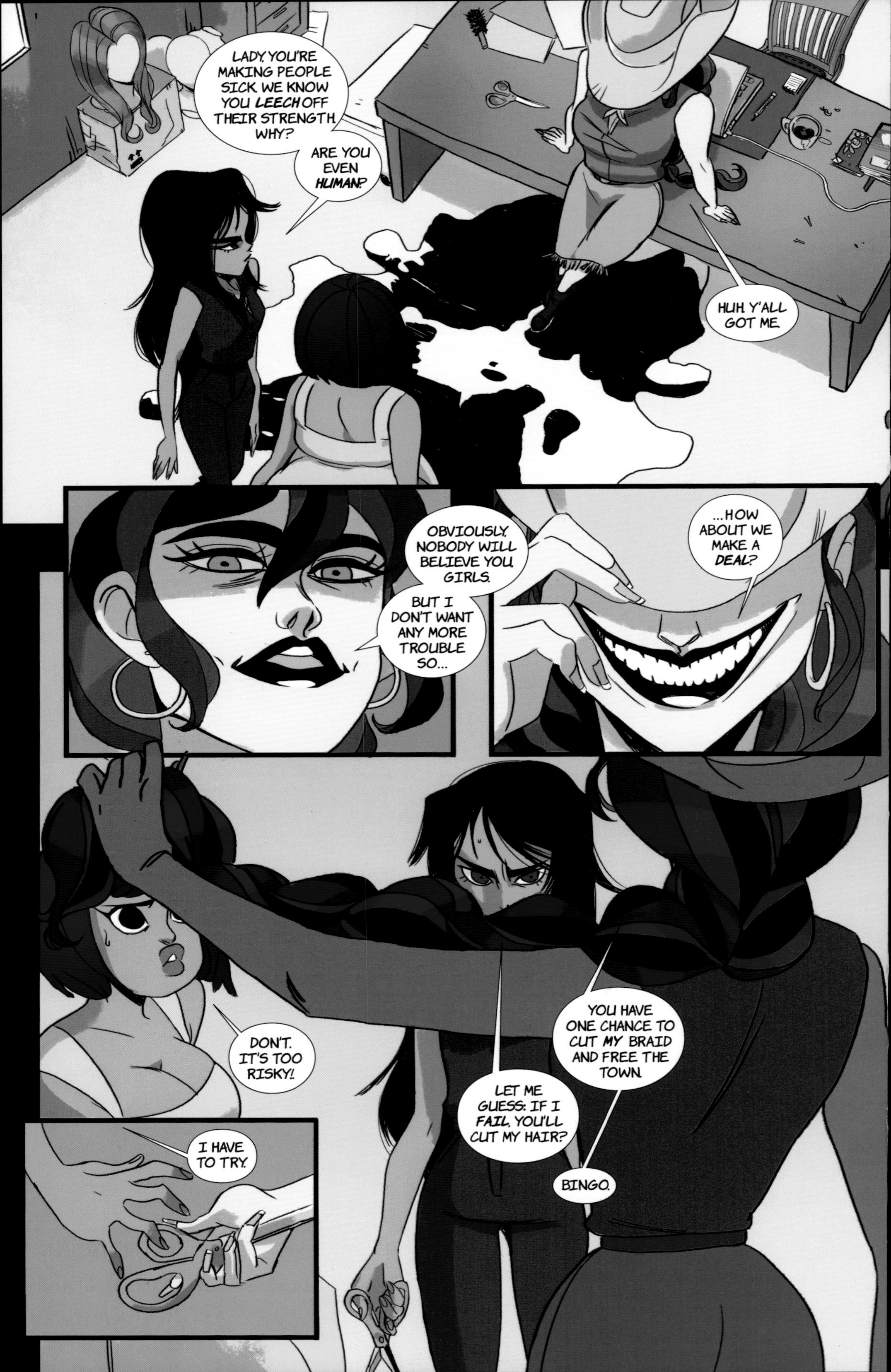
LADY, YOU'RE MAKING PEOPLE SICK. WE KNOW YOU LEECH OFF THEIR STRENGTH. WHY?
ARE YOU EVEN HUMAN?
HUH. Y'ALL GOT ME.
OBVIOUSLY, NOBODY WILL BELIEVE YOU, GIRLS.
BUT I DON'T WANT ANY MORE TROUBLE SO...
...HOW ABOUT WE MAKE A DEAL?
YOU HAVE ONE CHANCE TO CUT MY BRAID AND FREE THE TOWN.
DON'T. IT'S TOO RISKY!
LET ME GUESS: IF I FAIL, YOU'LL CUT MY HAIR?
BINGO.
I HAVE TO TRY.

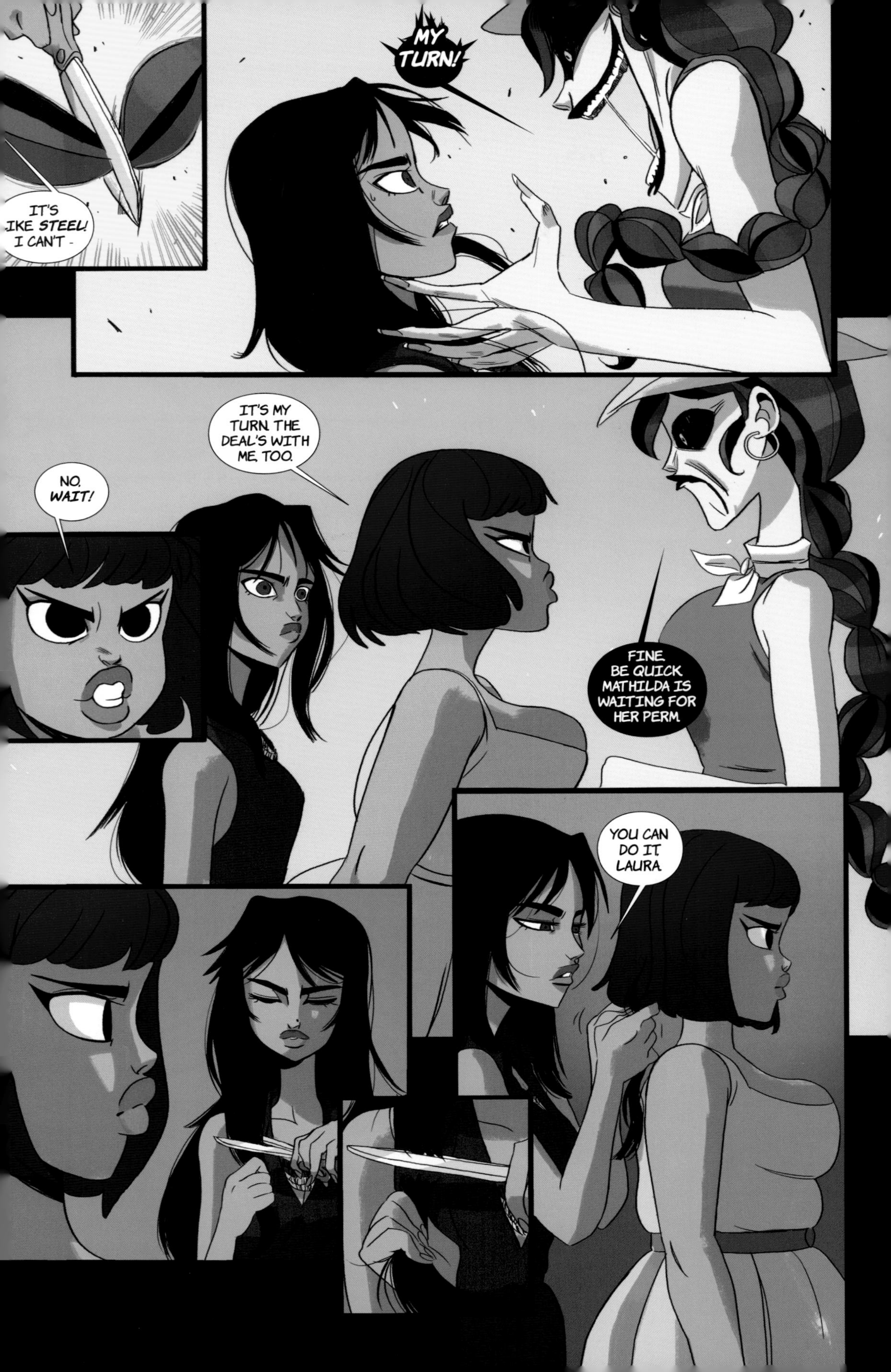
IT'S
LIKE STEEL! I CAN'T -
MY TURN!
IT'S MY TURN. THE DEAL'S WITH ME, TOO.
NO. WAIT!
FINE. BE QUICK. MATHILDA IS WAITING FOR HER PERM.
YOU CAN DO IT, LAURA.

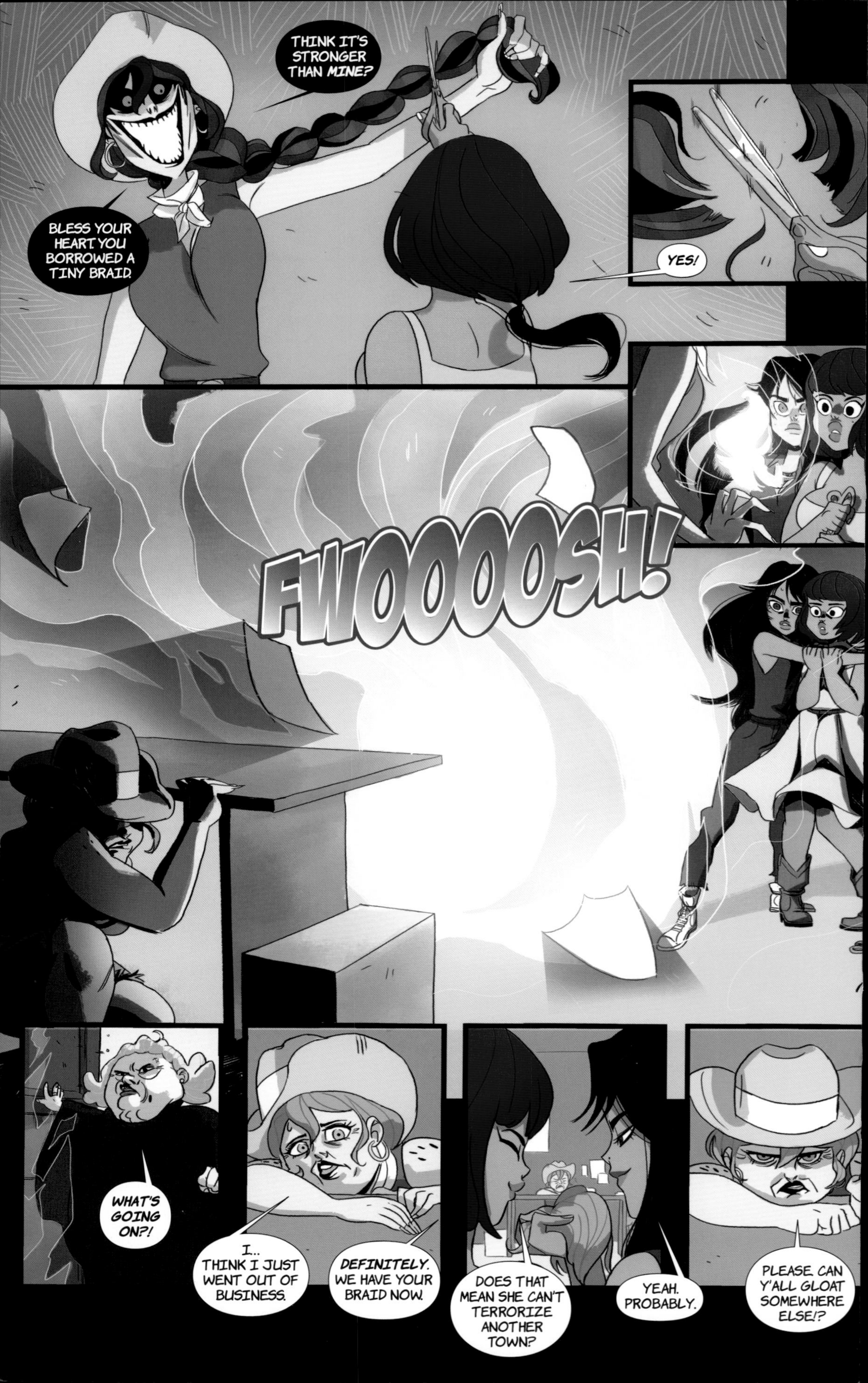
THINK IT'S STRONGER THAN MINE?
BLESS YOUR HEART. YOU BORROWED A TINY BRAID.
YES!
FWOOOOOSH!
WHAT'S GOING ON?!
I... THINK I JUST WENT OUT OF BUSINESS.
DEFINITELY. WE HAVE YOUR BRAID NOW.
DOES THAT MEAN SHE CAN'T TERRORIZE ANOTHER TOWN?
YEAH. PROBABLY.
PLEASE. CAN Y'ALL GLOAT SOMEWHERE ELSE!?

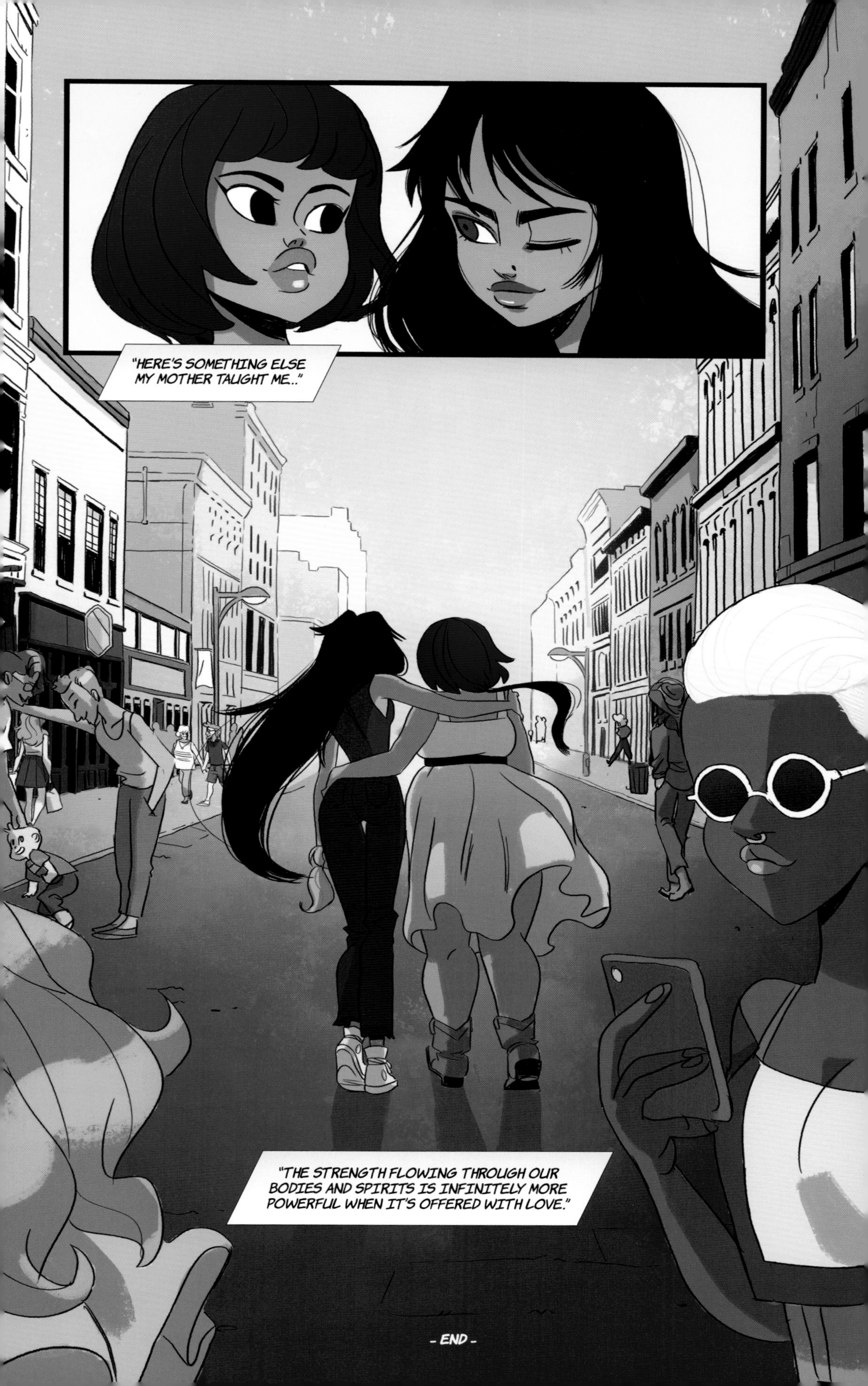
"HERE'S SOMETHING ELSE MY MOTHER TAUGHT ME..."
"THE STRENGTH FLOWING THROUGH OUR BODIES AND SPIRITS IS INFINITELY MORE POWERFUL WHEN IT'S OFFERED WITH LOVE."
- END -

Alina Pete's

KA'TEPWA: WHO CALLS?

Illustrated by Trudi Castle

BACKGROUND

The Calling Lakes are a series of four connected bodies of water in the Qu'Apelle Valley, Canada. The name (translated as "Who calls?" in English) was given to this region, located in south Saskatchewan, based on the Cree spirit known to call out from the river that connects the Calling Lakes. It is said the spirit calls, "Kâ-têpwêt?", which is Cree for "Who is calling?" Two of the lakes, Katepwa Lake ("Katepwa" is the Anglicized version of the traditional Cree word) and Echo Lake are named after this legend, as it is said that when someone calls out across the water, the spirit responds. The author is from nearby Little Pine First Nations, and her grandmother's people come from Cowessess First Nation in the Qu'Apelle Valley. The tale presented here is based on the stories heard through her own family's history.

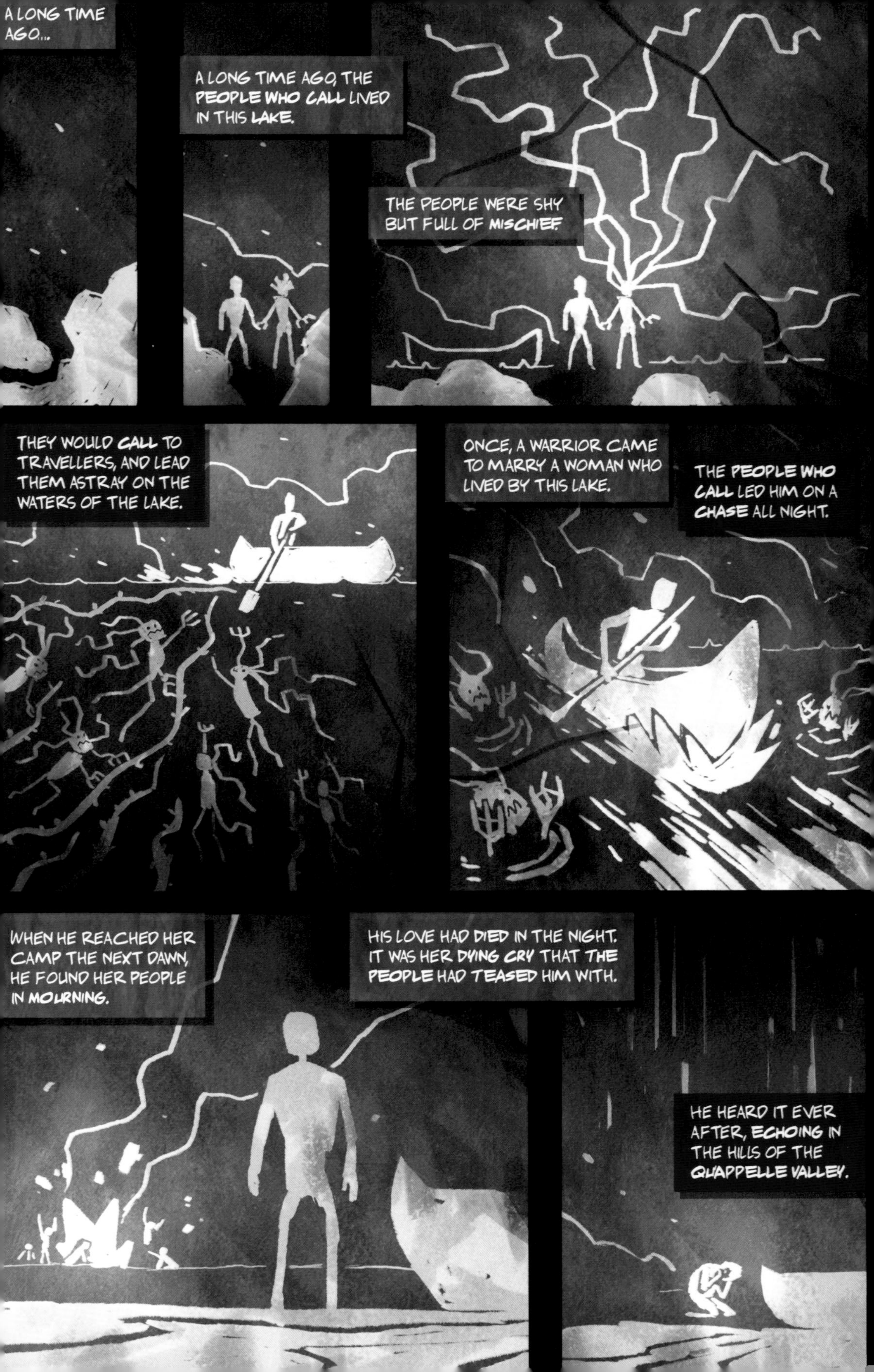
A LONG TIME AGO...
A LONG TIME AGO, THE PEOPLE WHO CALL LIVED IN THIS LAKE.
THE PEOPLE WERE SHY BUT FULL OF MISCHIEF.
THEY WOULD CALL TO TRAVELLERS, AND LEAD THEM ASTRAY ON THE WATERS OF THE LAKE.
ONCE, A WARRIOR CAME TO MARRY A WOMAN WHO LIVED BY THIS LAKE.
THE PEOPLE WHO CALL LED HIM ON A CHASE ALL NIGHT.
WHEN HE REACHED HER CAMP THE NEXT DAWN, HE FOUND HER PEOPLE IN MOURNING.
HIS LOVE HAD DIED IN THE NIGHT. IT WAS HER DYING CRY THAT THE PEOPLE HAD TEASED HIM WITH.
HE HEARD IT EVER AFTER, ECHOING IN THE HILLS OF THE QU'APPELLE VALLEY.

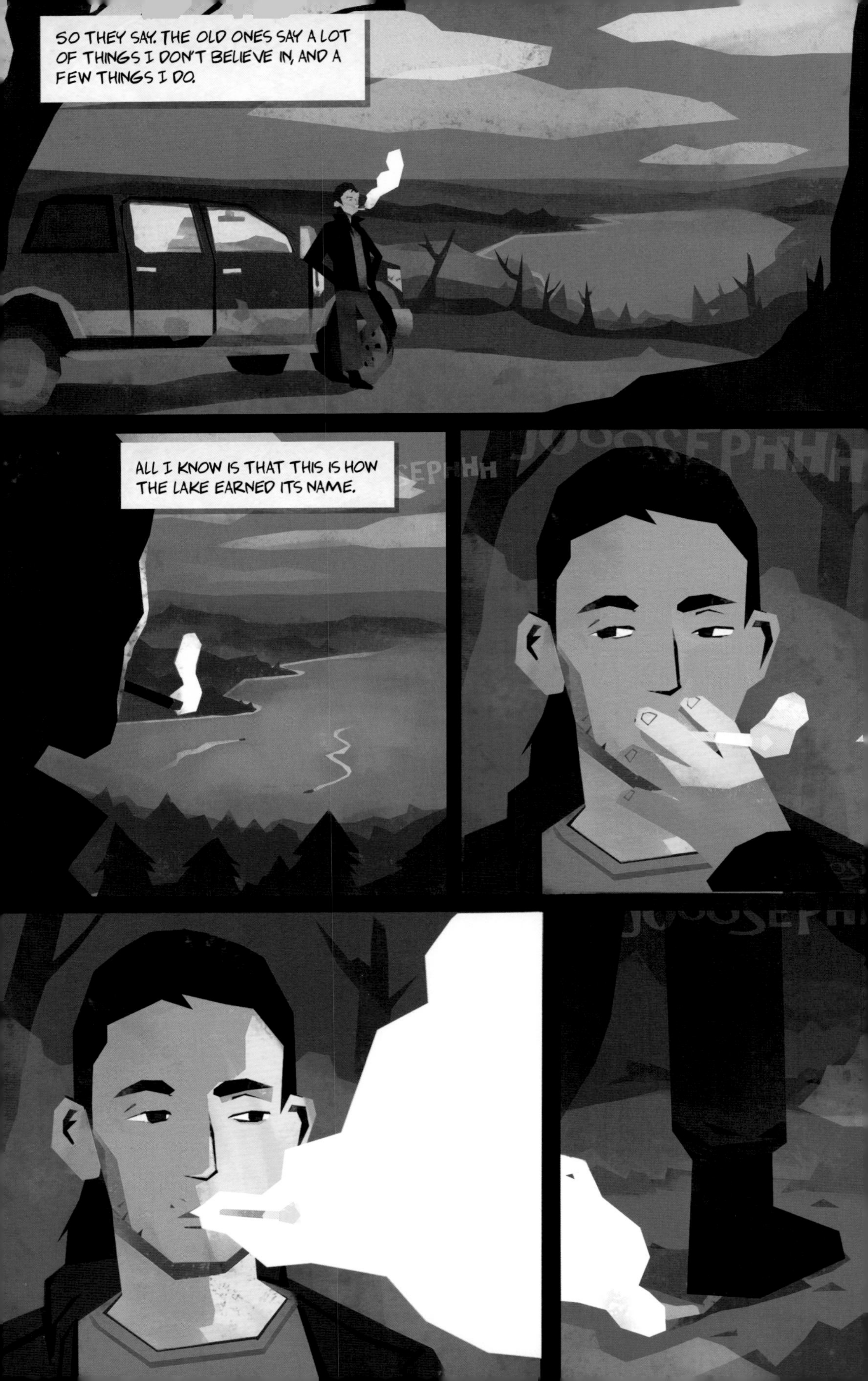
SO THEY SAY. THE OLD ONES SAY A LOT OF THINGS I DON'T BELIEVE IN, AND A FEW THINGS I DO.
ALL I KNOW IS THAT THIS IS HOW THE LAKE EARNED ITS NAME.
SEPHHH
JOOOSEPHHH

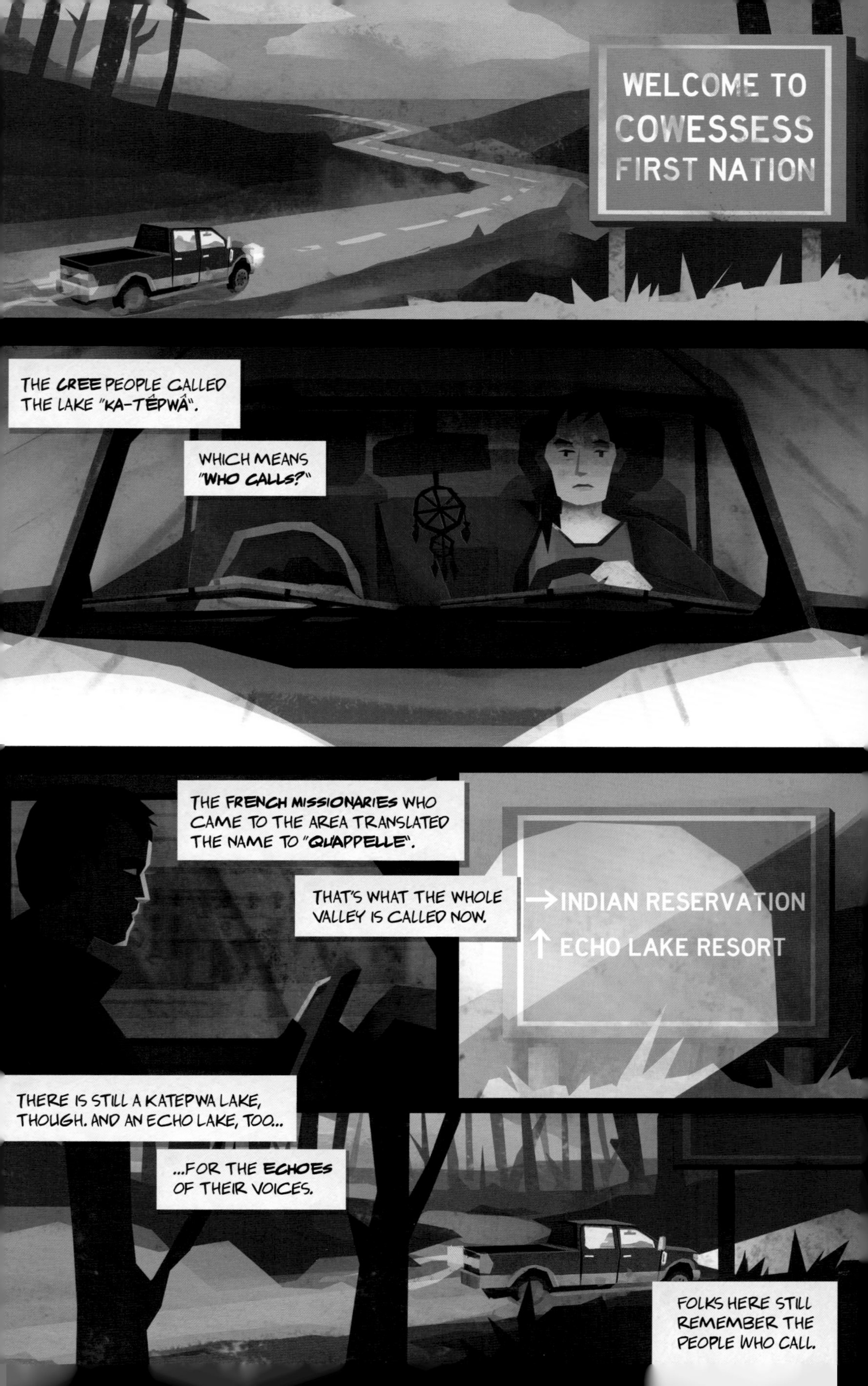

WELCOME TO COWESSESS FIRST NATION
THE **CREE** PEOPLE CALLED THE LAKE "**KA-TÊPWÂ**".
WHICH MEANS "**WHO CALLS?**"
THE **FRENCH MISSIONARIES** WHO CAME TO THE AREA TRANSLATED THE NAME TO "**QU'APPELLE**".
THAT'S WHAT THE WHOLE VALLEY IS CALLED NOW.
→INDIAN RESERVATION
↑ ECHO LAKE RESORT
THERE IS STILL A KATEPWA LAKE, THOUGH. AND AN ECHO LAKE, TOO...
...FOR THE **ECHOES** OF THEIR VOICES.
FOLKS HERE STILL REMEMBER THE PEOPLE WHO CALL.

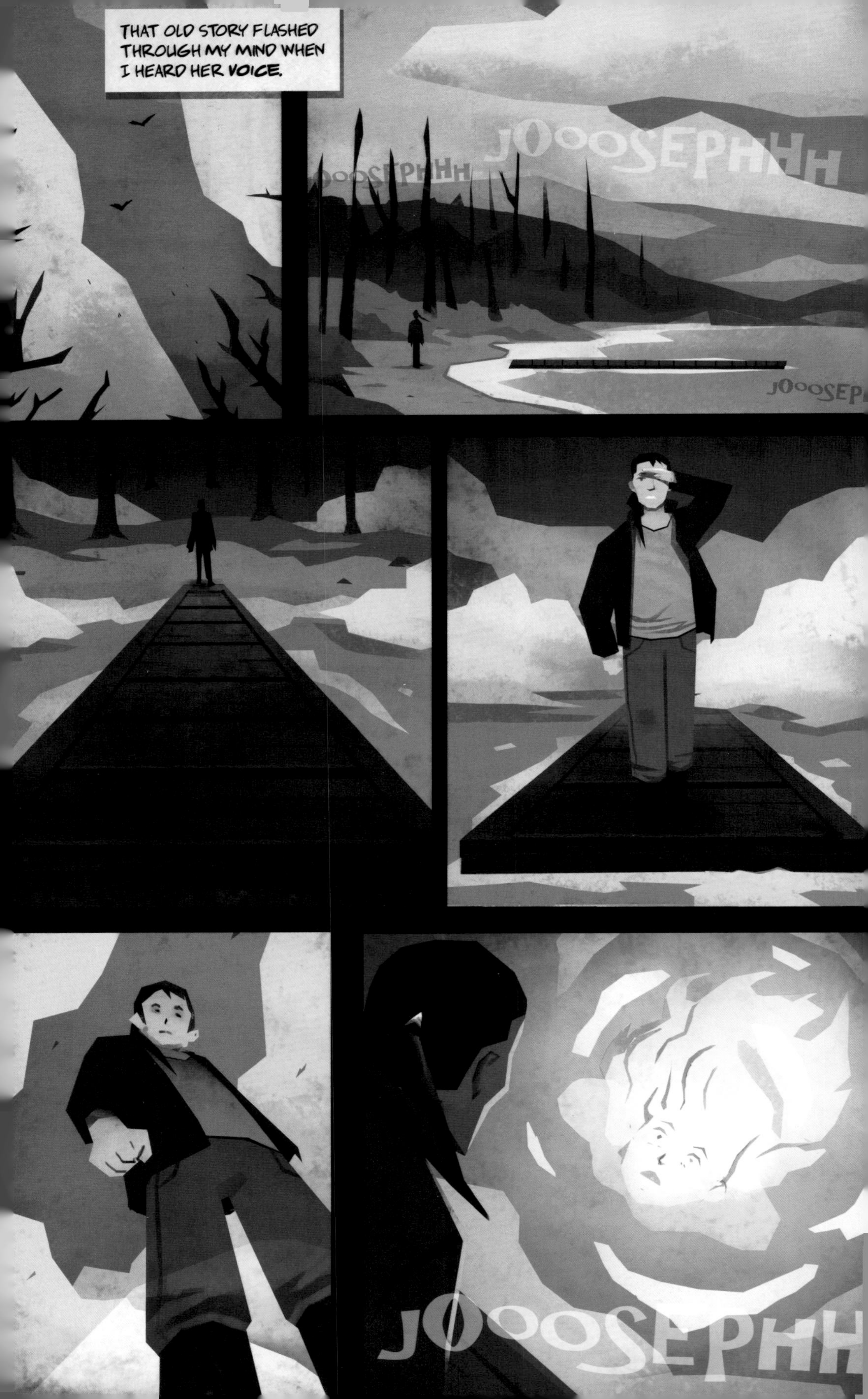

THAT OLD STORY FLASHED THROUGH MY MIND WHEN I HEARD HER VOICE.
JOOOSEPHHH
JOOOSEPHHH
JOOOSEP
JOOOSEPHH

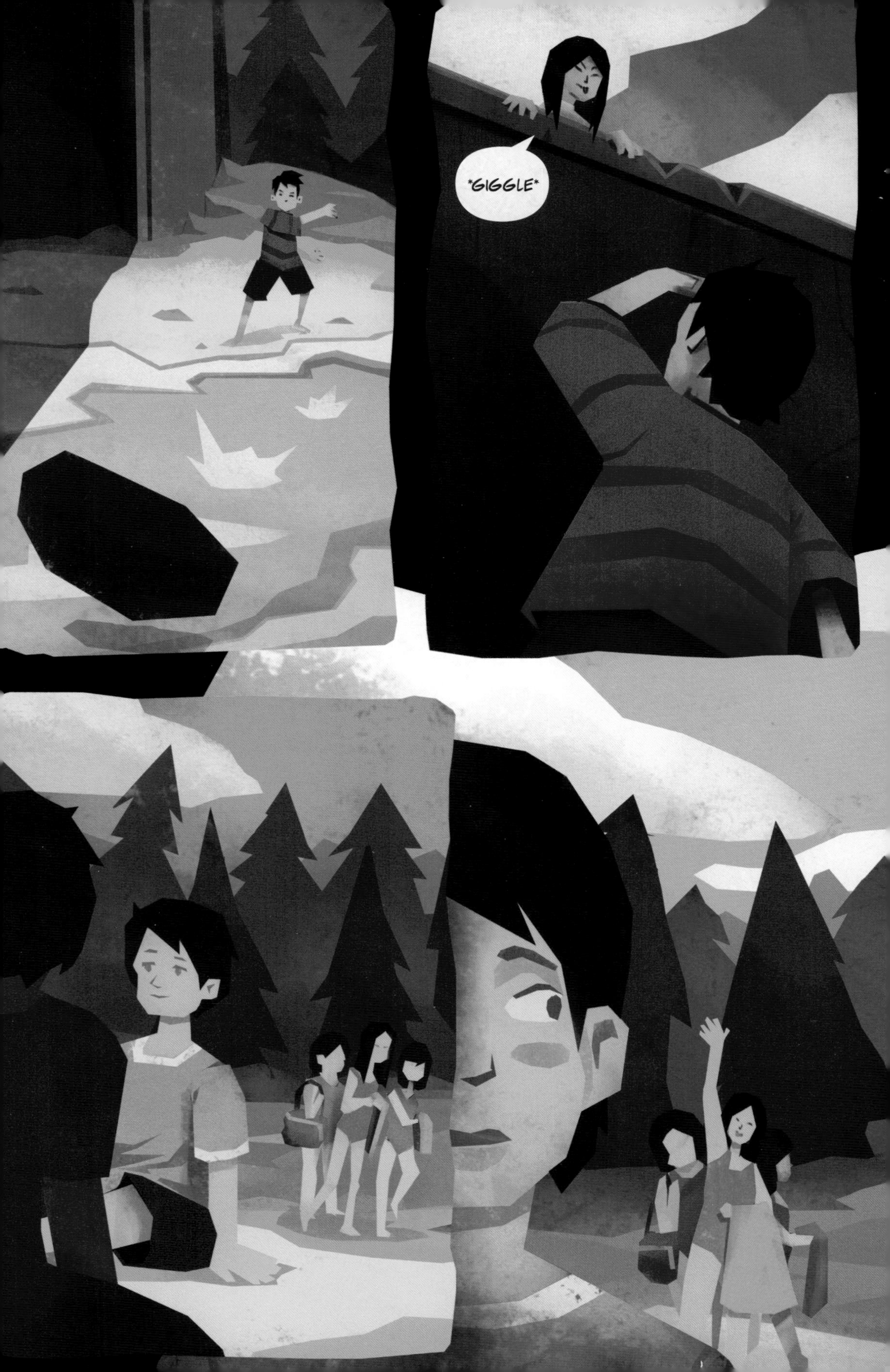
GIGGLE

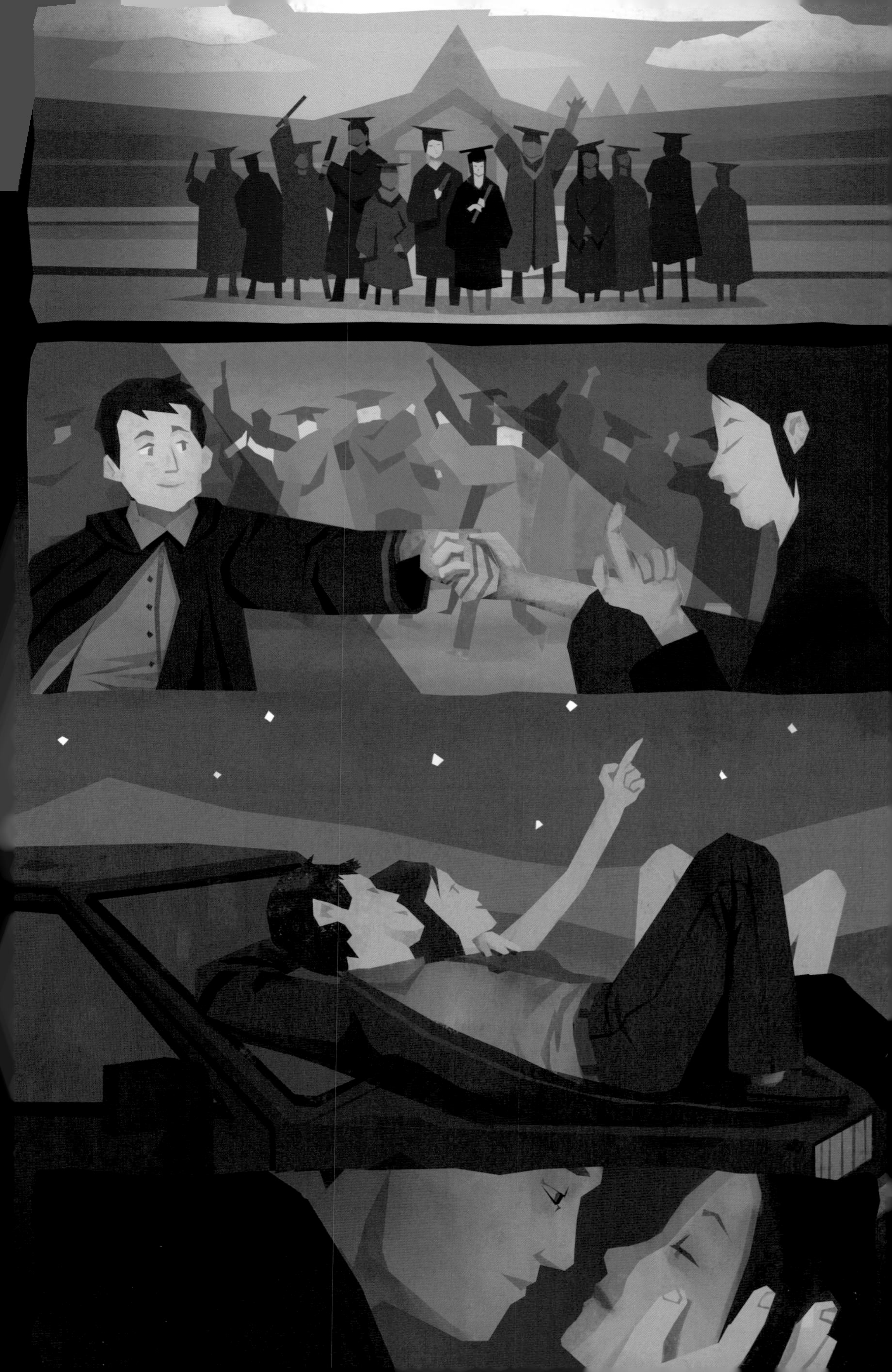

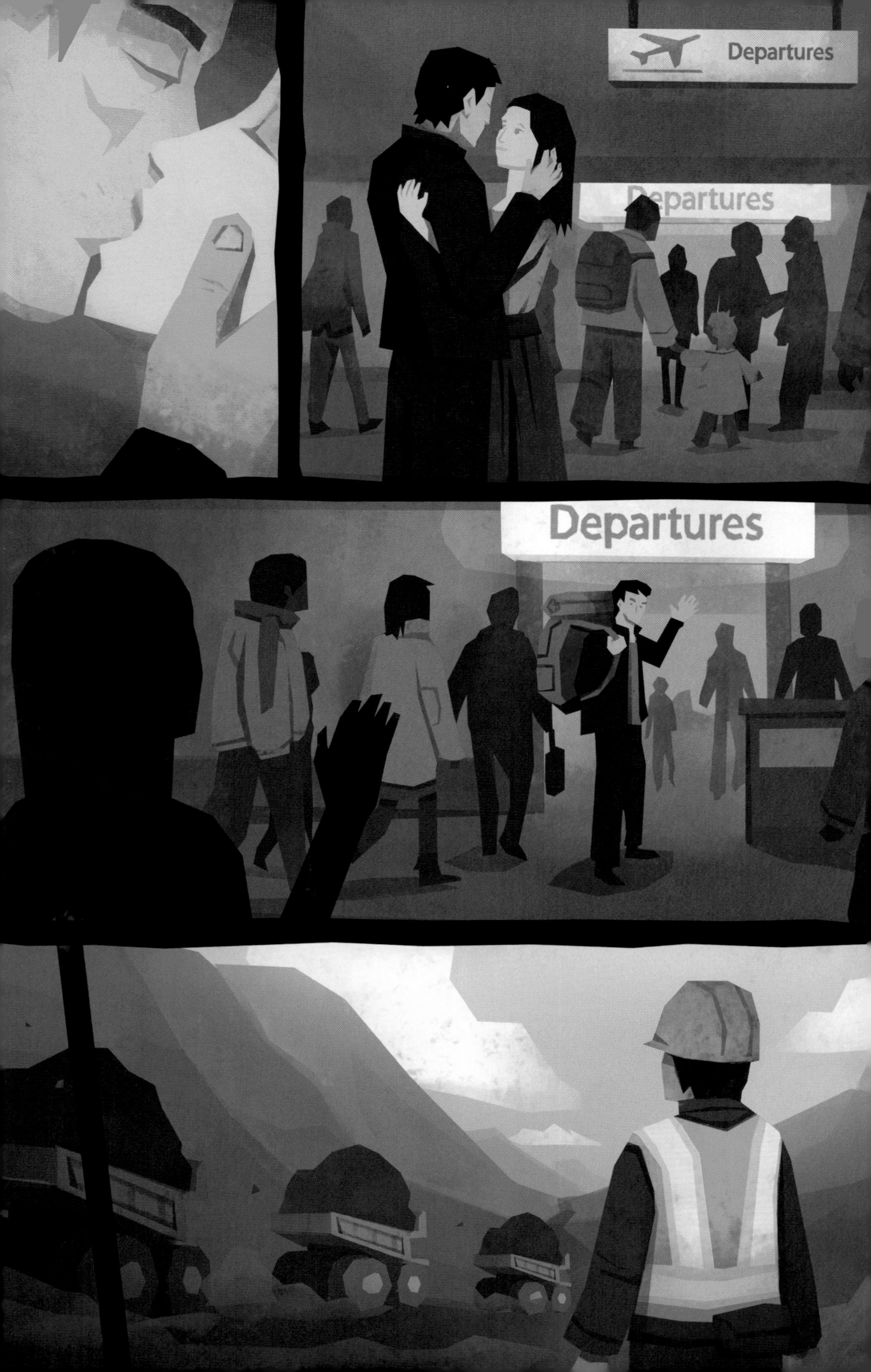
Departures
Departures
Departures

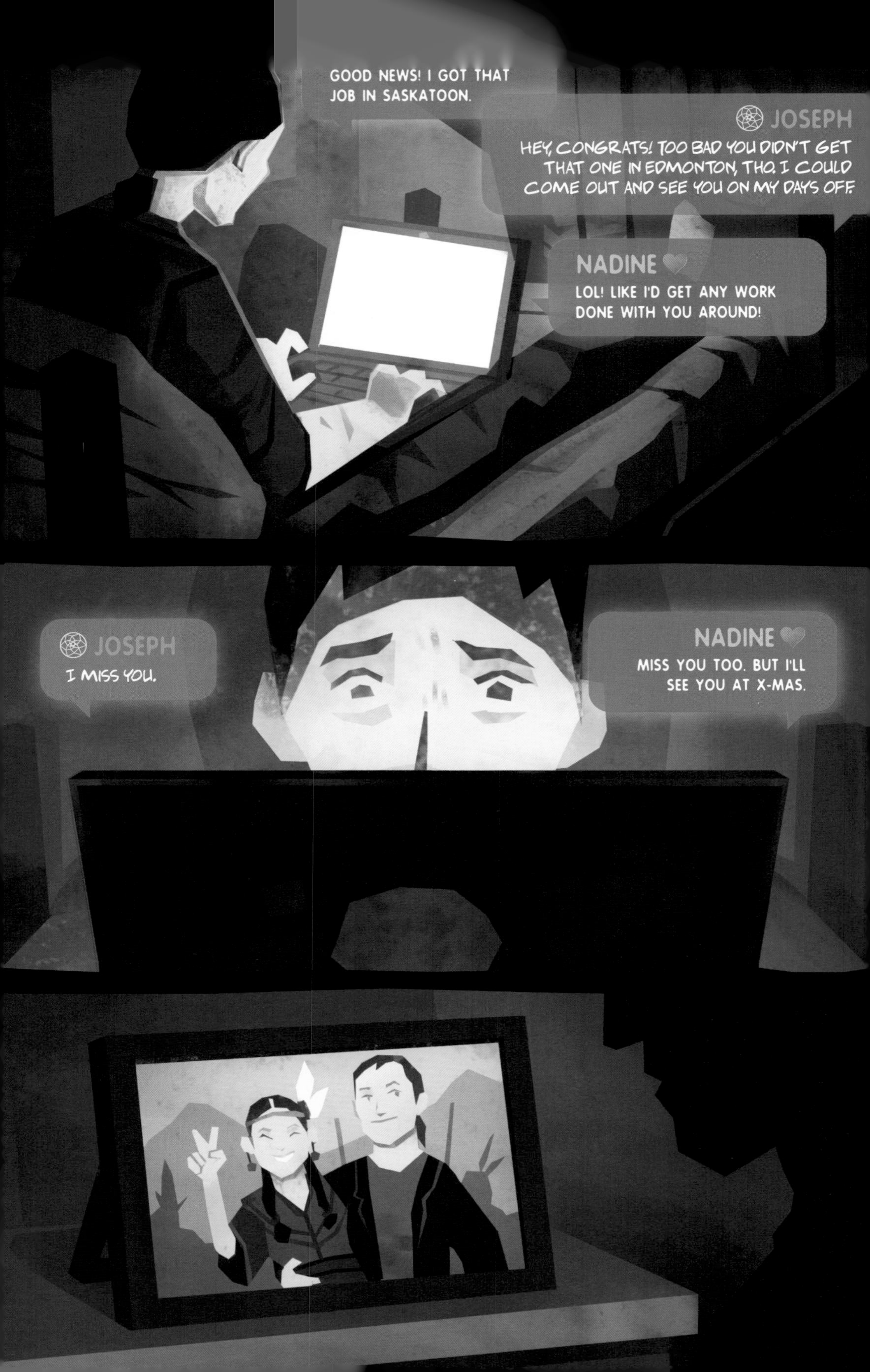
GOOD NEWS! I GOT THAT JOB IN SASKATOON.
JOSEPH
HEY, CONGRATS! TOO BAD YOU DIDN'T GET THAT ONE IN EDMONTON, THO. I COULD COME OUT AND SEE YOU ON MY DAYS OFF.
NADINE
LOL! LIKE I'D GET ANY WORK DONE WITH YOU AROUND!
JOSEPH
I MISS YOU.
NADINE
MISS YOU TOO. BUT I'LL SEE YOU AT X-MAS.

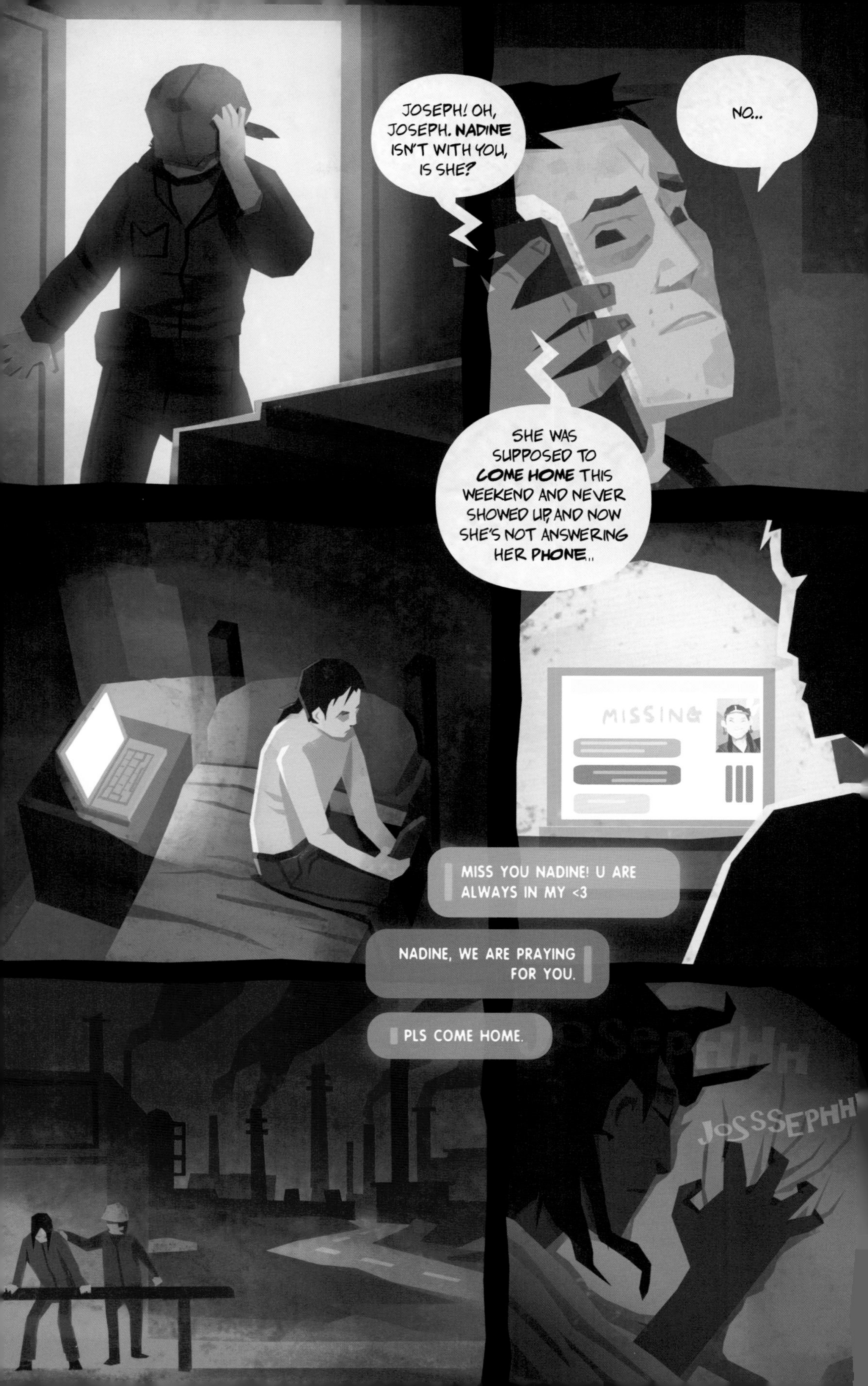
JOSEPH! OH, JOSEPH. NADINE ISN'T WITH YOU, IS SHE?
NO...
SHE WAS SUPPOSED TO COME HOME THIS WEEKEND AND NEVER SHOWED UP, AND NOW SHE'S NOT ANSWERING HER PHONE...
MISSING
MISS YOU NADINE! U ARE ALWAYS IN MY <3
NADINE, WE ARE PRAYING FOR YOU.
PLS COME HOME.
JOSSSEPHHH
JOSSSEPHH

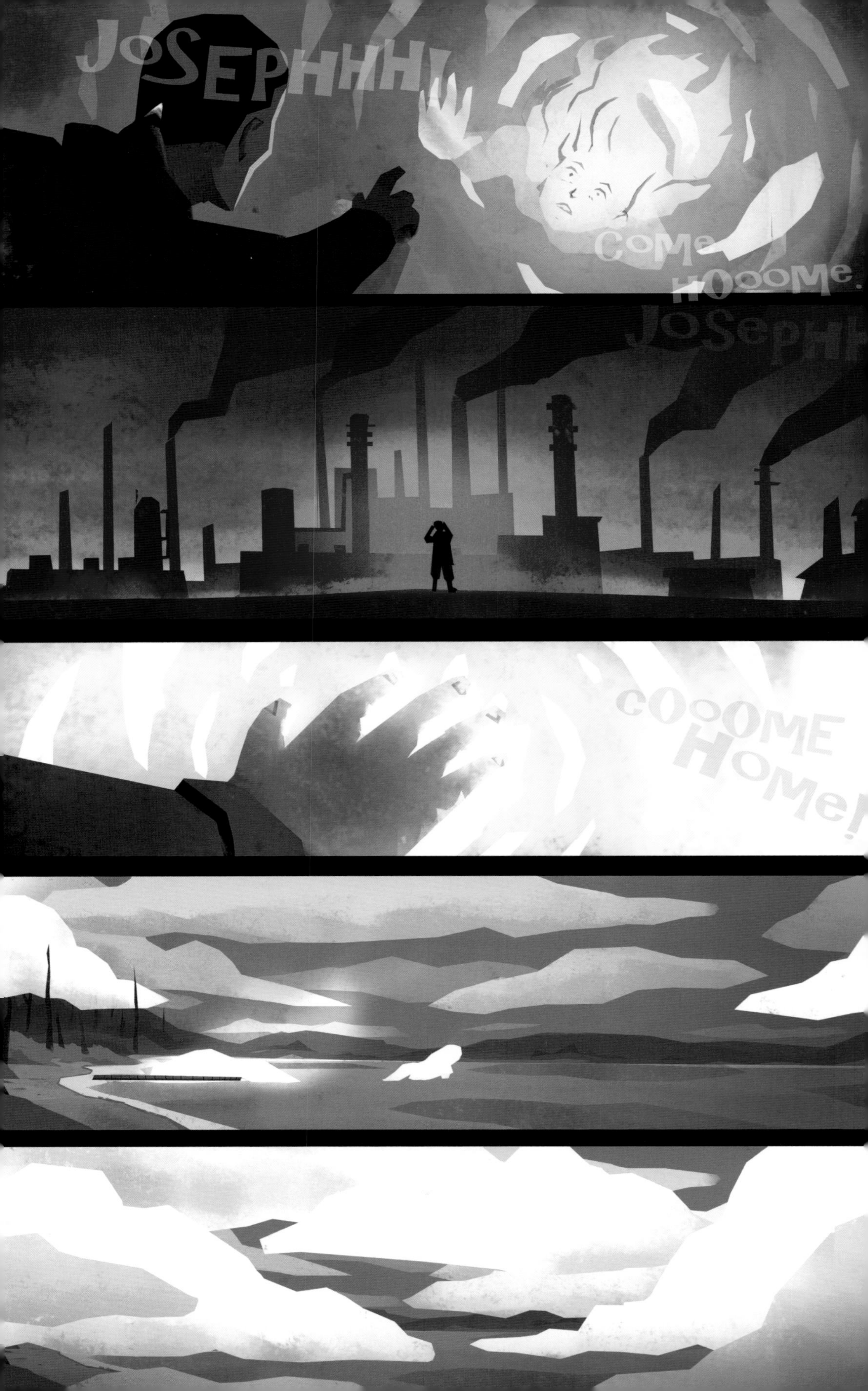
JOSEPHHH!
COME HOOOME.
JOSEPHH
COOOME HOME!

David Alexander Robertson's

BOOKMARK

Illustrated by Natasha Alterici

BACKGROUND

The creation story told within this piece recounts how Wisakicak used the four elements – earth, water, fire, and air – to make humans. It was an act that both symbolizes our connection to all matter around us and recognizes our individuality and uniqueness. Some still find it difficult to seek out a connection or ask for help when help is needed. "Bookmark" was written in consultation with suicide prevention specialists and three Elders regarding the suicide epidemic in First Nations communities. The Elders, from Wasagamack (Ojibway-Cree) in Manitoba, South Indian Lake, and Norway House Cree Nation, discussed with the author what solutions might be gained by seeking knowledge from a traditional perspective, and how the practical applications of those Indigenous teachings can be presented through story and legend.

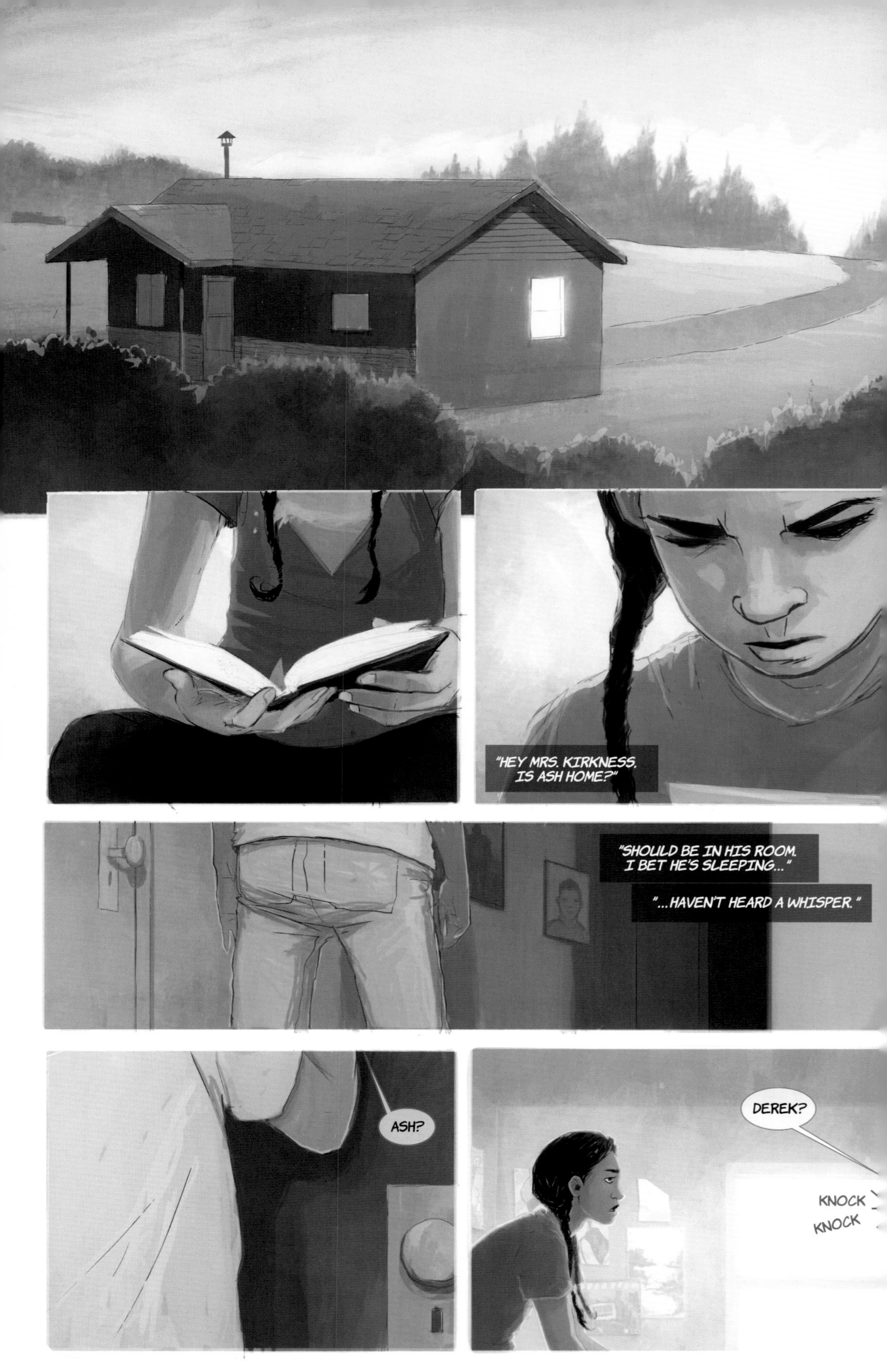
"HEY MRS. KIRKNESS, IS ASH HOME?"
"SHOULD BE IN HIS ROOM. I BET HE'S SLEEPING..."
"...HAVEN'T HEARD A WHISPER."
ASH?
DEREK?
KNOCK
KNOCK

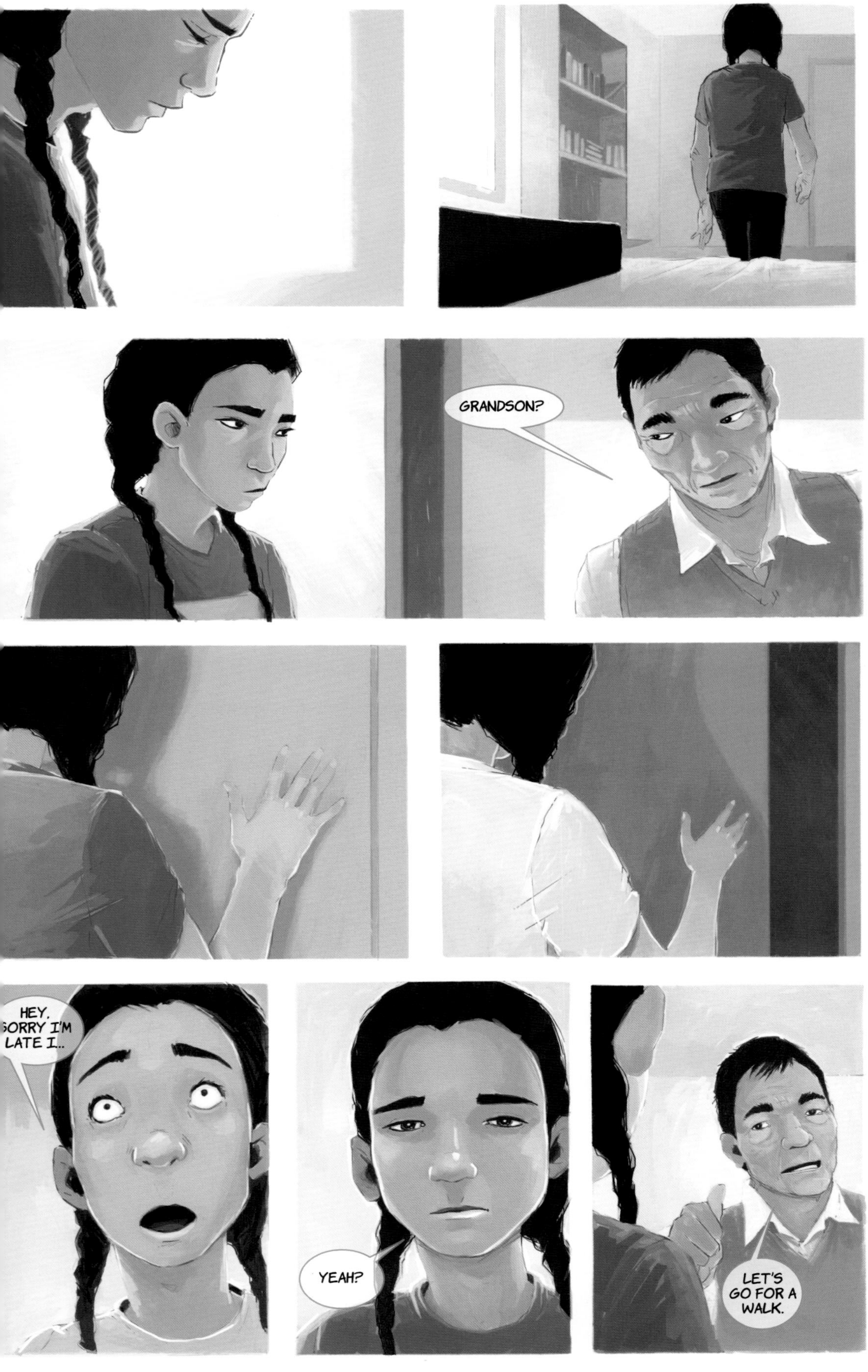
GRANDSON?
HEY, SORRY I'M LATE I..
YEAH?
LET'S GO FOR A WALK.

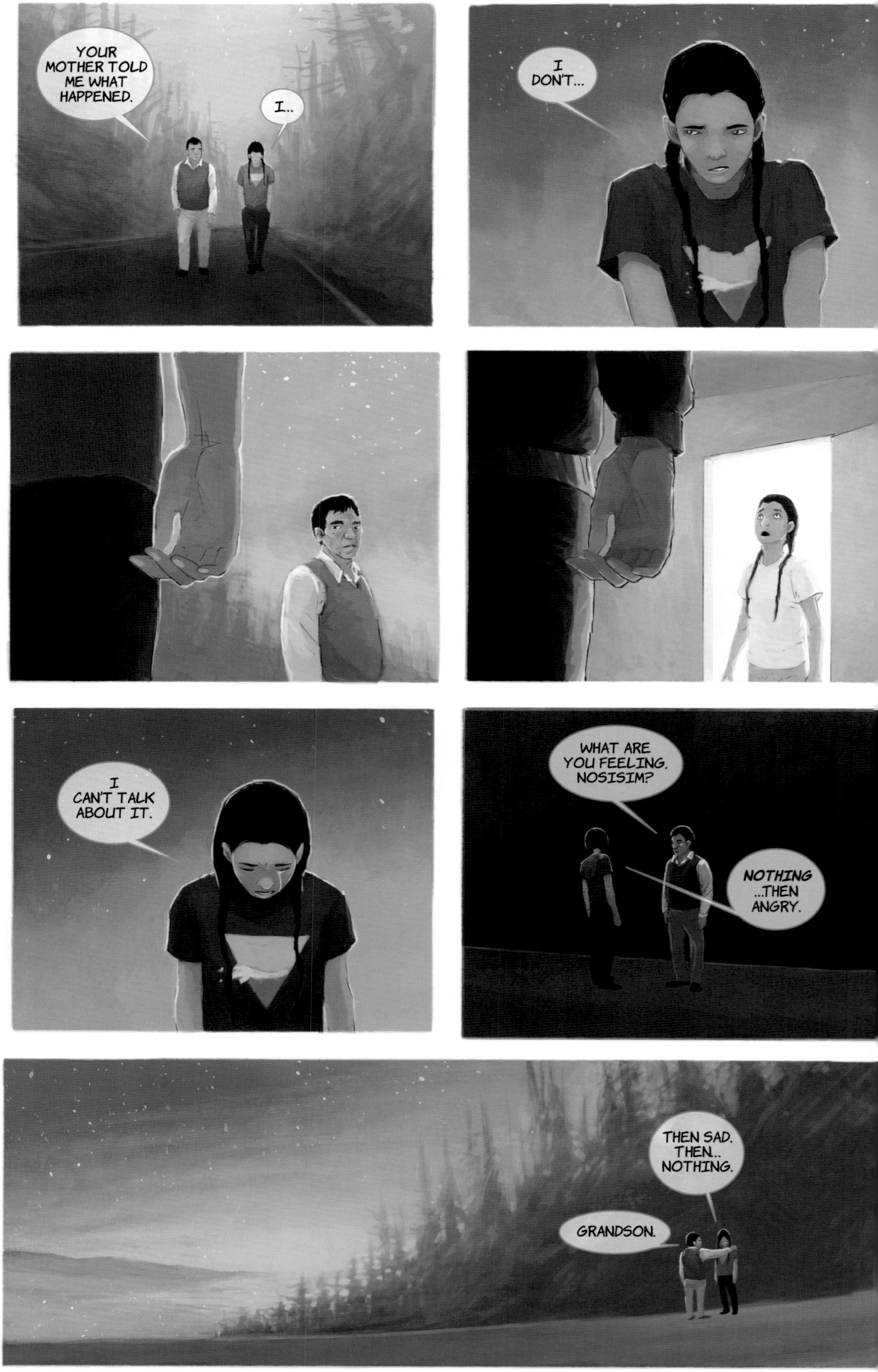

YOUR MOTHER TOLD ME WHAT HAPPENED.
I..
I DON'T...
I CAN'T TALK ABOUT IT.
WHAT ARE YOU FEELING, NOSISIM?
NOTHING ...THEN ANGRY.
THEN SAD. THEN.. NOTHING.
GRANDSON.

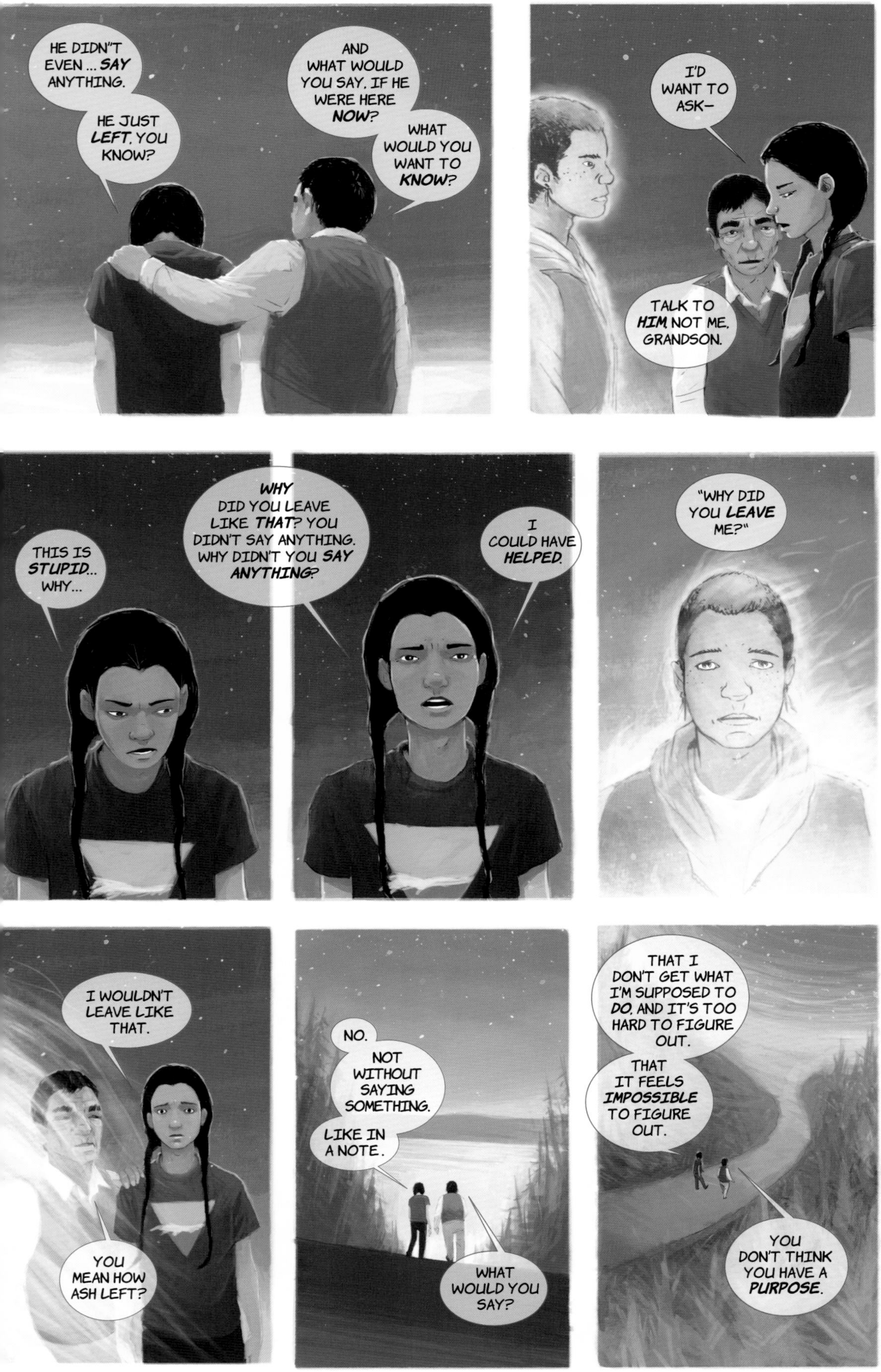
HE DIDN'T EVEN ... SAY ANYTHING.
HE JUST LEFT, YOU KNOW?
AND WHAT WOULD YOU SAY, IF HE WERE HERE NOW?
WHAT WOULD YOU WANT TO KNOW?
I'D WANT TO ASK–
TALK TO HIM, NOT ME, GRANDSON.
THIS IS STUPID... WHY...
WHY DID YOU LEAVE LIKE THAT? YOU DIDN'T SAY ANYTHING. WHY DIDN'T YOU SAY ANYTHING?
I COULD HAVE HELPED.
"WHY DID YOU LEAVE ME?"
I WOULDN'T LEAVE LIKE THAT.
YOU MEAN HOW ASH LEFT?
NO.
NOT WITHOUT SAYING SOMETHING.
LIKE IN A NOTE.
WHAT WOULD YOU SAY?
THAT I DON'T GET WHAT I'M SUPPOSED TO DO, AND IT'S TOO HARD TO FIGURE OUT.
THAT IT FEELS IMPOSSIBLE TO FIGURE OUT.
YOU DON'T THINK YOU HAVE A PURPOSE.

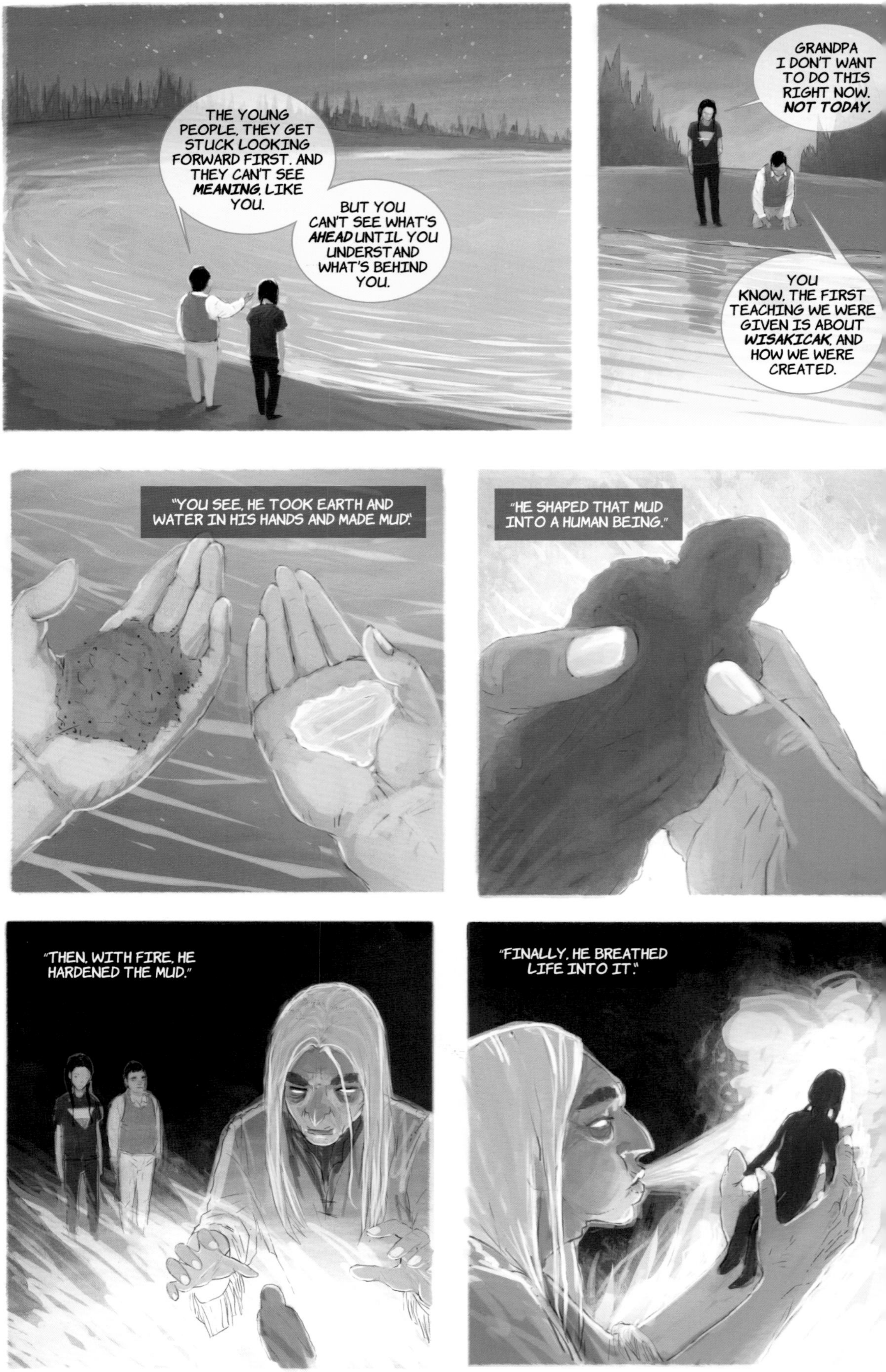
THE YOUNG PEOPLE, THEY GET STUCK LOOKING FORWARD FIRST. AND THEY CAN'T SEE MEANING, LIKE YOU.
BUT YOU CAN'T SEE WHAT'S AHEAD UNTIL YOU UNDERSTAND WHAT'S BEHIND YOU.
GRANDPA I DON'T WANT TO DO THIS RIGHT NOW. NOT TODAY.
YOU KNOW, THE FIRST TEACHING WE WERE GIVEN IS ABOUT WISAKICAK, AND HOW WE WERE CREATED.
"YOU SEE, HE TOOK EARTH AND WATER IN HIS HANDS AND MADE MUD."
"HE SHAPED THAT MUD INTO A HUMAN BEING."
"THEN, WITH FIRE, HE HARDENED THE MUD."
"FINALLY, HE BREATHED LIFE INTO IT."

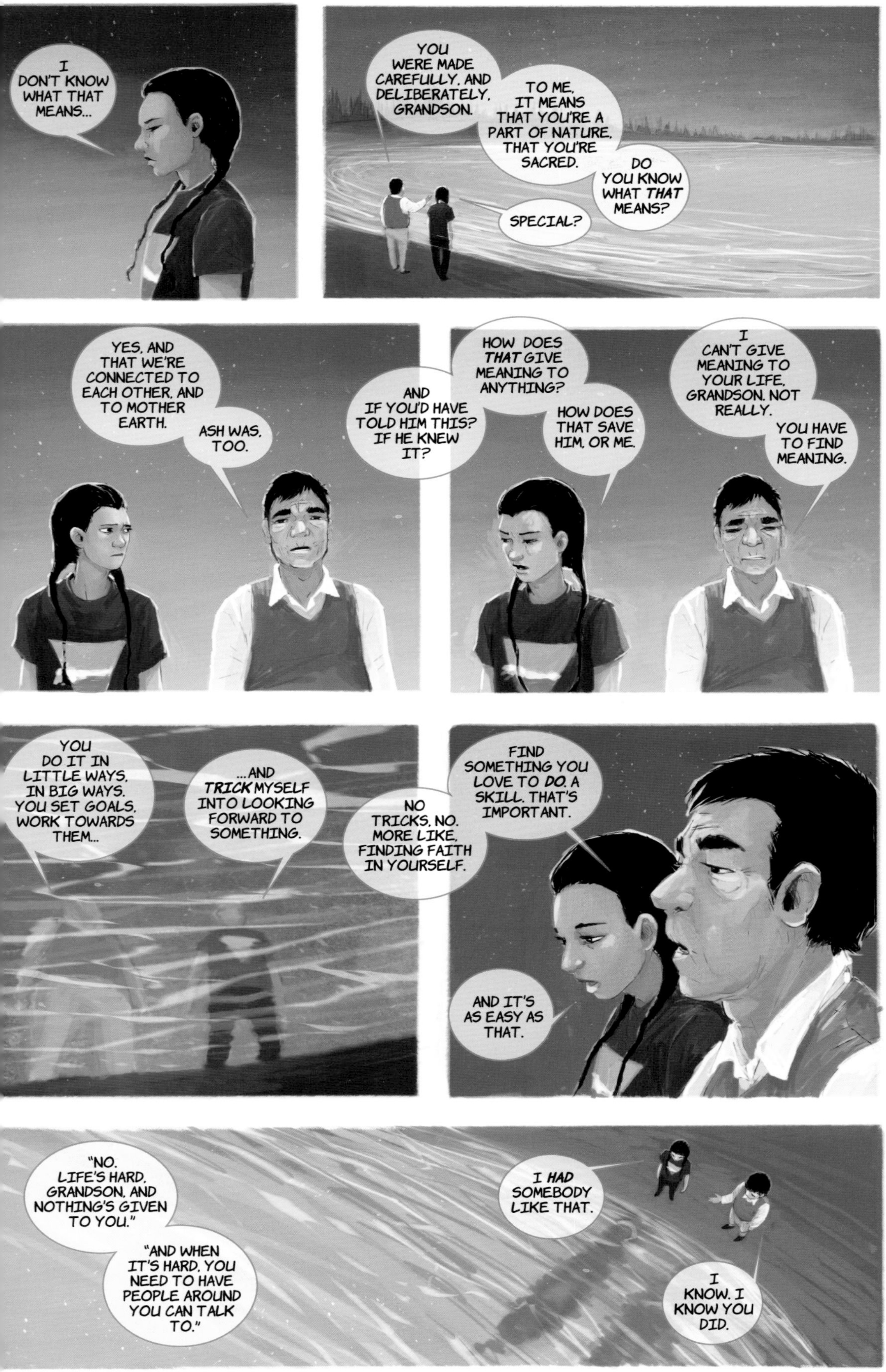
I DON'T KNOW WHAT THAT MEANS...
YOU WERE MADE CAREFULLY, AND DELIBERATELY, GRANDSON.
TO ME, IT MEANS THAT YOU'RE A PART OF NATURE, THAT YOU'RE SACRED.
DO YOU KNOW WHAT *THAT* MEANS?
SPECIAL?
YES, AND THAT WE'RE CONNECTED TO EACH OTHER, AND TO MOTHER EARTH.
ASH WAS, TOO.
AND IF YOU'D HAVE TOLD HIM THIS? IF HE KNEW IT?
HOW DOES *THAT* GIVE MEANING TO ANYTHING?
HOW DOES THAT SAVE HIM, OR ME.
I CAN'T GIVE MEANING TO YOUR LIFE, GRANDSON. NOT REALLY.
YOU HAVE TO FIND MEANING.
YOU DO IT IN LITTLE WAYS, IN BIG WAYS. YOU SET GOALS, WORK TOWARDS THEM...
...AND *TRICK* MYSELF INTO LOOKING FORWARD TO SOMETHING.
NO TRICKS, NO. MORE LIKE, FINDING FAITH IN YOURSELF.
FIND SOMETHING YOU LOVE TO *DO*, A SKILL. THAT'S IMPORTANT.
AND IT'S AS EASY AS THAT.
"NO. LIFE'S HARD, GRANDSON, AND NOTHING'S GIVEN TO YOU."
"AND WHEN IT'S HARD, YOU NEED TO HAVE PEOPLE AROUND YOU CAN TALK TO."
I *HAD* SOMEBODY LIKE THAT.
I KNOW. I KNOW YOU DID.

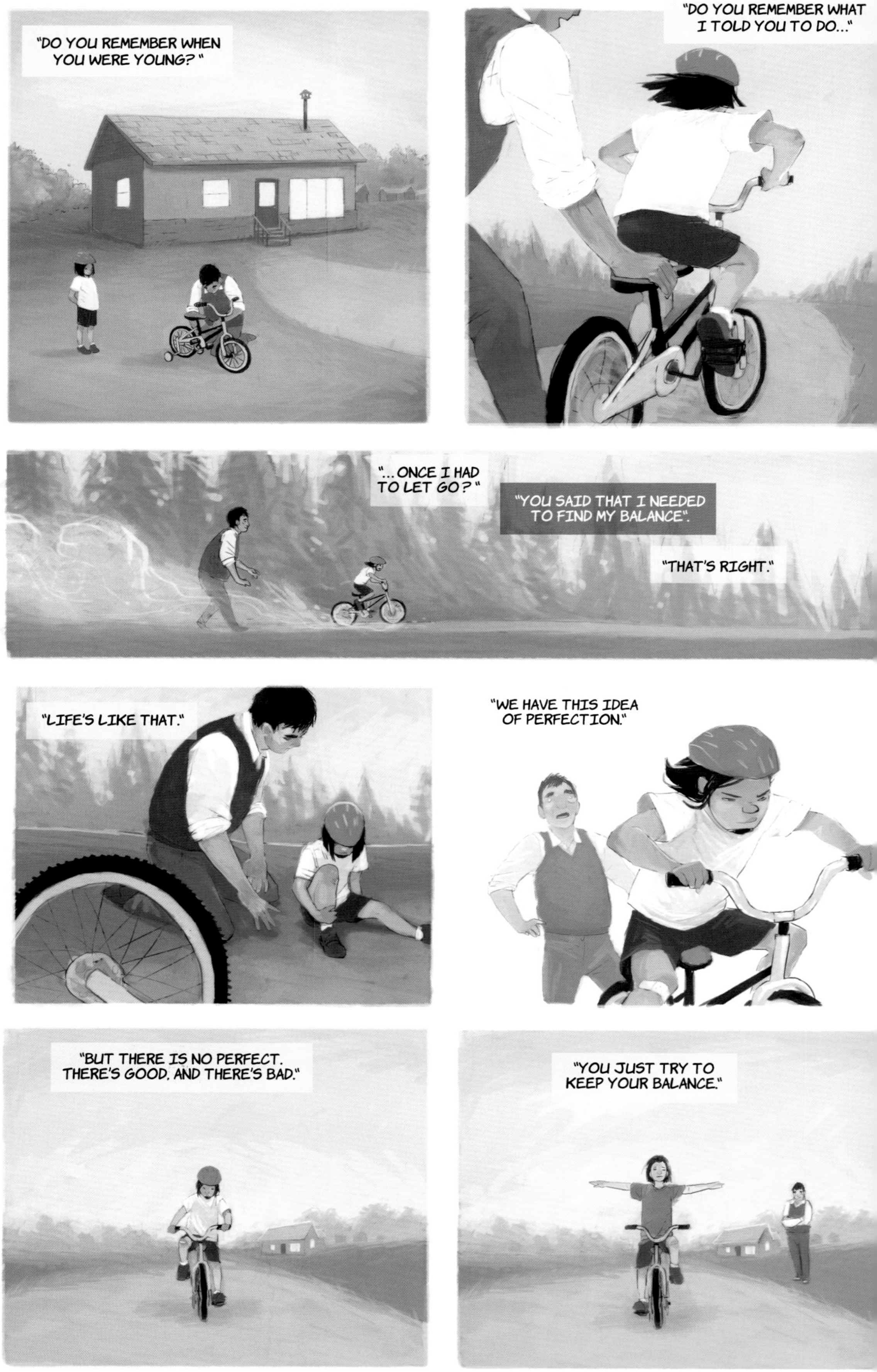
"DO YOU REMEMBER WHEN YOU WERE YOUNG? "
"DO YOU REMEMBER WHAT I TOLD YOU TO DO..."
"...ONCE I HAD TO LET GO? "
"YOU SAID THAT I NEEDED TO FIND MY BALANCE".
"THAT'S RIGHT."
"LIFE'S LIKE THAT."
"WE HAVE THIS IDEA OF PERFECTION."
"BUT THERE IS NO PERFECT. THERE'S GOOD, AND THERE'S BAD."
"YOU JUST TRY TO KEEP YOUR BALANCE."

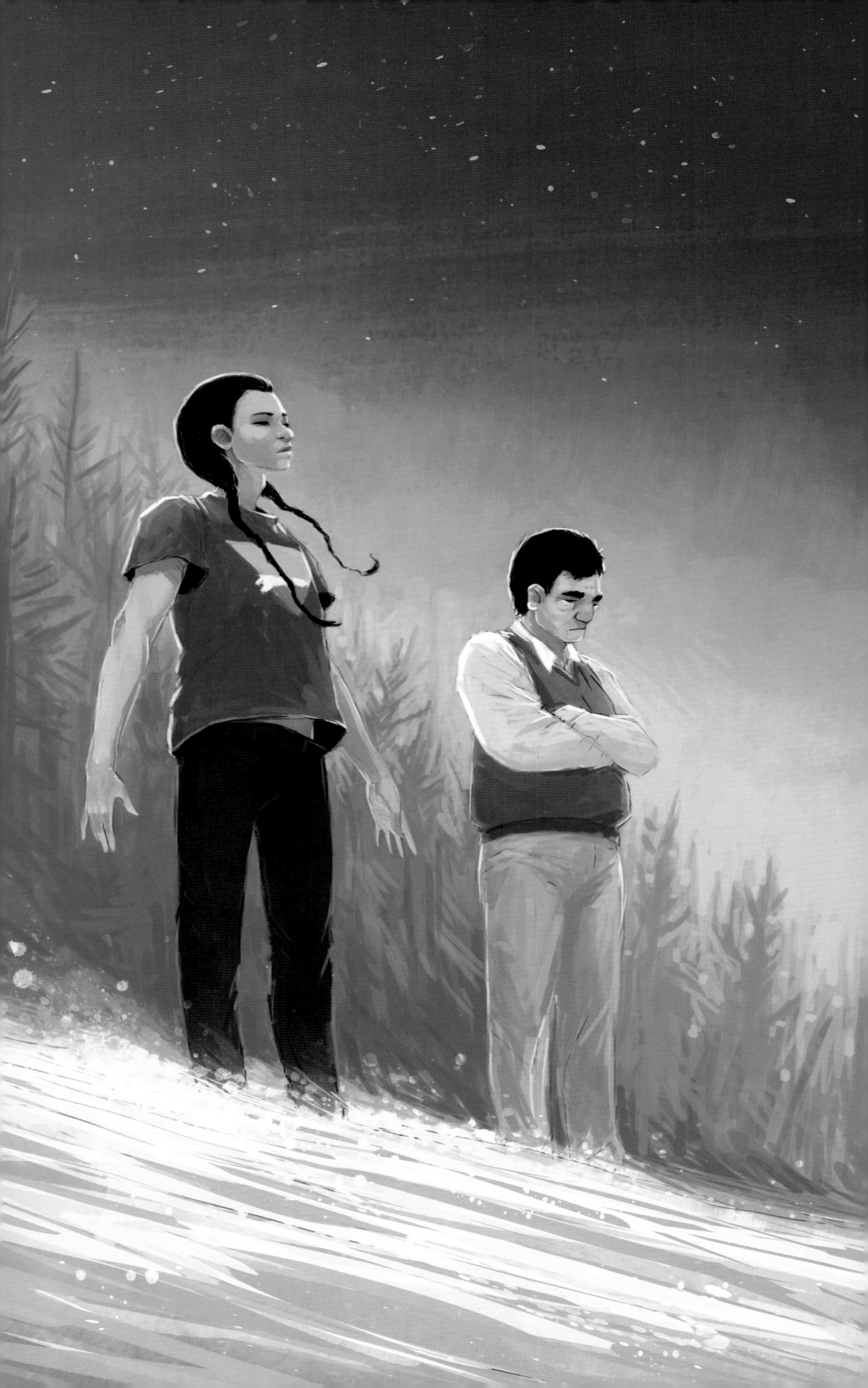

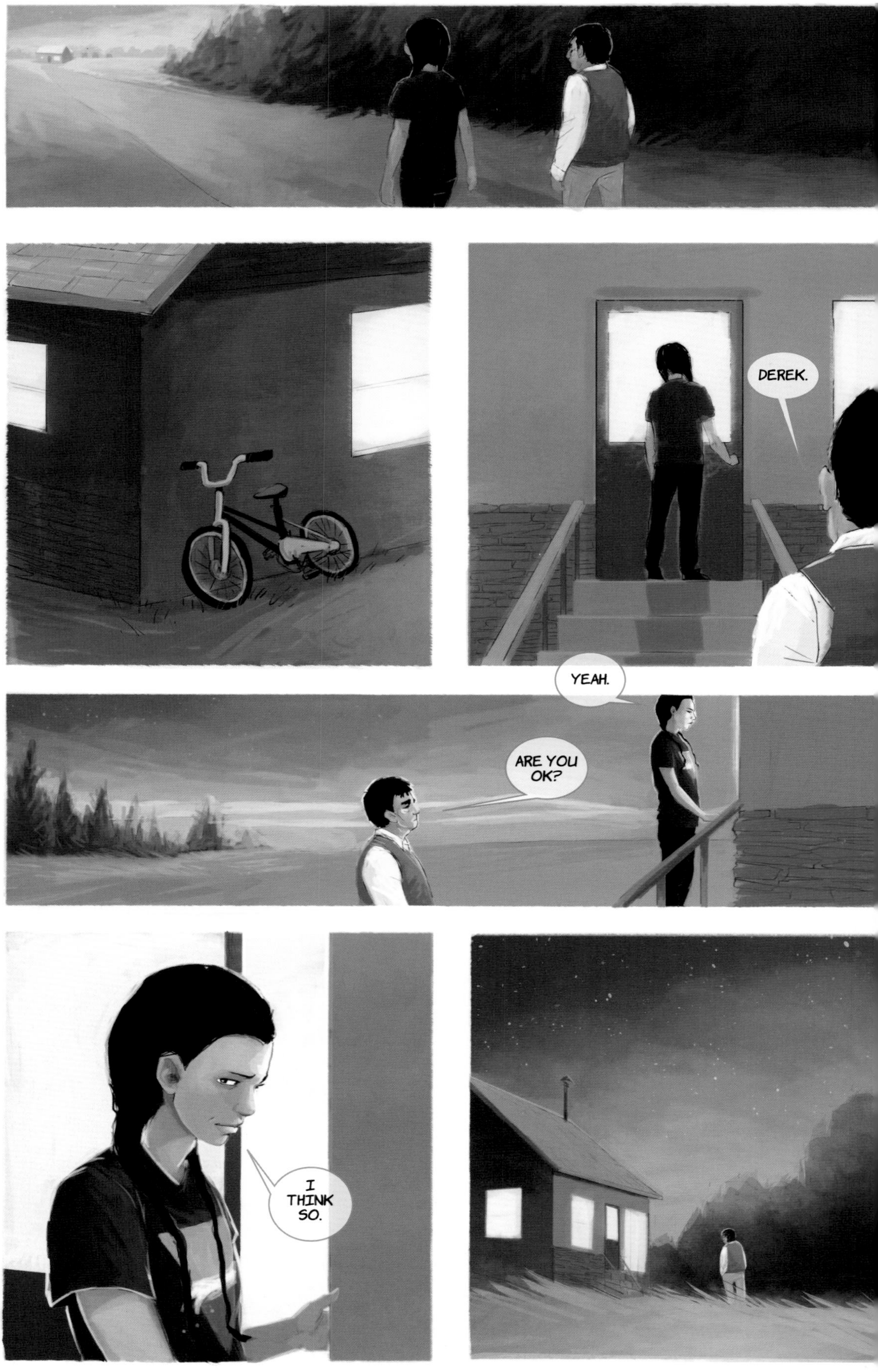
DEREK.
YEAH.
ARE YOU OK?
I THINK SO.

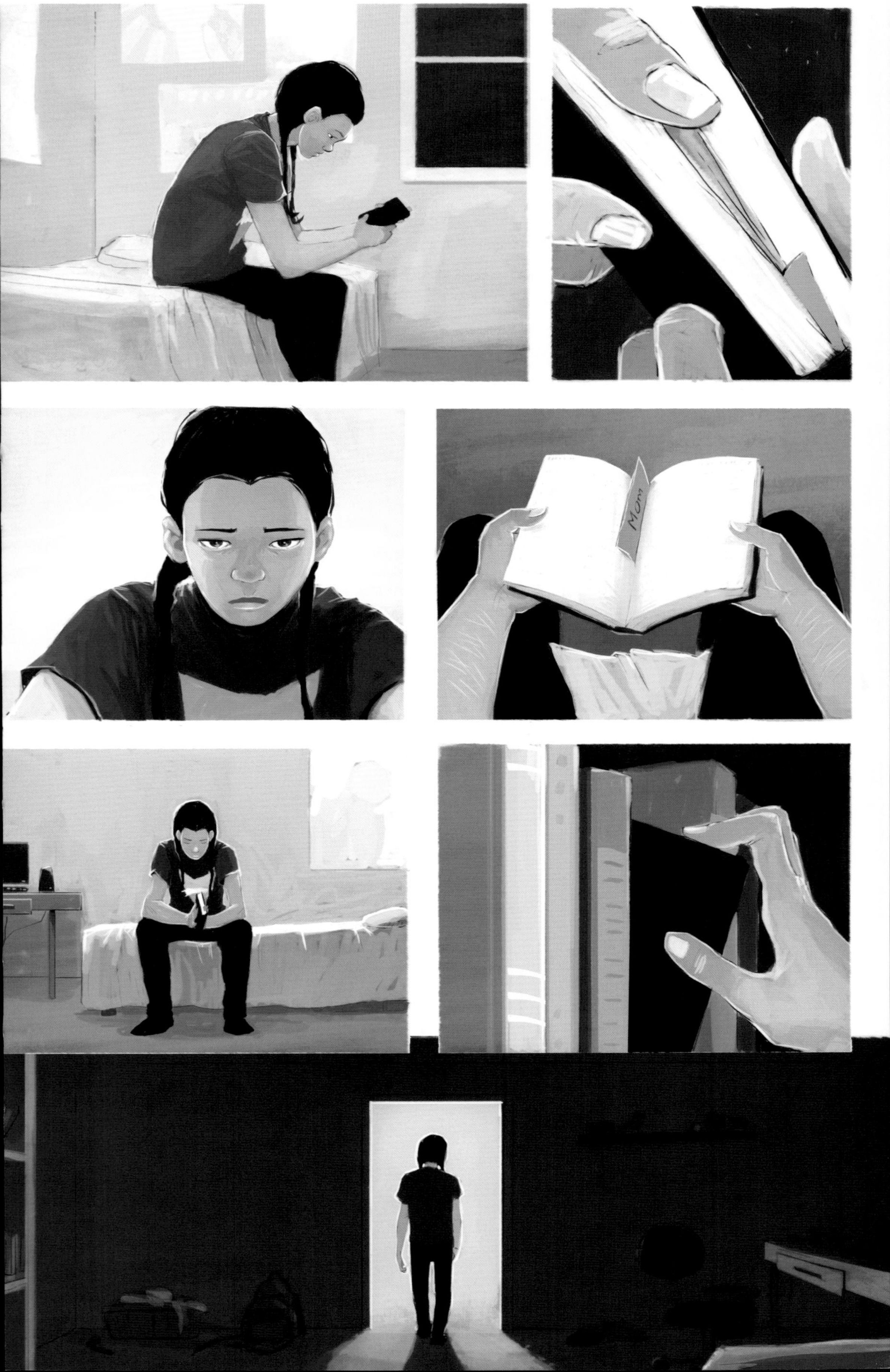
Mom

Armand Garnet Ruffo's

THE
AWAKENING

Illustrated by David Cutler

BACKGROUND

This story was inspired by the work of Ojibway Elder Arthur Solomon, who led the way in the 1980s for Indigenous cultural practices to be accepted into the Canadian federal prison system. Federal prisons in Canada have a critical overrepresentation of Indigenous inmates, and Elder Solomon believed that by returning to the ways given to Indigenous people by the Creator, they could find healing. Likewise, with these sacred teachings, incarcerated youths and adults could understand the oppressive circumstances that led them to where they are, and help them to work their way through it. "The Awakening" introduces us to one Indigenous youth who ends up on the wrong side of the law. This story teaches that even in the most dismal of situations, the rituals and beliefs of one's community can lead that person to light. One of the traditions presented in this piece involves the use of tobacco, placed into fire as a means of communication with the ancestors and protectors, to offer strength and guidance for those in need.

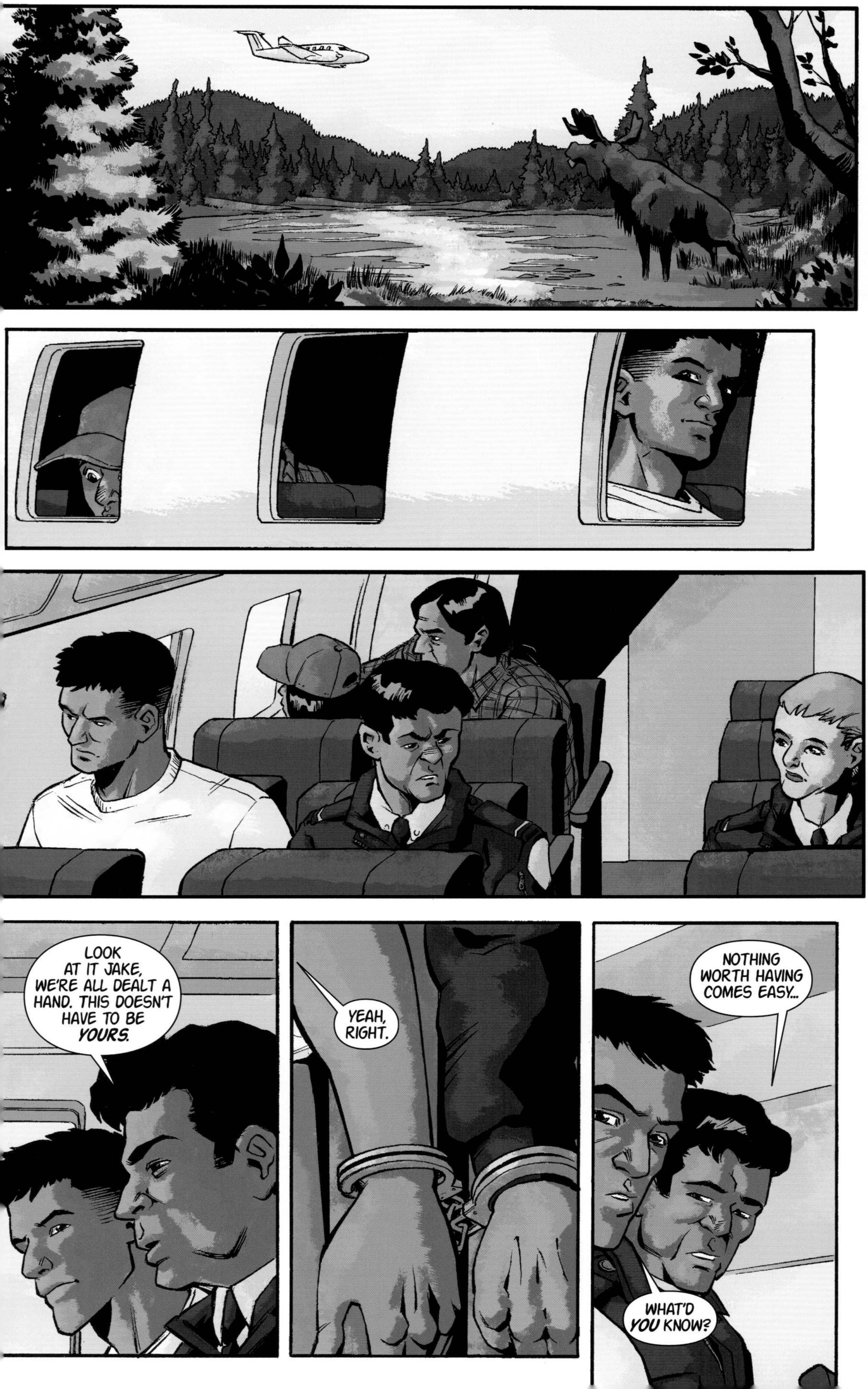
LOOK AT IT JAKE, WE'RE ALL DEALT A HAND. THIS DOESN'T HAVE TO BE YOURS.
YEAH, RIGHT.
NOTHING WORTH HAVING COMES EASY...
WHAT'D YOU KNOW?

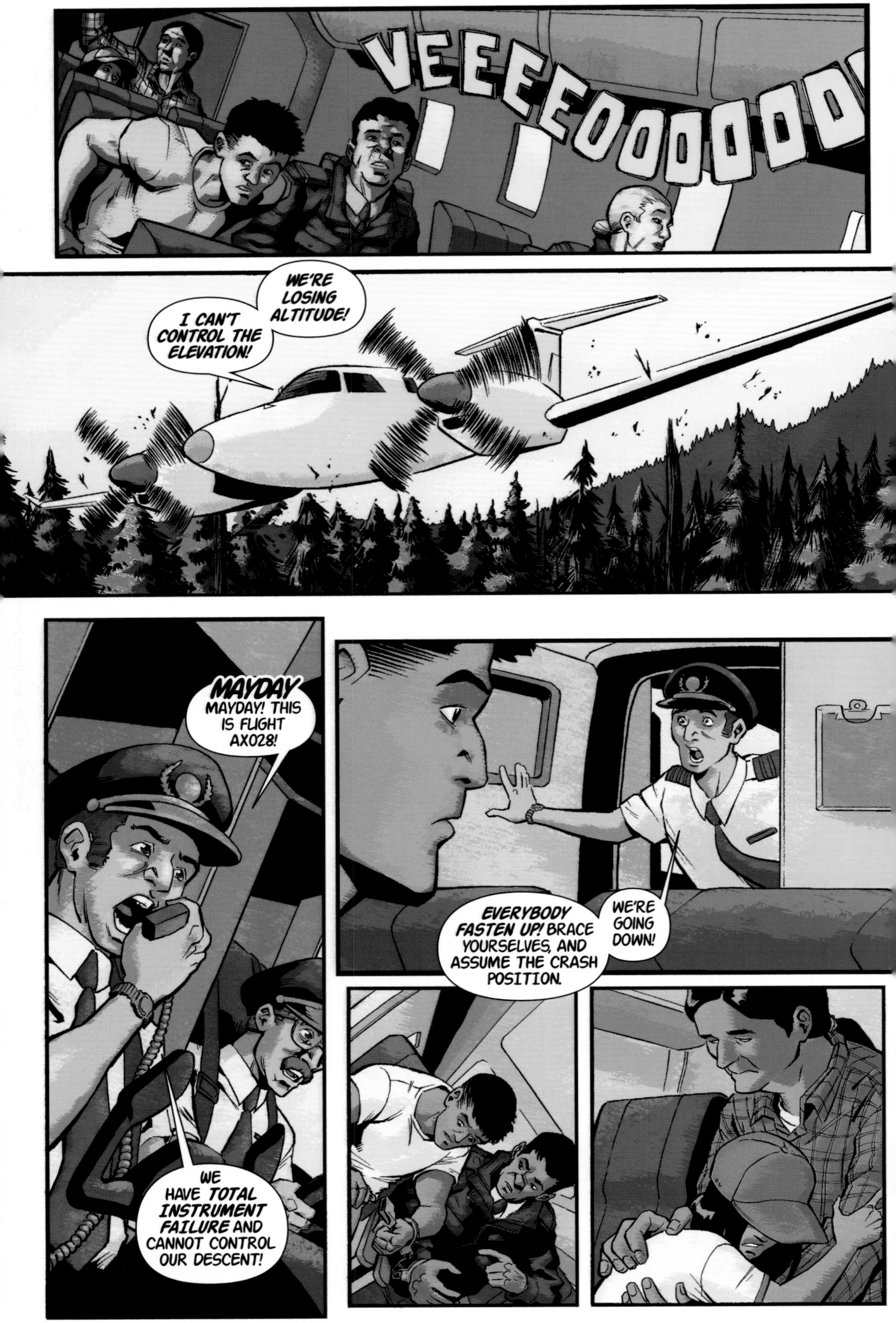
VEEEEOOOOOOO
I CAN'T CONTROL THE ELEVATION!
WE'RE LOSING ALTITUDE!
MAYDAY MAYDAY! THIS IS FLIGHT AX028!
WE HAVE TOTAL INSTRUMENT FAILURE AND CANNOT CONTROL OUR DESCENT!
WE'RE GOING DOWN!
EVERYBODY FASTEN UP! BRACE YOURSELVES, AND ASSUME THE CRASH POSITION.

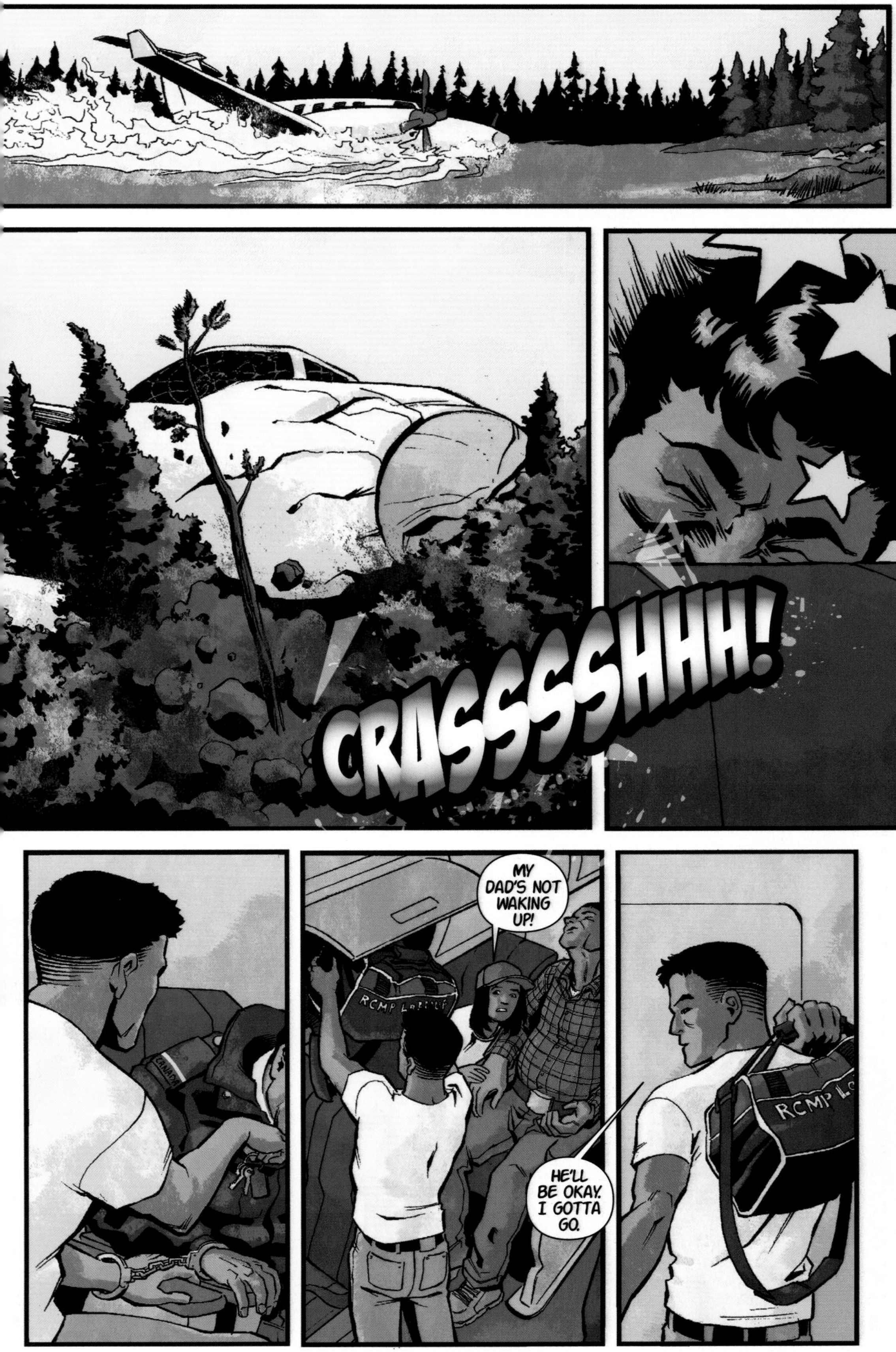
CRASSSSHHH!
MY DAD'S NOT WAKING UP!
HE'LL BE OKAY. I GOTTA GO.

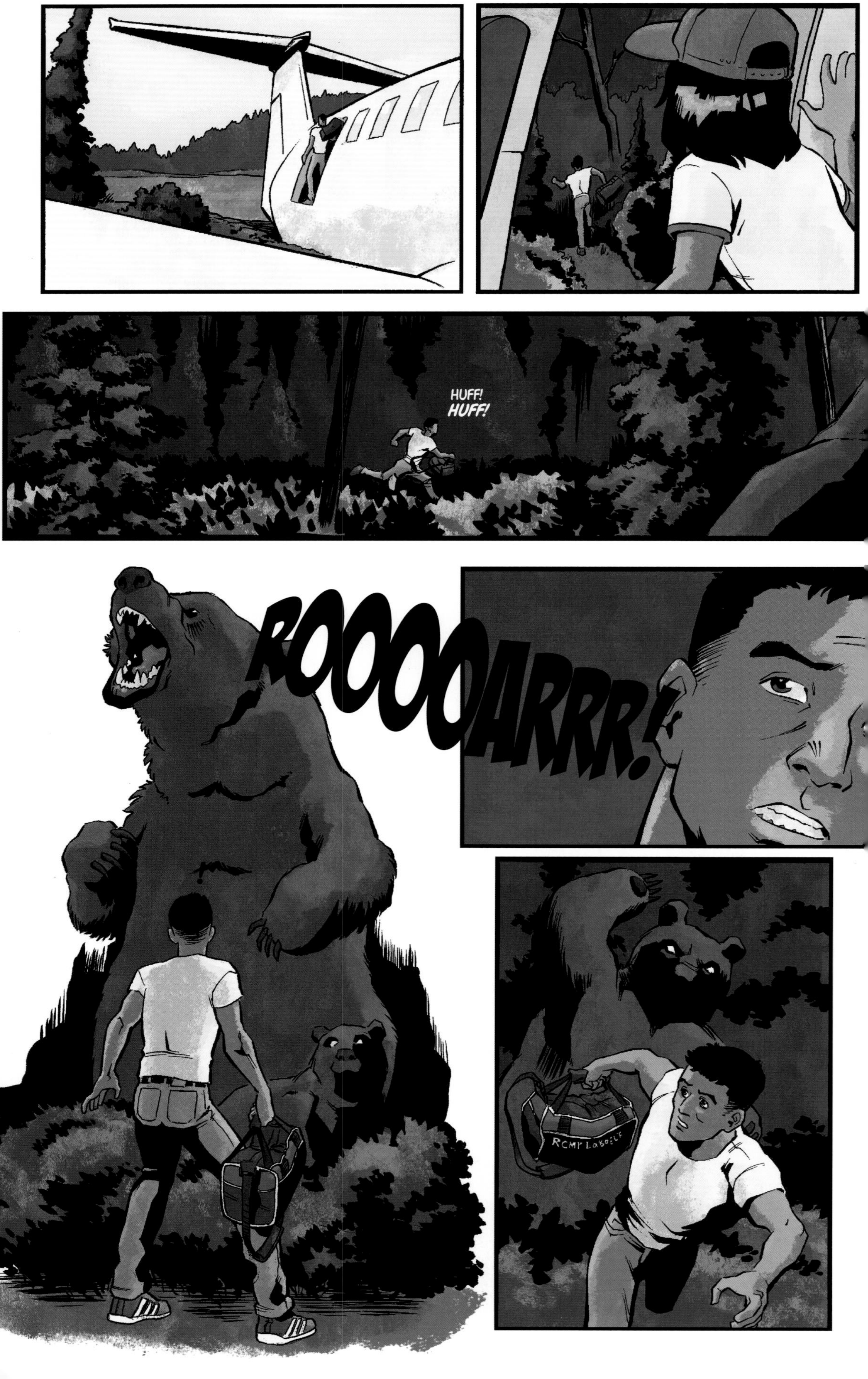
HUFF!
HUFF!
ROOOOARRR!
RCMP

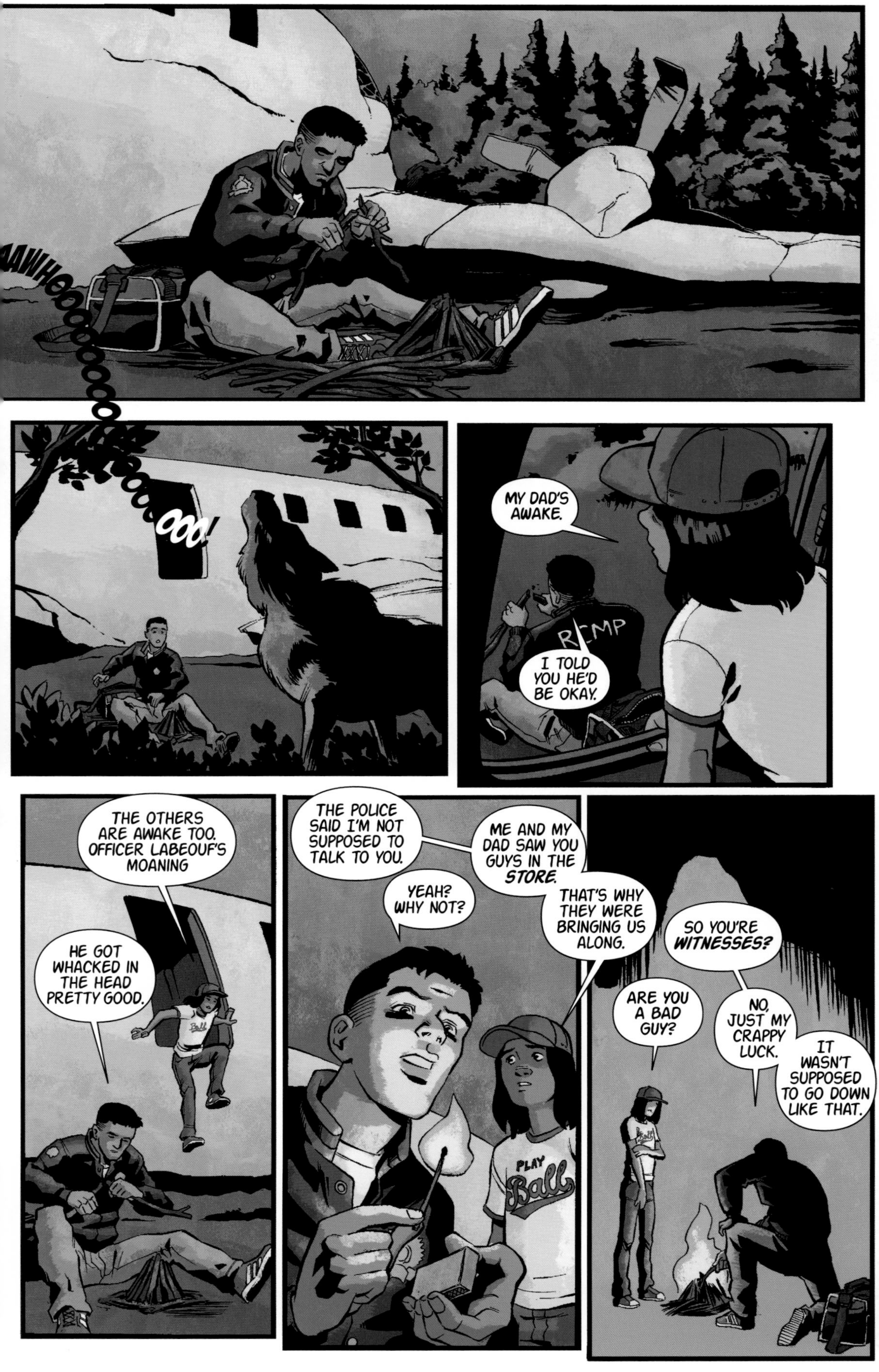
AAWHOOOOOOOOOOOOOOOOOOOOOO!
MY DAD'S AWAKE.
I TOLD YOU HE'D BE OKAY.
RCMP
THE OTHERS ARE AWAKE TOO. OFFICER LABEOUF'S MOANING
HE GOT WHACKED IN THE HEAD PRETTY GOOD.
THE POLICE SAID I'M NOT SUPPOSED TO TALK TO YOU.
YEAH? WHY NOT?
ME AND MY DAD SAW YOU GUYS IN THE STORE.
THAT'S WHY THEY WERE BRINGING US ALONG.
PLAY Ball
SO YOU'RE WITNESSES?
ARE YOU A BAD GUY?
NO, JUST MY CRAPPY LUCK.
IT WASN'T SUPPOSED TO GO DOWN LIKE THAT.

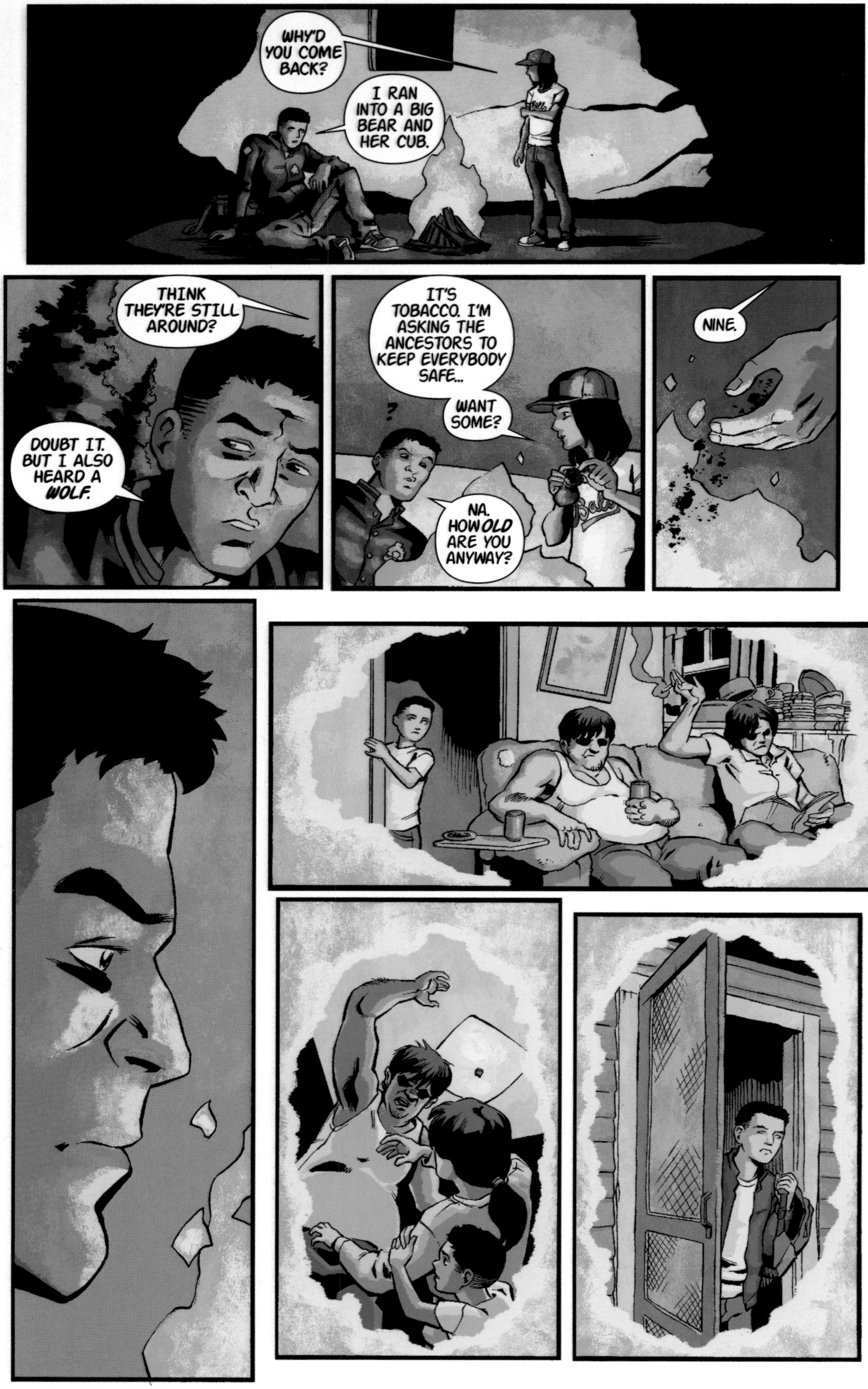
WHY'D YOU COME BACK?
I RAN INTO A BIG BEAR AND HER CUB.
THINK THEY'RE STILL AROUND?
DOUBT IT. BUT I ALSO HEARD A *WOLF*.
IT'S TOBACCO. I'M ASKING THE ANCESTORS TO KEEP EVERYBODY SAFE...
WANT SOME?
?
NA. HOW *OLD* ARE YOU ANYWAY?
NINE.

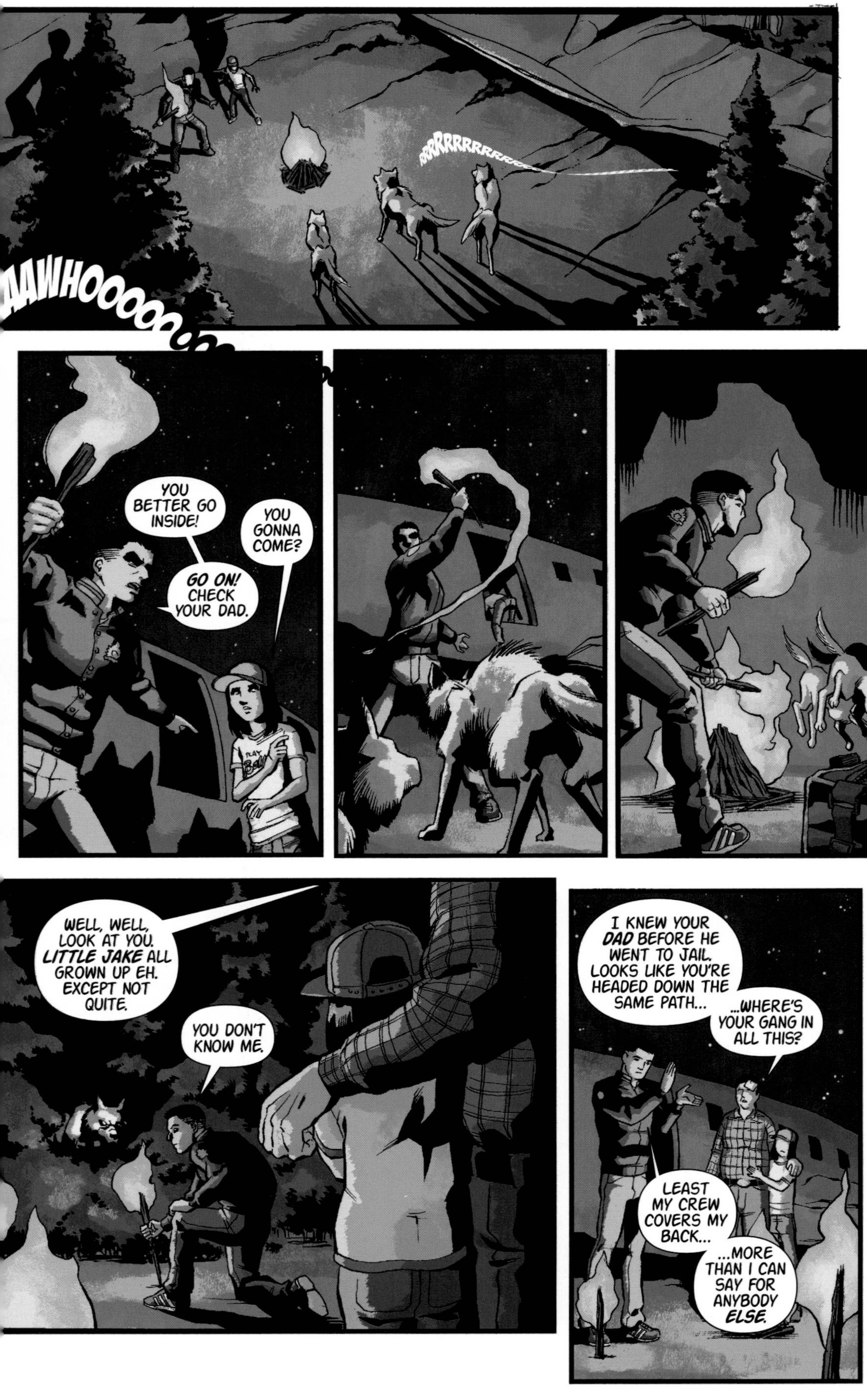
RRRRRRRRRRRR
AAWHOOOOOOO
YOU BETTER GO INSIDE!
YOU GONNA COME?
GO ON! CHECK YOUR DAD.
WELL, WELL, LOOK AT YOU. LITTLE JAKE ALL GROWN UP EH. EXCEPT NOT QUITE.
YOU DON'T KNOW ME.
I KNEW YOUR DAD BEFORE HE WENT TO JAIL. LOOKS LIKE YOU'RE HEADED DOWN THE SAME PATH...
...WHERE'S YOUR GANG IN ALL THIS?
LEAST MY CREW COVERS MY BACK...
...MORE THAN I CAN SAY FOR ANYBODY ELSE.

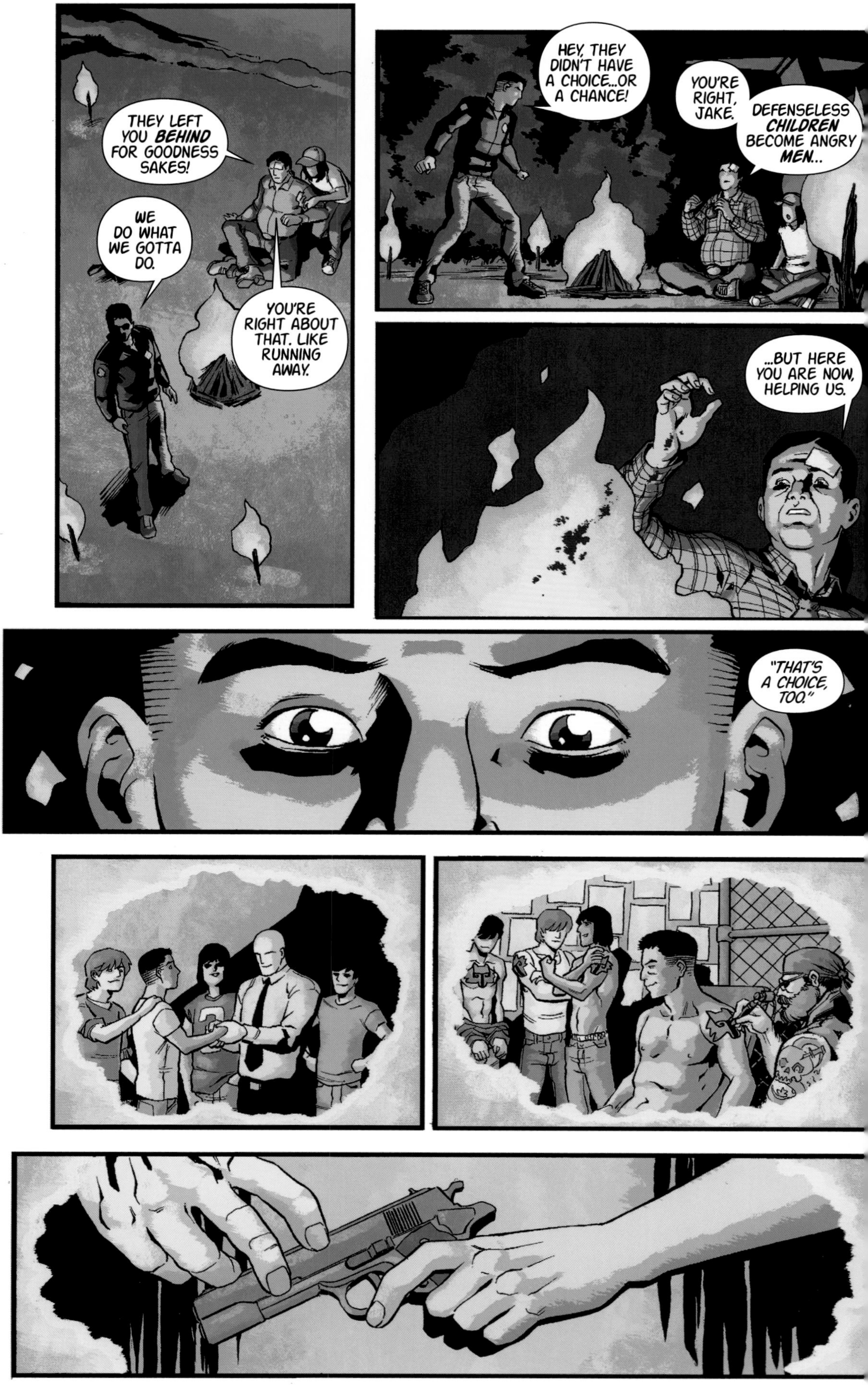
THEY LEFT YOU BEHIND FOR GOODNESS SAKES!
WE DO WHAT WE GOTTA DO.
YOU'RE RIGHT ABOUT THAT. LIKE RUNNING AWAY.
HEY, THEY DIDN'T HAVE A CHOICE...OR A CHANCE!
YOU'RE RIGHT, JAKE.
DEFENSELESS CHILDREN BECOME ANGRY MEN...
...BUT HERE YOU ARE NOW, HELPING US.
"THAT'S A CHOICE, TOO."

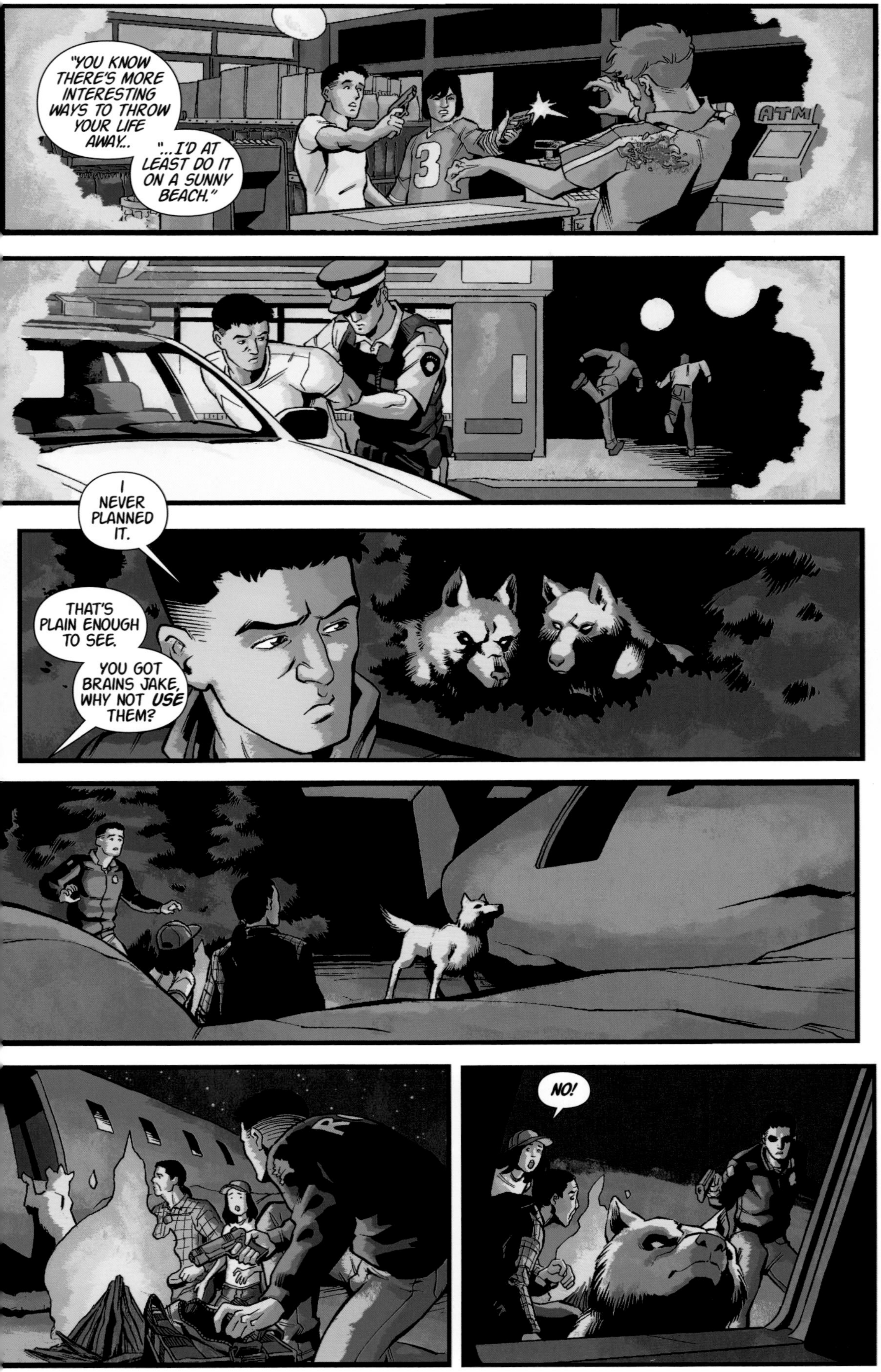
"YOU KNOW THERE'S MORE INTERESTING WAYS TO THROW YOUR LIFE AWAY...
"...I'D AT LEAST DO IT ON A SUNNY BEACH."
ATM
I NEVER PLANNED IT.
THAT'S PLAIN ENOUGH TO SEE.
YOU GOT BRAINS JAKE, WHY NOT USE THEM?
NO!

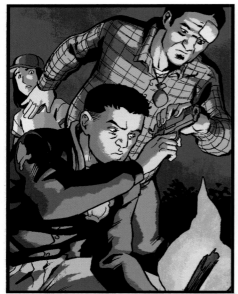

MIIGWETCH. THANKS.

I'M GLAD YOU DIDN'T SHOOT.

AH, THEY'RE JUST HERE TO *SURVIVE*.

...GRAB WHAT THEY CAN.

RECOGNIZE YOURSELF DO YOU?

I GUESS.

THEN YOU'VE ALREADY MOVED ON.

EVEN *WOLVES* CAN TEACH US THINGS.

LOOK, *THE GREAT BEAR*, WHO'S REALLY A SHE-BEAR.

I'VE BEEN LEARNING ABOUT STARS IN SCHOOL.

THERE SHOULD BE A CONSTELLATION WITH A BEAR *AND* A WOLF!

A SIGN OF *COURAGE* AND *STRENGTH*.

THAT'D BE A GOOD ONE.

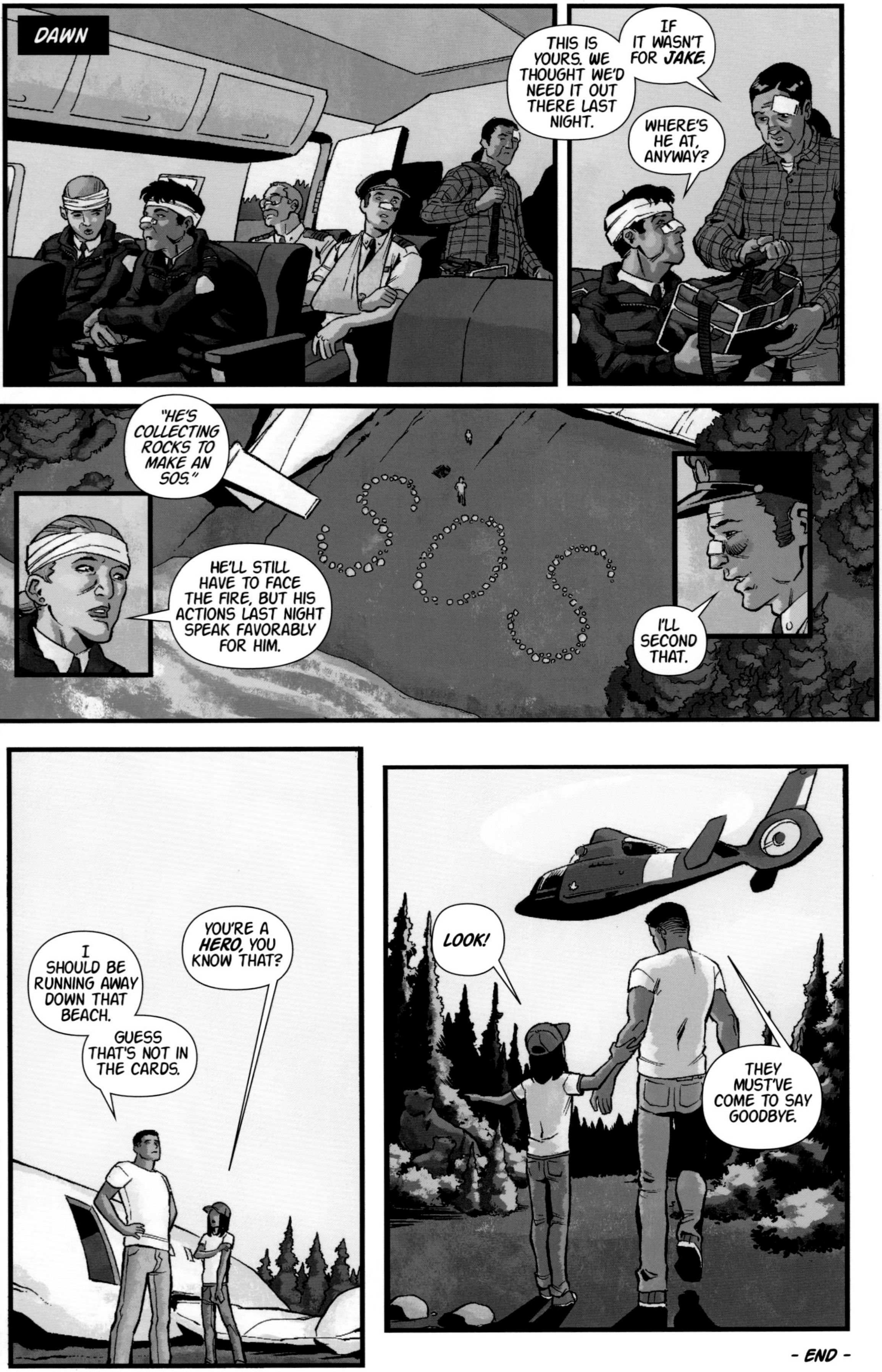
DAWN
THIS IS YOURS. WE THOUGHT WE'D NEED IT OUT THERE LAST NIGHT.
IF IT WASN'T FOR JAKE.
WHERE'S HE AT, ANYWAY?
"HE'S COLLECTING ROCKS TO MAKE AN SOS."
HE'LL STILL HAVE TO FACE THE FIRE, BUT HIS ACTIONS LAST NIGHT SPEAK FAVORABLY FOR HIM.
I'LL SECOND THAT.
I SHOULD BE RUNNING AWAY DOWN THAT BEACH.
GUESS THAT'S NOT IN THE CARDS.
YOU'RE A HERO, YOU KNOW THAT?
LOOK!
THEY MUST'VE COME TO SAY GOODBYE.

- END -

Richard Van Camp's

THE MAGIC OF WOLVERINES

Illustrated by Scott Henderson

BACKGROUND

Throughout North America, the wolverine is revered in a multitude of ways. In Indigenous populations in both Canada and the US, the wolverine is known as a trickster spirit. In mid-Eastern Canadian communities, this figure is part of their Creation stories, having helped shape the Earth itself. In Northern Canadian Nations – such as the author's own Tlicho Dene First Nations – the wolverine is connected to the cosmos and represents an unending source of strength. An existing tradition in some of these communities sees parents place wolverine teeth on cribs and baskets for protection for newborns. With this, the wolverine is involved in the full circle of life for people from across the continent. It is this connection to all people that inspired the author to write this story. From Elders to grandfathers, from teens to toddlers, the wolverine is an important physical presence in Indigenous traditions today, and spiritually represents the most important facets of life in our universe – beauty, strength, and respect.

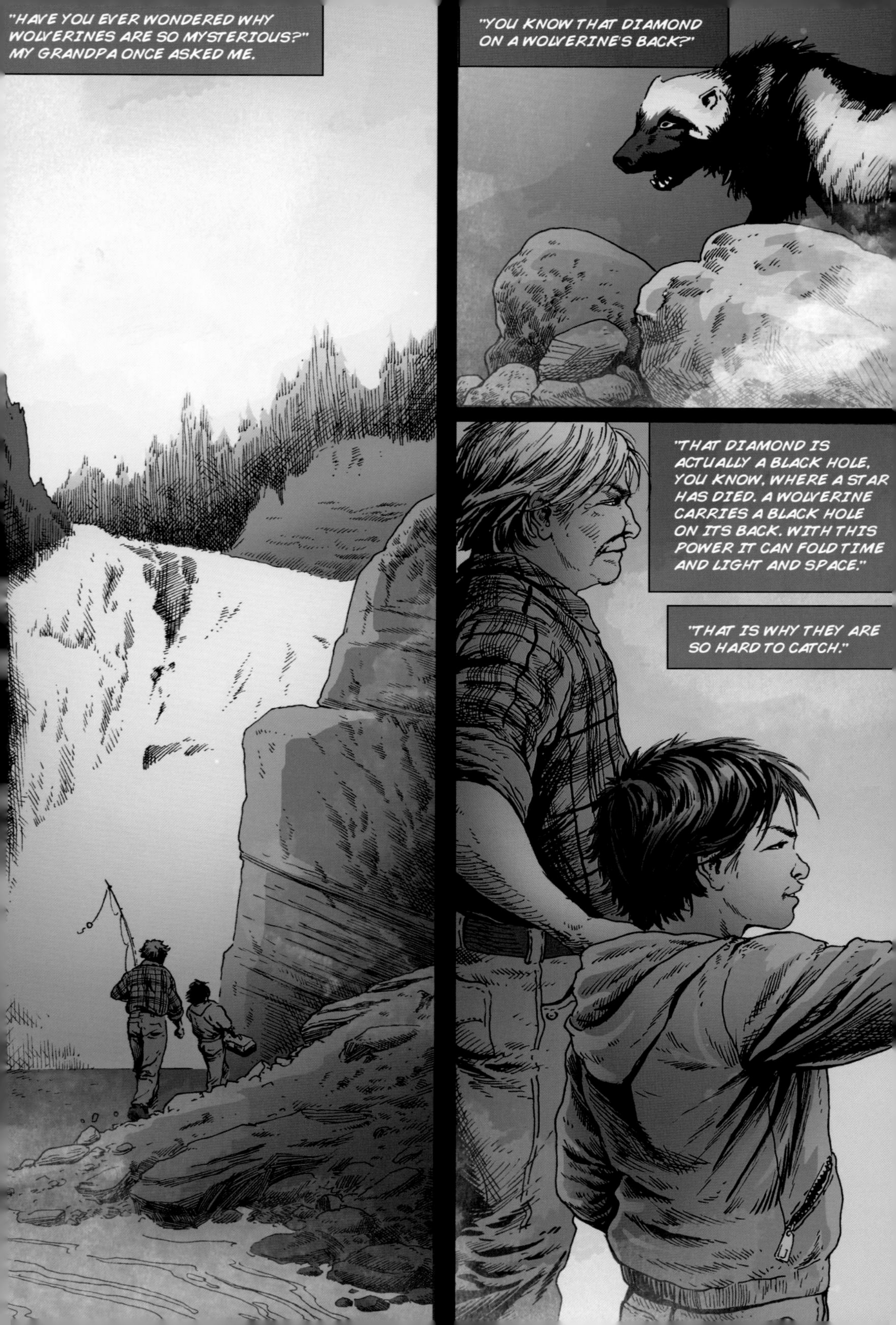
"HAVE YOU EVER WONDERED WHY WOLVERINES ARE SO MYSTERIOUS?" MY GRANDPA ONCE ASKED ME.
"YOU KNOW THAT DIAMOND ON A WOLVERINE'S BACK?"
"THAT DIAMOND IS ACTUALLY A BLACK HOLE, YOU KNOW, WHERE A STAR HAS DIED. A WOLVERINE CARRIES A BLACK HOLE ON ITS BACK. WITH THIS POWER IT CAN FOLD TIME AND LIGHT AND SPACE."
"THAT IS WHY THEY ARE SO HARD TO CATCH."

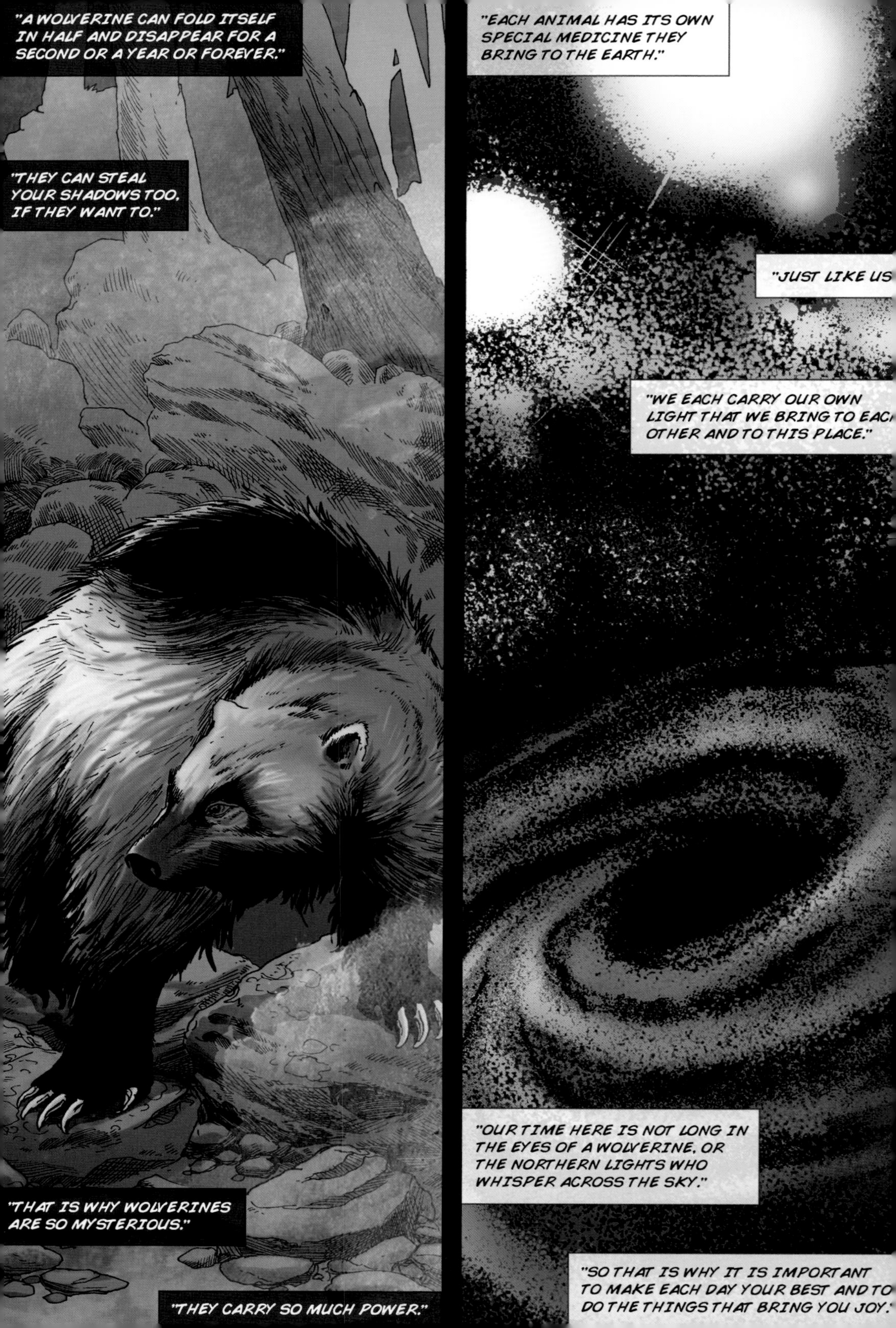
"A WOLVERINE CAN FOLD ITSELF IN HALF AND DISAPPEAR FOR A SECOND OR A YEAR OR FOREVER."
"THEY CAN STEAL YOUR SHADOWS TOO, IF THEY WANT TO."
"THAT IS WHY WOLVERINES ARE SO MYSTERIOUS."
"THEY CARRY SO MUCH POWER."
"EACH ANIMAL HAS ITS OWN SPECIAL MEDICINE THEY BRING TO THE EARTH."
"JUST LIKE US
"WE EACH CARRY OUR OWN LIGHT THAT WE BRING TO EAC OTHER AND TO THIS PLACE."
"OUR TIME HERE IS NOT LONG IN THE EYES OF A WOLVERINE, OR THE NORTHERN LIGHTS WHO WHISPER ACROSS THE SKY."
"SO THAT IS WHY IT IS IMPORTANT TO MAKE EACH DAY YOUR BEST AND TO DO THE THINGS THAT BRING YOU JOY."

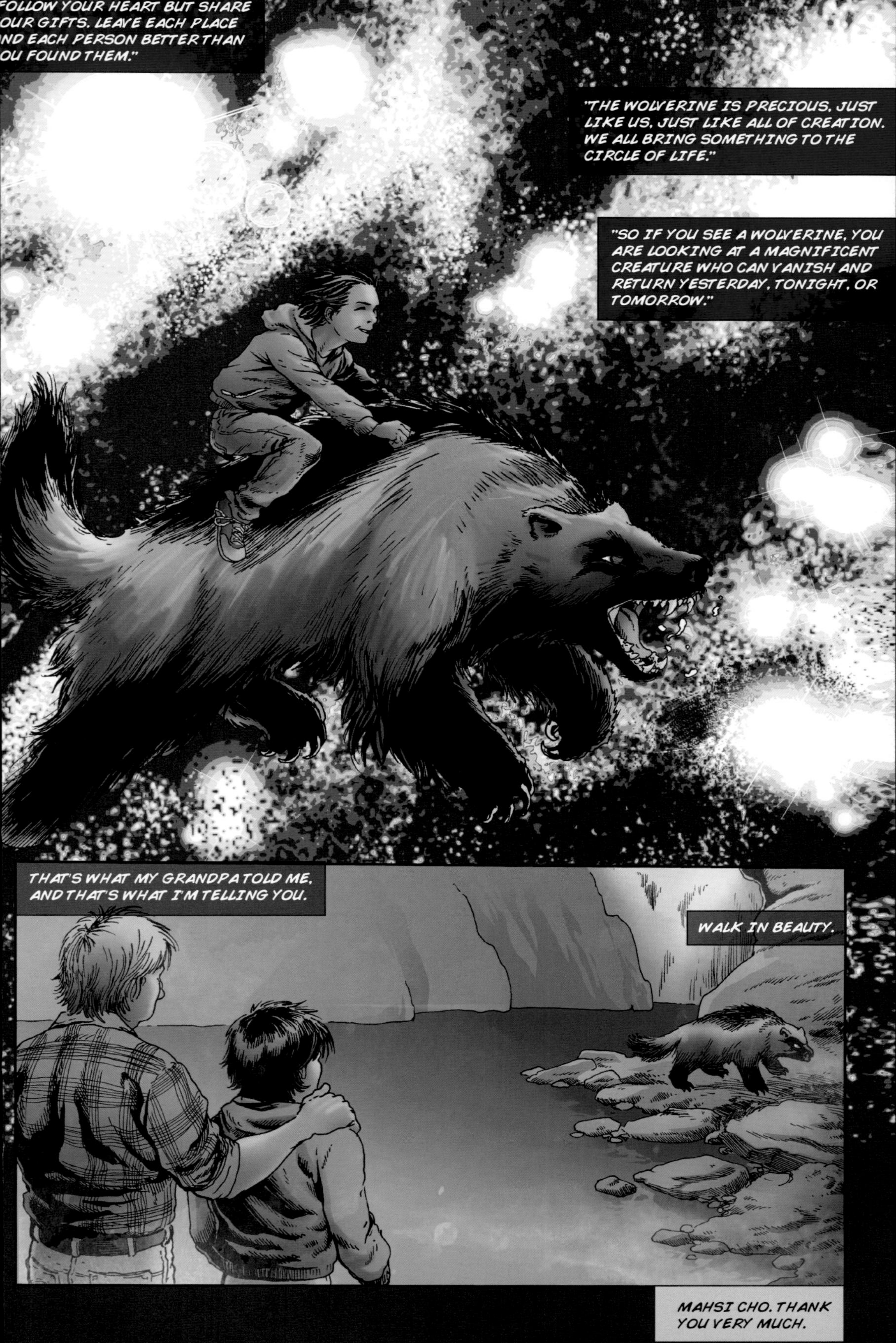
FOLLOW YOUR HEART BUT SHARE OUR GIFTS. LEAVE EACH PLACE ND EACH PERSON BETTER THAN OU FOUND THEM."
"THE WOLVERINE IS PRECIOUS, JUST LIKE US, JUST LIKE ALL OF CREATION. WE ALL BRING SOMETHING TO THE CIRCLE OF LIFE."
"SO IF YOU SEE A WOLVERINE, YOU ARE LOOKING AT A MAGNIFICENT CREATURE WHO CAN VANISH AND RETURN YESTERDAY, TONIGHT, OR TOMORROW."
THAT'S WHAT MY GRANDPA TOLD ME, AND THAT'S WHAT I'M TELLING YOU.
WALK IN BEAUTY.
MAHSI CHO. THANK YOU VERY MUCH.

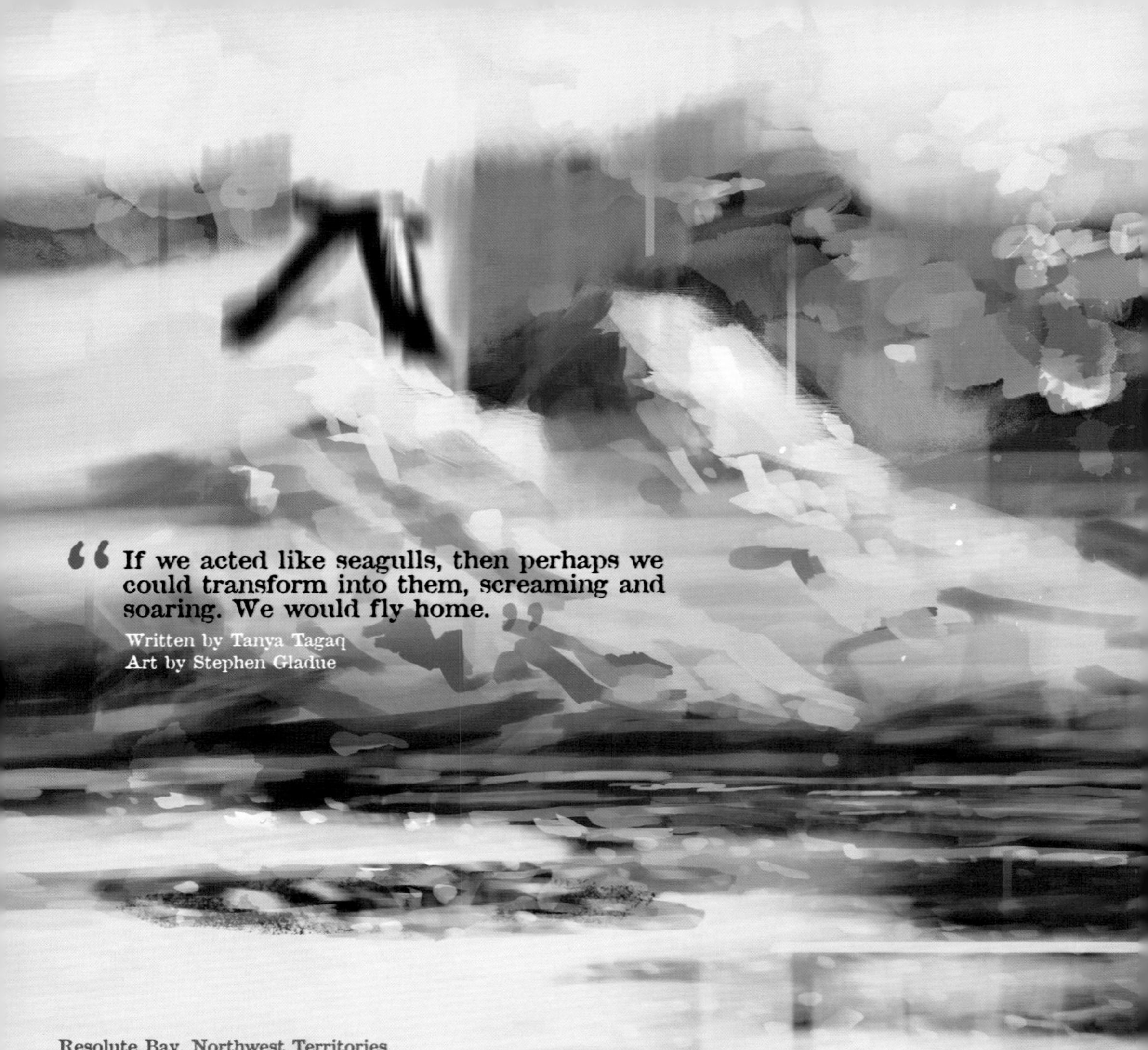

> "If we acted like seagulls, then perhaps we could transform into them, screaming and soaring. We would fly home."

Written by Tanya Tagaq
Art by Stephen Gladue

Resolute Bay, Northwest Territories

My little cousin, you were only seven years old. I was eleven, the big girl. We pilfered money from our parents and went to the store. The Resolute Bay Co-op always had a particular smell. It smelled dry, a little like mildew and a lot like dust. The aisles seemed so long, with all the possibilities in the world contained in the form of candy. After intense negotiation of what to buy, we left with two giant plastic bags of junk food. Cokes, M&M's, salt and vinegar potato chips, the weird pink popcorn with an elephant on the package, Popeye's brand candy cigarettes, and even a few real cigarettes. We lit the cigarettes behind the old A-Framed house near the playground, hoping that our mothers would not see us. We had already been caught smoking under the porch while eating a bottle of Flintstones vitamins. Nobody was happy with us on that day. I was aware of being the bad influence, but could never keep you from following me from place to place. Sometimes I would trick you and run away, and then feel bad and come back, your little tear-stained face making me feel like I had no soul. I never let you tag along while hanging out with the big boys, because we were always up to no good. You were too small for all of that chaos. I did my best to protect you. I still do.

It was getting late, but it didn't matter. The twenty-four-hour sun was blazing high in the sky, and the cold wind kept us alert. Three months of bright light meant that there was no curfew, no time constraints. We wanted an adventure, which usually meant a hike out of town. There were a few interesting places we could go on our trek, considering the vastness of the tundra. The river was relatively close, where we would balance a two-by-four between the jagged rocks of the rapids and cross, praying our makeshift bridge would not falter. We could go to the beach. The shore was ripe with seaweed and their treasures. Remember that time we found a sea snake, its bloated corpse so cold and lonely? The playground was all right, but inevitably one particular gas-sniffing jerk would come along and pester us. Best to get out of town. We marched out on our own, feeling like big girls, teenage girls. You trailed behind on your tiny legs. Signal Hill was the best option today. Making it to the transmission tower was good, but I wanted the cliffs. It was a steep climb and our breath was heavy when we reached the top. We ate half of our food as we sat on the summit, our feet dangling over the precipice as we kept our eye out for polar bears. Uncle Nathaniel used to slide down this hill in the winter. I remember thinking that he was the coolest, and hoped I would reach that level of awesomeness when I grew up.

We decided to try to make it to Nine Mile Lake. It seemed like just a few kilometres from the top of the hill. This is when I learned that on the tundra, everything is much farther away than it seems. The treeless expanse lends itself to illusion. We could handle it. The most daunting task was passing the seagull nests. There was no going around them; we had to run through their nesting zone. I recall that being one of the scariest things I had to do to date, draw up my courage and run as quickly as possible, your little hand in mine. Seagulls scream and dive when you get near their nests. I held my fist up into the sky and waved it as we ran, so they would go for the highest point of contact. I could feel

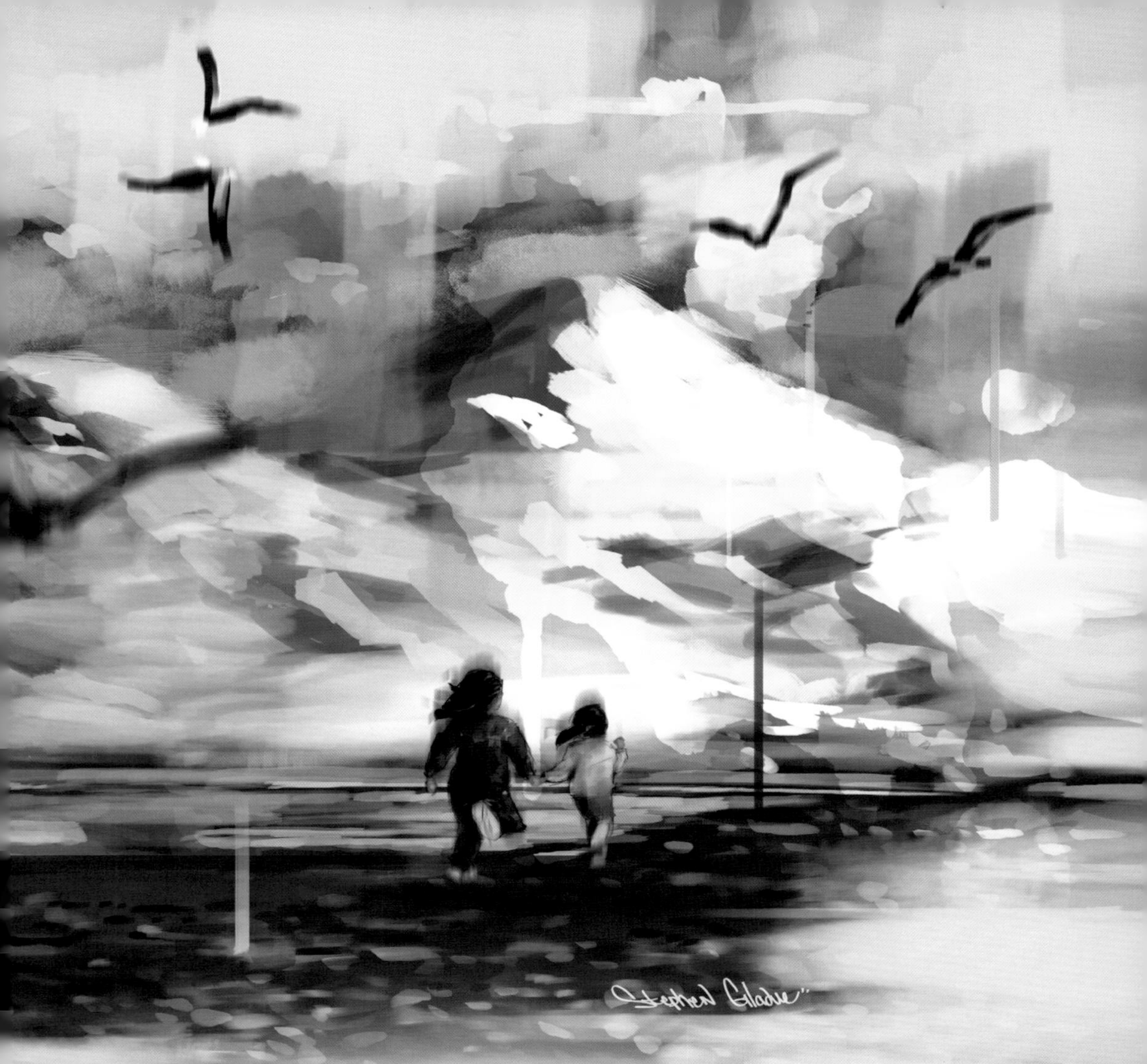
Stephen Gladue

their beaks pecking through my thin glove. We ran as quickly as we could, even losing a few bags of chips from our precious rations. We were red-faced and laughing once we made it through. I will never forget your sweet little face that day, proud and exhilarated with our accomplishment. I carried your heart in mine. I still do.

The tundra is sparse, rocky, no trees and hardly any dirt. The lichens take hundreds of years to grow. They grow and die and eventually collect to make up the soil. We were surrounded by shale rock, dry and sharp under the feet. The clean and hollow sound of walking on shale is still one of my favorite sounds. Random pieces of plywood were lying on the ground. They must have blown away from some construction site during a blast of fierce winds. It was fun to flip these over, because lemmings and other creatures used them for shelter in the unforgiving landscape. We would chase and catch the lemmings, eventually letting them go after holding them long enough to calm their little heartbeats. We felt like heroes when we calmed them down, not realizing if we just left them unmolested it would have been better for their well being.

One piece of plywood we lifted had a snow bunting's nest under it. Three bald baby birds screamed at us. They were so small, newly hatched. The veins under their still-closed eyelids were purple and throbbing, their necks barely strong enough to hold up their heads. Shrill cries filled the air, and a panic arose. We wanted to make them happy! Were they hungry? We opened up the elephant popcorn. We fed the little mouths. In horror, we watched as each one of them choked and died on the popcorn. We could see the kernels through their little transparent throats. There was nothing we could do. The mother came back from her insect hunt and made us cry even harder. We left in defeat, feeling like demons and hoping neither of us would speak of it again. I made the biggest mistakes with you. I still do.

Finally arriving at Nine Mile Lake, we were thankful that the wind had died down a bit. This is good because polar bears can't smell you as easily. The water was vast and clean. Thirst is easily quenched by fresh Arctic water. Around the periphery of the lake, there were small pools that held baby trout. I trapped one and put it in my mouth. I let it swim down my esophagus. Upon swallowing another one, its tail tickled all the way down to my tummy. It was delightful. The flesh was so fresh. Something awoke in me, an old memory; an ancient memory, of eating live flesh. It is a true joining of flesh to flesh. My spine straightened. When flesh is eaten live, you glean the spirit with the energy. That is why wild predators are so strong. The farther away you get from the time of death, the less energy meat carries. We pretended to be seagulls, not even chewing the fish and feeling them swim down our throats. We gorged ourselves on them. The energy of the fish's life was readily absorbed into my body, and its death throes became a shining and swimming beacon into the sky.

If we acted like seagulls, than perhaps we could transform into them, screaming and soaring. We would fly home.

End.

Daniel Heath Justice's

THE BOYS WHO BECAME THE HUMMINGBIRDS

Illustrated by Weshoyot Alvitre

BACKGROUND

There are multiple versions of a Cherokee story that tell of a sick People who have had their sacred medicine – tobacco – stolen (or selfishly possessed) by dangerous guardians. It is the swift Hummingbird who is able to return the medicine to the People and helps heal their sickness. In one account, Hummingbird is a medicine man who uses the bird's skin to transform himself, thus evading capture and taking back the tobacco. The Cherokee Nation author of the story you are about to read, loosely inspired by that original tale, tells of the fierce beauty and unexpected resilience of the hummingbird in a two-spirit parable about a different kind of sickness, and an altogether different kind of healing.

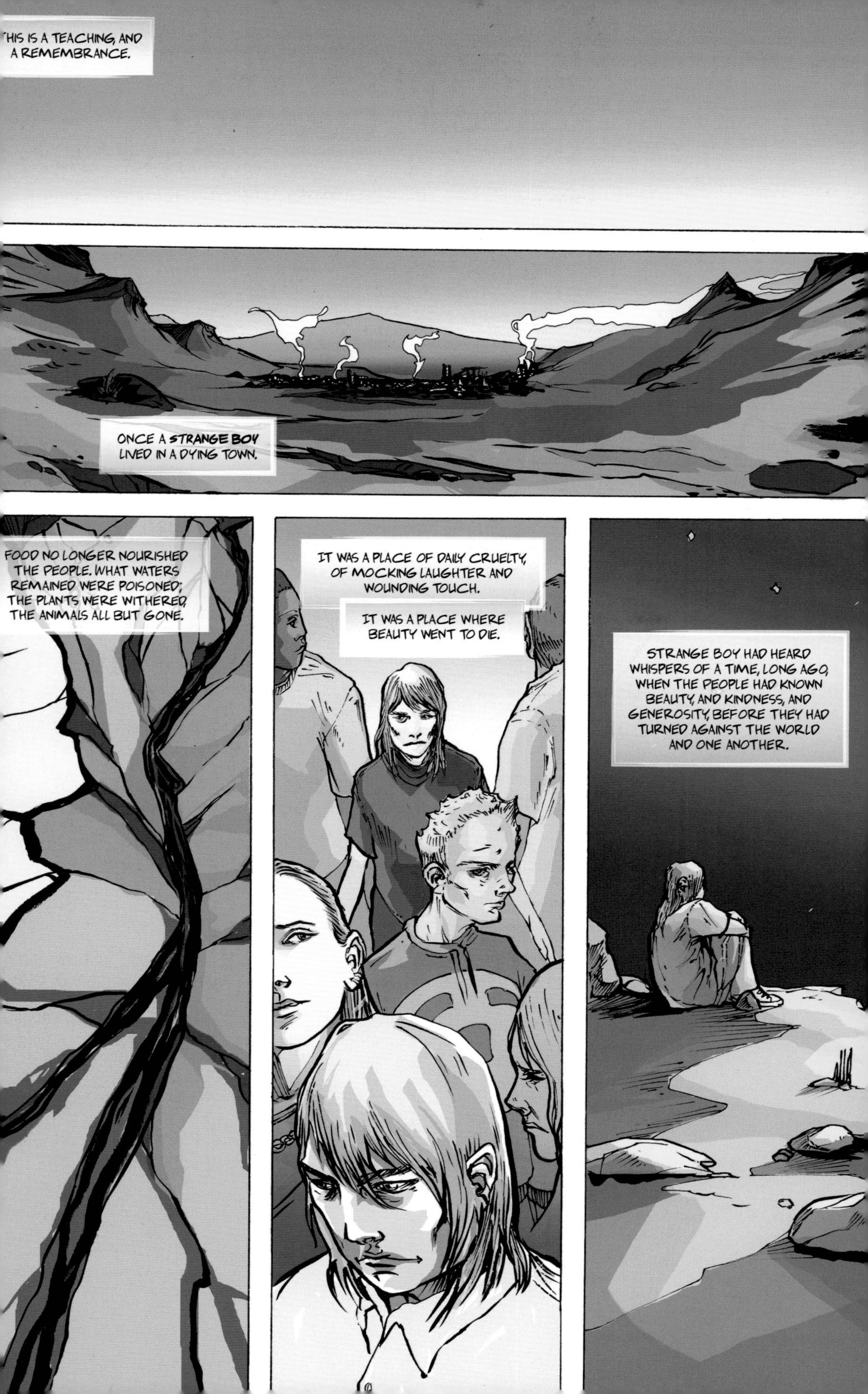
THIS IS A TEACHING, AND A REMEMBRANCE.
ONCE A STRANGE BOY LIVED IN A DYING TOWN.
FOOD NO LONGER NOURISHED THE PEOPLE. WHAT WATERS REMAINED WERE POISONED; THE PLANTS WERE WITHERED, THE ANIMALS ALL BUT GONE.
IT WAS A PLACE OF DAILY CRUELTY, OF MOCKING LAUGHTER AND WOUNDING TOUCH.
IT WAS A PLACE WHERE BEAUTY WENT TO DIE.
STRANGE BOY HAD HEARD WHISPERS OF A TIME, LONG AGO, WHEN THE PEOPLE HAD KNOWN BEAUTY, AND KINDNESS, AND GENEROSITY, BEFORE THEY HAD TURNED AGAINST THE WORLD AND ONE ANOTHER.

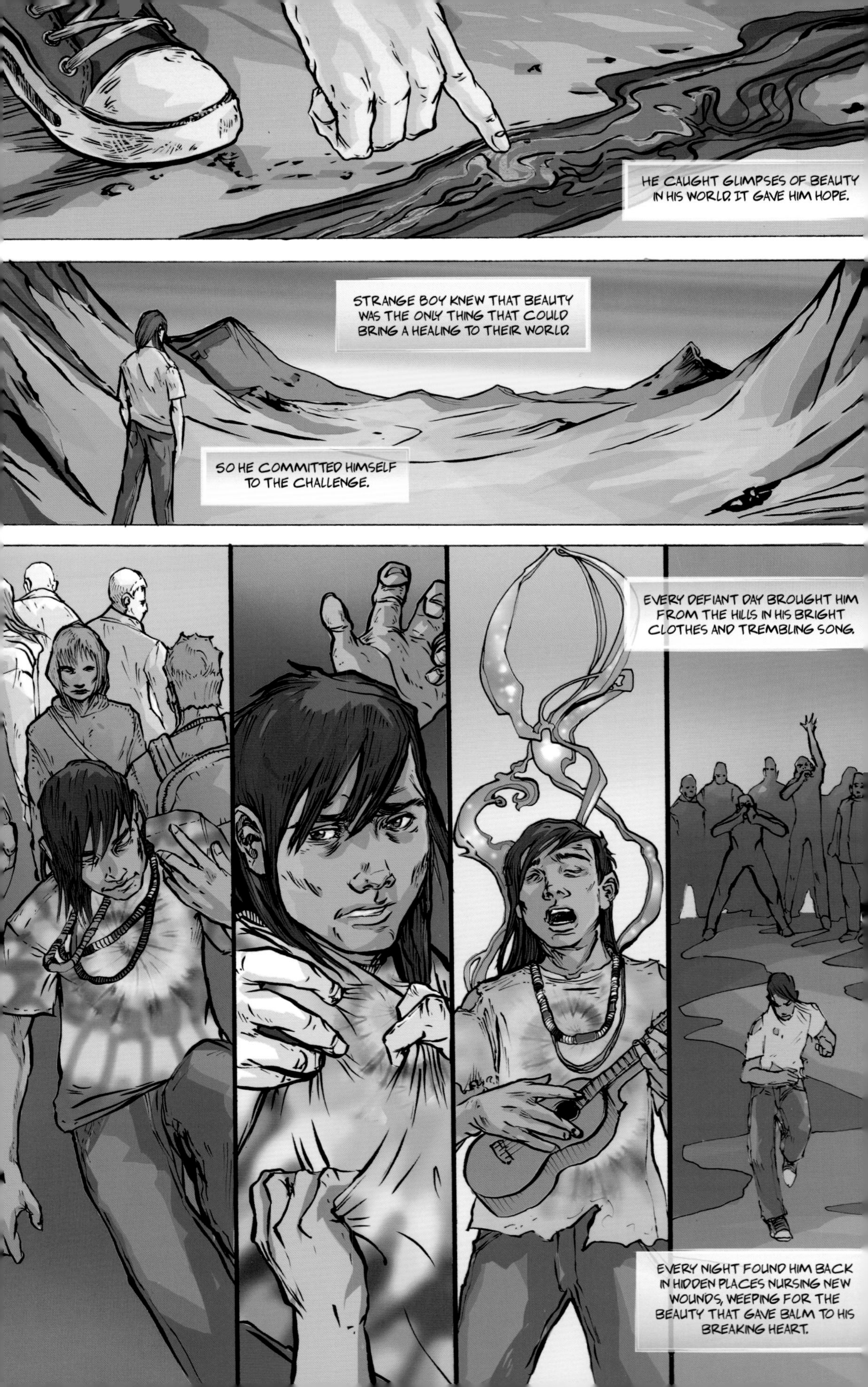
HE CAUGHT GLIMPSES OF BEAUTY IN HIS WORLD. IT GAVE HIM HOPE.
STRANGE BOY KNEW THAT BEAUTY WAS THE ONLY THING THAT COULD BRING A HEALING TO THEIR WORLD.
SO HE COMMITTED HIMSELF TO THE CHALLENGE.
EVERY DEFIANT DAY BROUGHT HIM FROM THE HILLS IN HIS BRIGHT CLOTHES AND TREMBLING SONG.
EVERY NIGHT FOUND HIM BACK IN HIDDEN PLACES NURSING NEW WOUNDS, WEEPING FOR THE BEAUTY THAT GAVE BALM TO HIS BREAKING HEART.

OCCASIONALLY HE FOUND A COMPANION IN THE WELCOMING DARKNESS AND TASTED SWEET, FLEETING MOMENTS OF WHAT COULD BE.

BUT THE NIGHT'S DELIGHTS NEVER LASTED UNTIL MORNING, AND HE ALWAYS AWOKE ALONE.

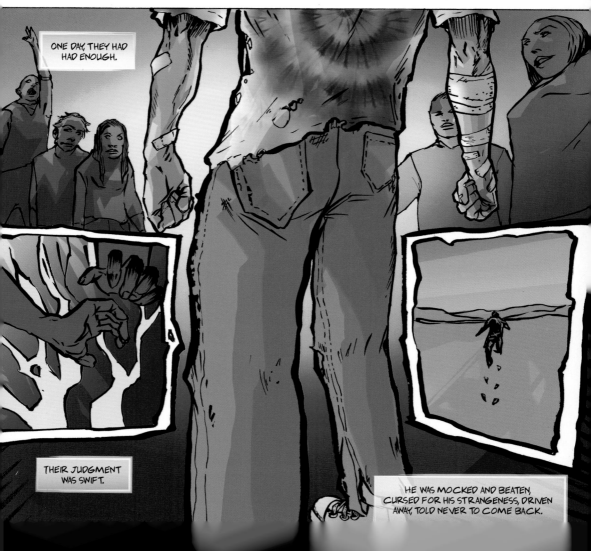

ONE DAY, THEY HAD HAD ENOUGH.

THEIR JUDGMENT WAS SWIFT.

HE WAS MOCKED AND BEATEN, CURSED FOR HIS STRANGENESS, DRIVEN AWAY, TOLD NEVER TO COME BACK.

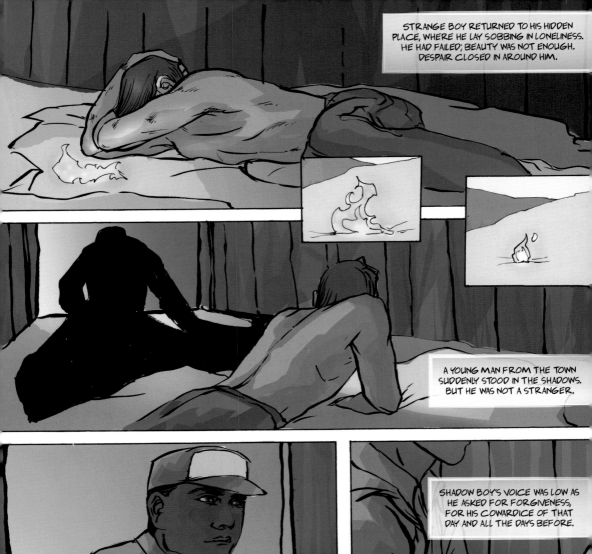

STRANGE BOY RETURNED TO HIS HIDDEN PLACE, WHERE HE LAY SOBBING IN LONELINESS. HE HAD FAILED; BEAUTY WAS NOT ENOUGH. DESPAIR CLOSED IN AROUND HIM.

A YOUNG MAN FROM THE TOWN SUDDENLY STOOD IN THE SHADOWS. BUT HE WAS NOT A STRANGER.

THEY HAD SHARED MORE THAN ONE TENDER MOMENT IN THE DARKNESS, BUT IN THE DAYLIGHT THE ONE CALLED **SHADOW BOY** HAD STOOD IN SILENCE AS THE CROWD INFLICTED ITS CRUELTIES.

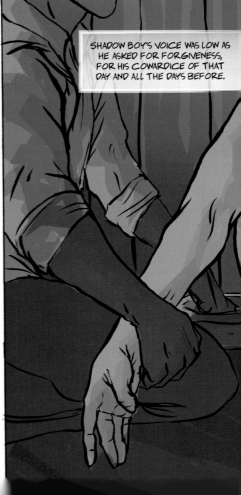

SHADOW BOY'S VOICE WAS LOW AS HE ASKED FOR FORGIVENESS, FOR HIS COWARDICE OF THAT DAY AND ALL THE DAYS BEFORE.

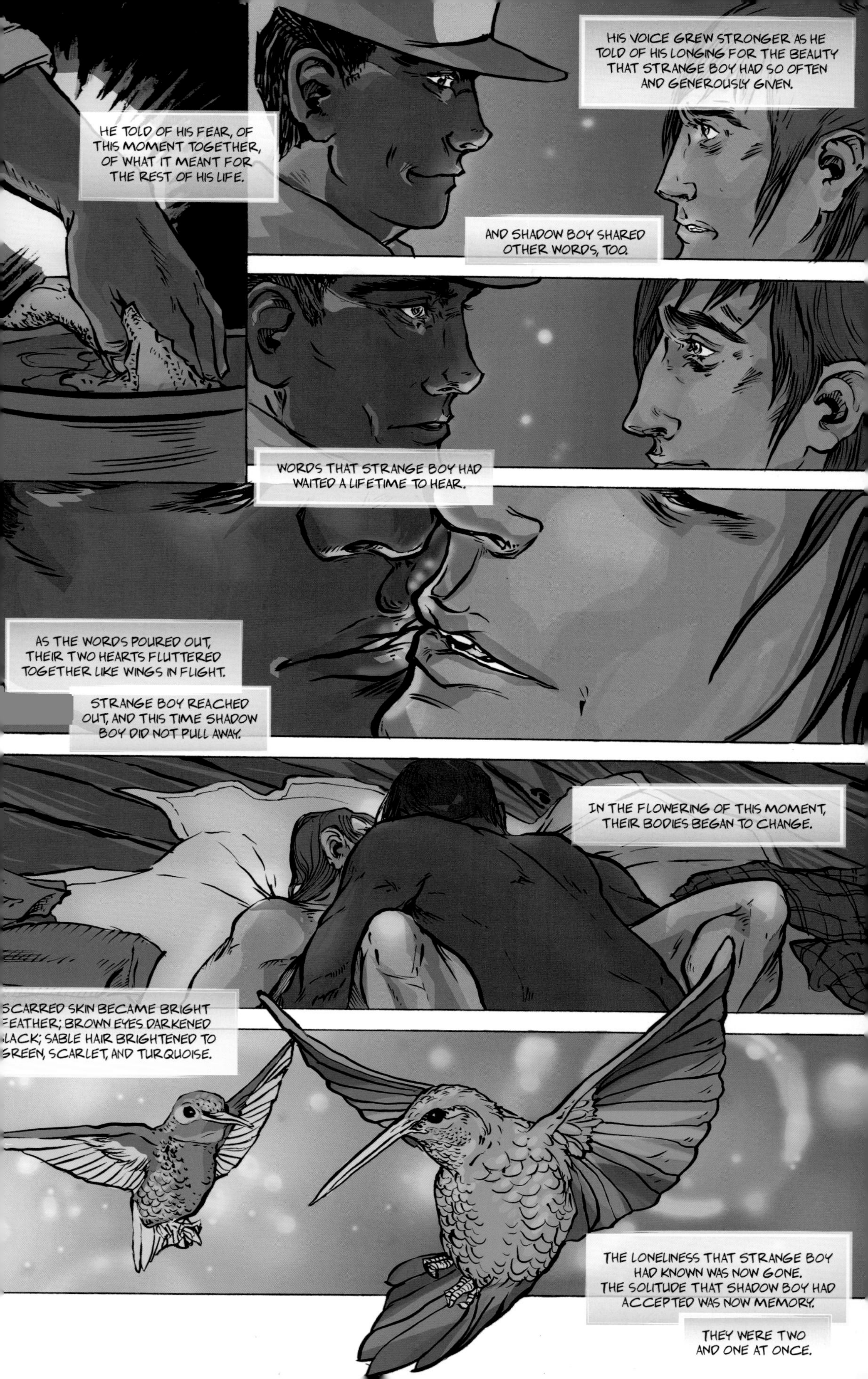
HE TOLD OF HIS FEAR, OF THIS MOMENT TOGETHER, OF WHAT IT MEANT FOR THE REST OF HIS LIFE.
HIS VOICE GREW STRONGER AS HE TOLD OF HIS LONGING FOR THE BEAUTY THAT STRANGE BOY HAD SO OFTEN AND GENEROUSLY GIVEN.
AND SHADOW BOY SHARED OTHER WORDS, TOO.
WORDS THAT STRANGE BOY HAD WAITED A LIFETIME TO HEAR.
AS THE WORDS POURED OUT, THEIR TWO HEARTS FLUTTERED TOGETHER LIKE WINGS IN FLIGHT.
STRANGE BOY REACHED OUT, AND THIS TIME SHADOW BOY DID NOT PULL AWAY.
IN THE FLOWERING OF THIS MOMENT, THEIR BODIES BEGAN TO CHANGE.
SCARRED SKIN BECAME BRIGHT FEATHER; BROWN EYES DARKENED BLACK; SABLE HAIR BRIGHTENED TO GREEN, SCARLET, AND TURQUOISE.
THE LONELINESS THAT STRANGE BOY HAD KNOWN WAS NOW GONE. THE SOLITUDE THAT SHADOW BOY HAD ACCEPTED WAS NOW MEMORY.
THEY WERE TWO AND ONE AT ONCE.

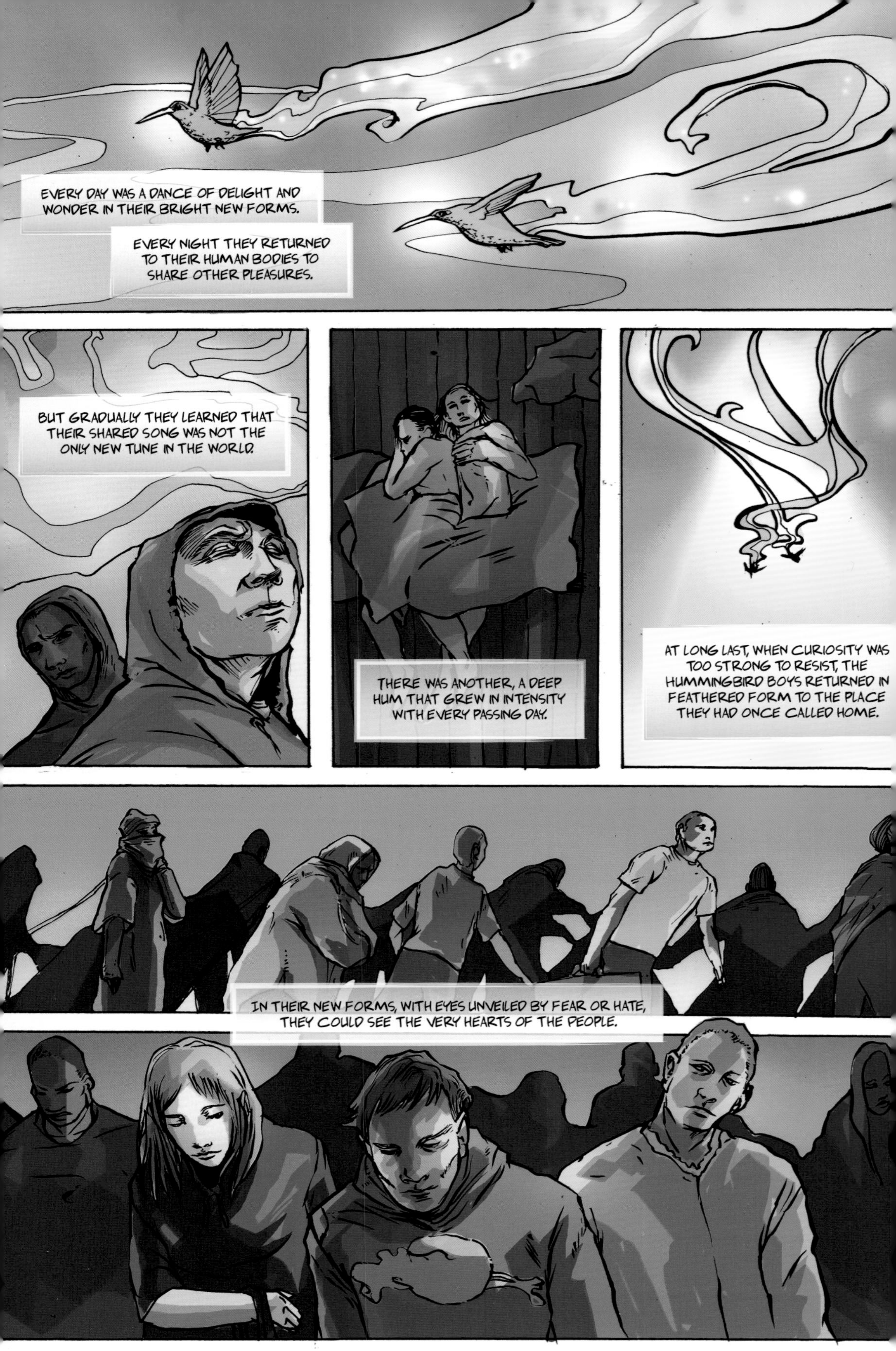
EVERY DAY WAS A DANCE OF DELIGHT AND WONDER IN THEIR BRIGHT NEW FORMS.
EVERY NIGHT THEY RETURNED TO THEIR HUMAN BODIES TO SHARE OTHER PLEASURES.
BUT GRADUALLY THEY LEARNED THAT THEIR SHARED SONG WAS NOT THE ONLY NEW TUNE IN THE WORLD.
THERE WAS ANOTHER, A DEEP HUM THAT GREW IN INTENSITY WITH EVERY PASSING DAY.
AT LONG LAST, WHEN CURIOSITY WAS TOO STRONG TO RESIST, THE HUMMINGBIRD BOYS RETURNED IN FEATHERED FORM TO THE PLACE THEY HAD ONCE CALLED HOME.
IN THEIR NEW FORMS, WITH EYES UNVEILED BY FEAR OR HATE, THEY COULD SEE THE VERY HEARTS OF THE PEOPLE.

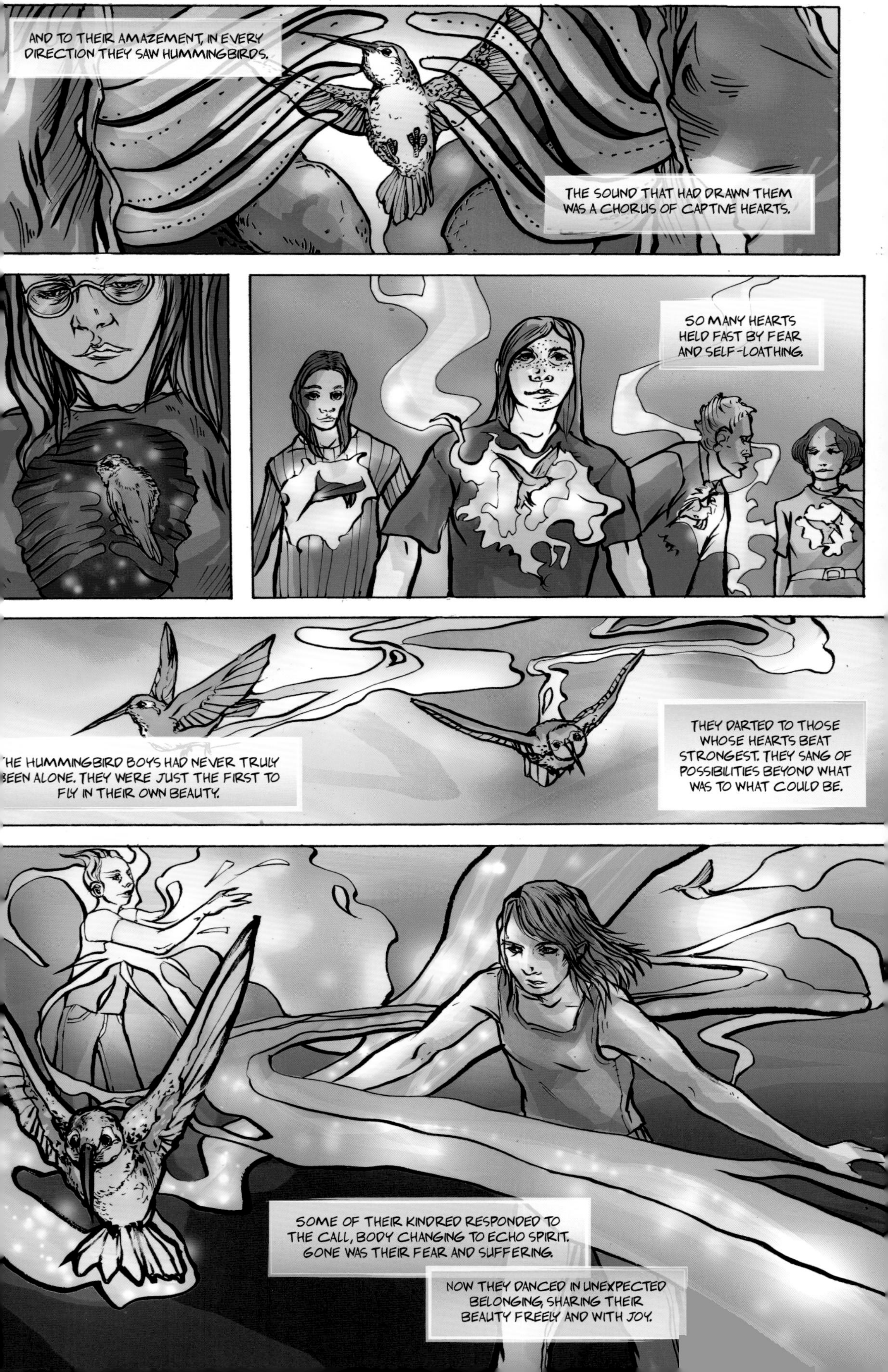
AND TO THEIR AMAZEMENT, IN EVERY DIRECTION THEY SAW HUMMINGBIRDS.
THE SOUND THAT HAD DRAWN THEM WAS A CHORUS OF CAPTIVE HEARTS.
SO MANY HEARTS HELD FAST BY FEAR AND SELF-LOATHING.
THE HUMMINGBIRD BOYS HAD NEVER TRULY BEEN ALONE. THEY WERE JUST THE FIRST TO FLY IN THEIR OWN BEAUTY.
THEY DARTED TO THOSE WHOSE HEARTS BEAT STRONGEST. THEY SANG OF POSSIBILITIES BEYOND WHAT WAS TO WHAT COULD BE.
SOME OF THEIR KINDRED RESPONDED TO THE CALL, BODY CHANGING TO ECHO SPIRIT. GONE WAS THEIR FEAR AND SUFFERING.
NOW THEY DANCED IN UNEXPECTED BELONGING, SHARING THEIR BEAUTY FREELY AND WITH JOY.

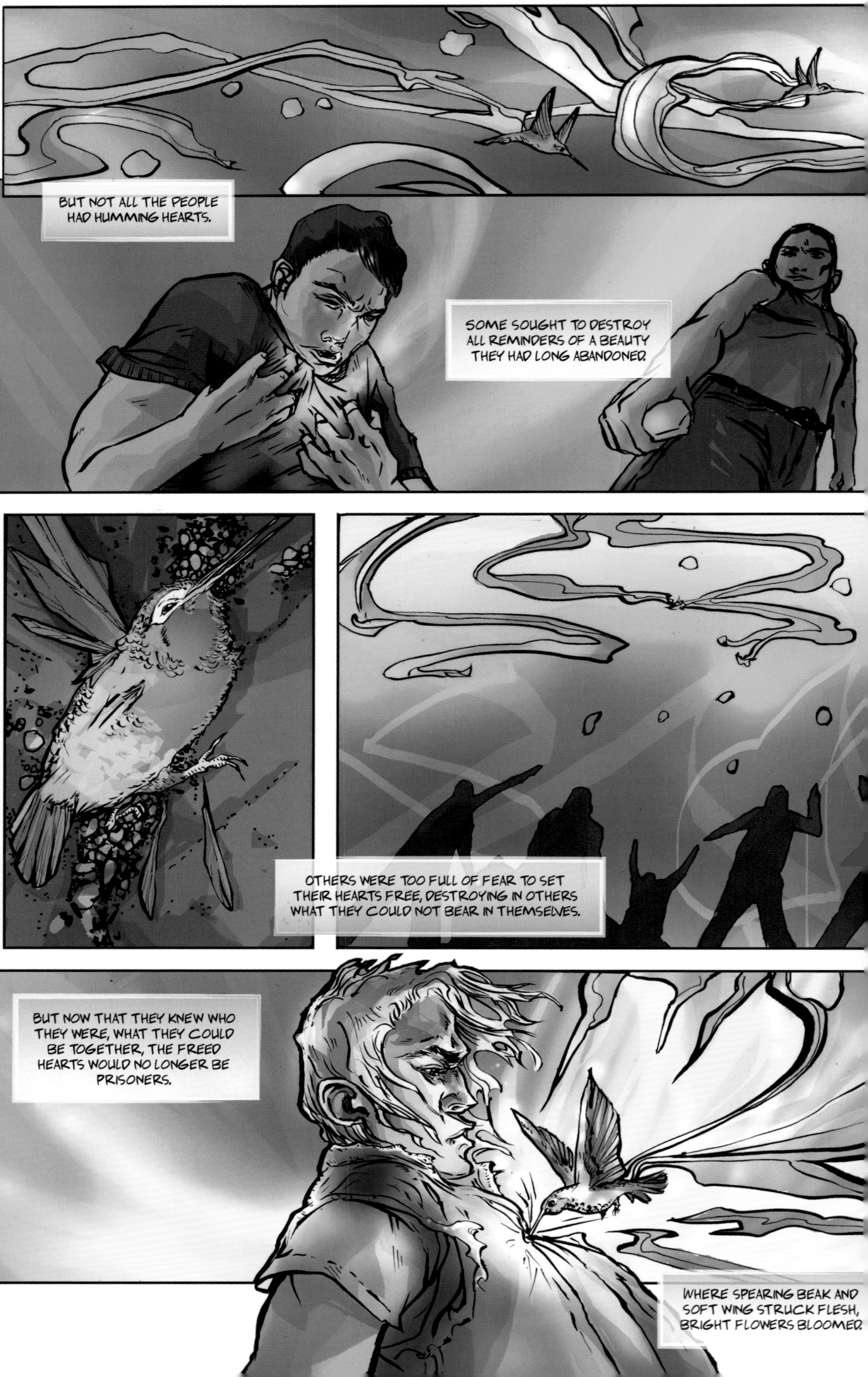
BUT NOT ALL THE PEOPLE HAD HUMMING HEARTS.
SOME SOUGHT TO DESTROY ALL REMINDERS OF A BEAUTY THEY HAD LONG ABANDONED.
OTHERS WERE TOO FULL OF FEAR TO SET THEIR HEARTS FREE, DESTROYING IN OTHERS WHAT THEY COULD NOT BEAR IN THEMSELVES.
BUT NOW THAT THEY KNEW WHO THEY WERE, WHAT THEY COULD BE TOGETHER, THE FREED HEARTS WOULD NO LONGER BE PRISONERS.
WHERE SPEARING BEAK AND SOFT WING STRUCK FLESH, BRIGHT FLOWERS BLOOMED.

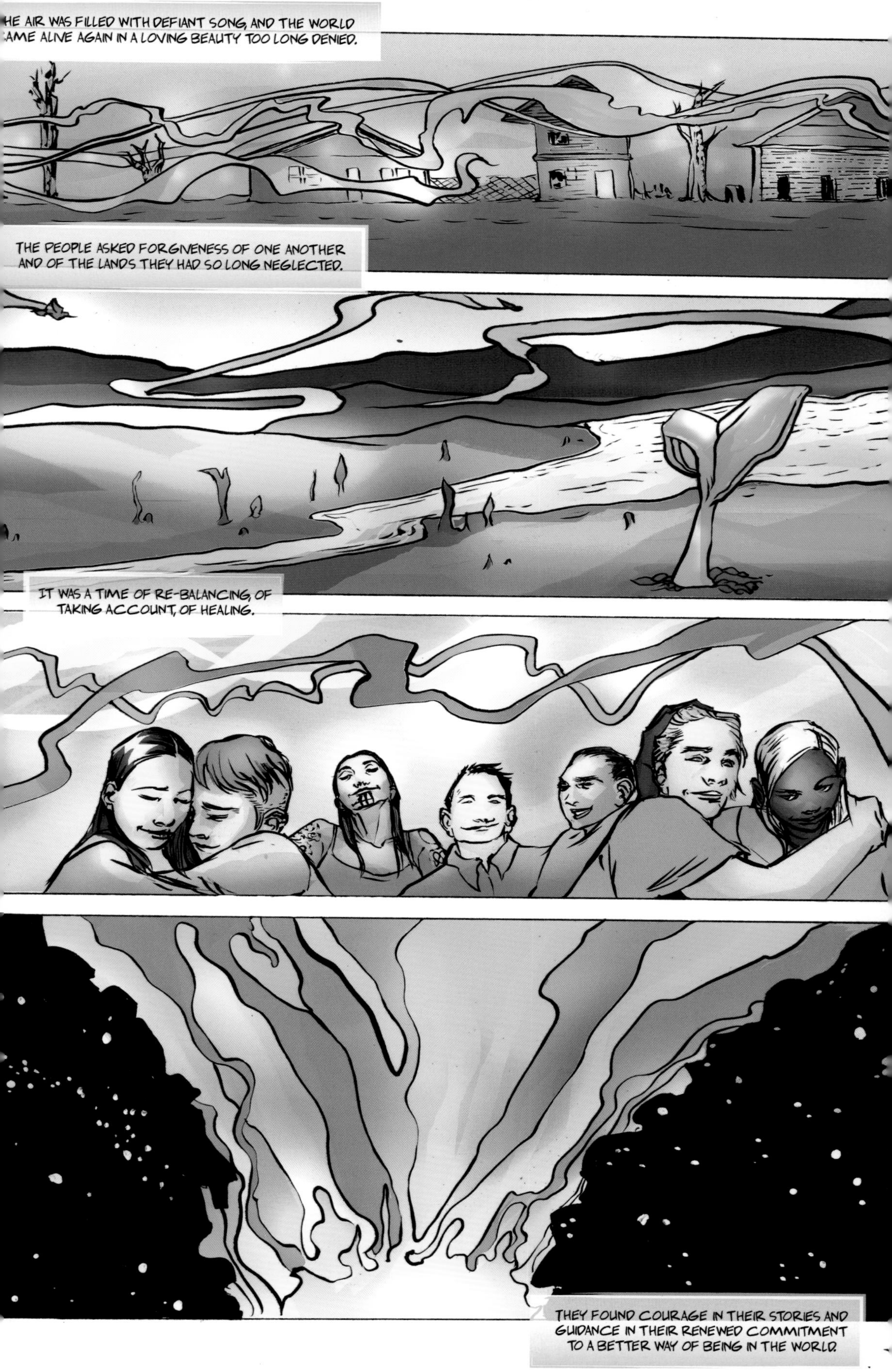
HE AIR WAS FILLED WITH DEFIANT SONG, AND THE WORLD
AME ALIVE AGAIN IN A LOVING BEAUTY TOO LONG DENIED.
THE PEOPLE ASKED FORGIVENESS OF ONE ANOTHER AND OF THE LANDS THEY HAD SO LONG NEGLECTED.
IT WAS A TIME OF RE-BALANCING, OF TAKING ACCOUNT, OF HEALING.
THEY FOUND COURAGE IN THEIR STORIES AND GUIDANCE IN THEIR RENEWED COMMITMENT TO A BETTER WAY OF BEING IN THE WORLD.

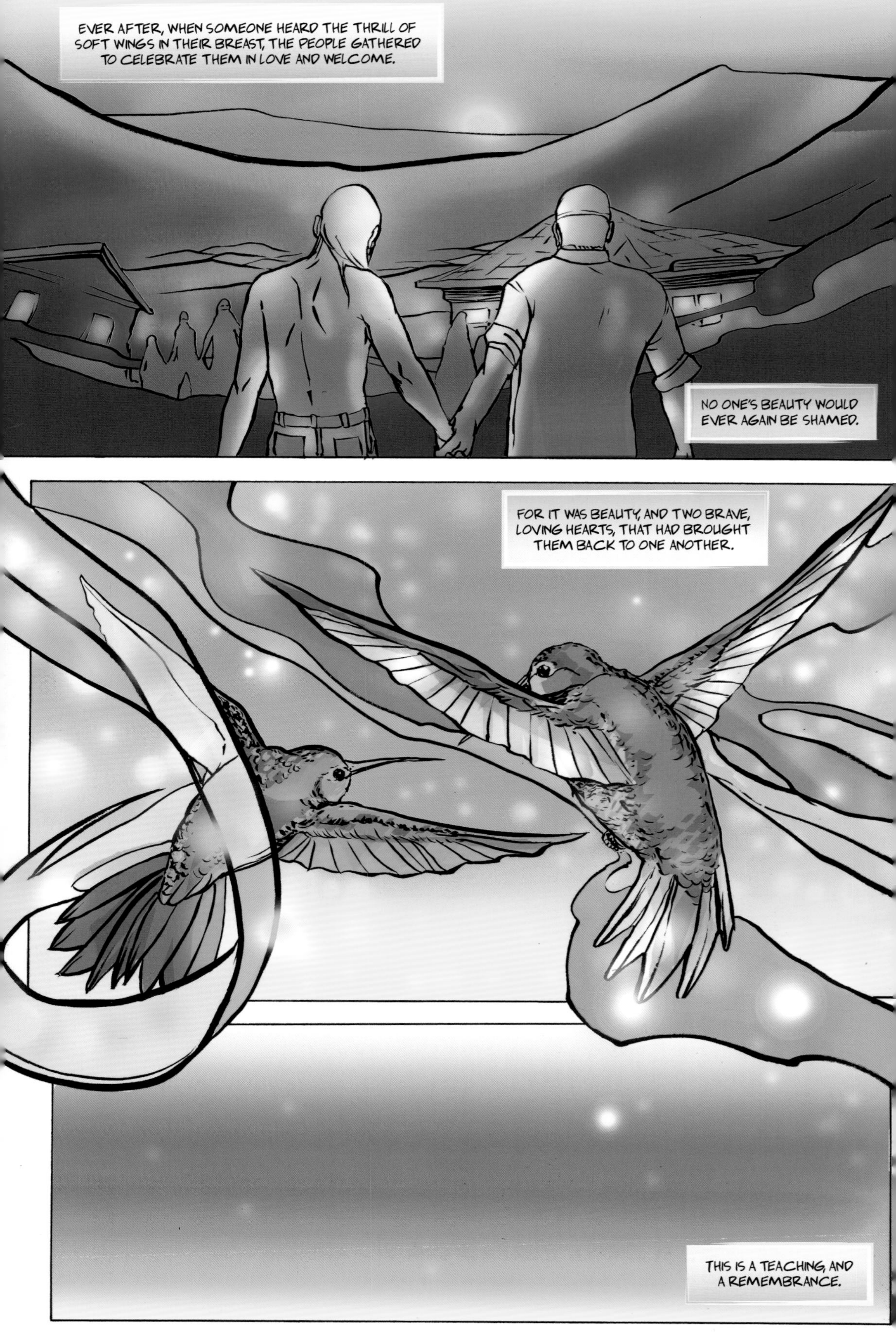
EVER AFTER, WHEN SOMEONE HEARD THE THRILL OF SOFT WINGS IN THEIR BREAST, THE PEOPLE GATHERED TO CELEBRATE THEM IN LOVE AND WELCOME.
NO ONE'S BEAUTY WOULD EVER AGAIN BE SHAMED.
FOR IT WAS BEAUTY, AND TWO BRAVE, LOVING HEARTS, THAT HAD BROUGHT THEM BACK TO ONE ANOTHER.
THIS IS A TEACHING, AND A REMEMBRANCE.

- END -

Richard Van Camp's

WATER
SPIRITS

Illustrated by Haiwei Hou

BACKGROUND

The history of the location and operations of the gold mining facility, as told by the fictional guide in this story, is true. This giant mine was an important part of Yellowknife's history, its prosperity and growth as a community. However, in its construction, the mine was also responsible for uprooting the Indigenous population and destroying the lands they protected for fish and other wildlife. The process used to extract gold leeched dangerous chemicals into the ground and water to such a large extent that the mine was shut down, known now as one of the most toxic industrial sites in Canada. It is this poisoning of the waters that inspired the author to create this piece, introducing readers to the Dene belief in the Water Spirits that exist in all vessels. The tradition of respecting the Spirits and never placing drinking cups directly on the ground, as described in the story, is typically told by Elders to youth only in the spoken word, making this story a unique experience.

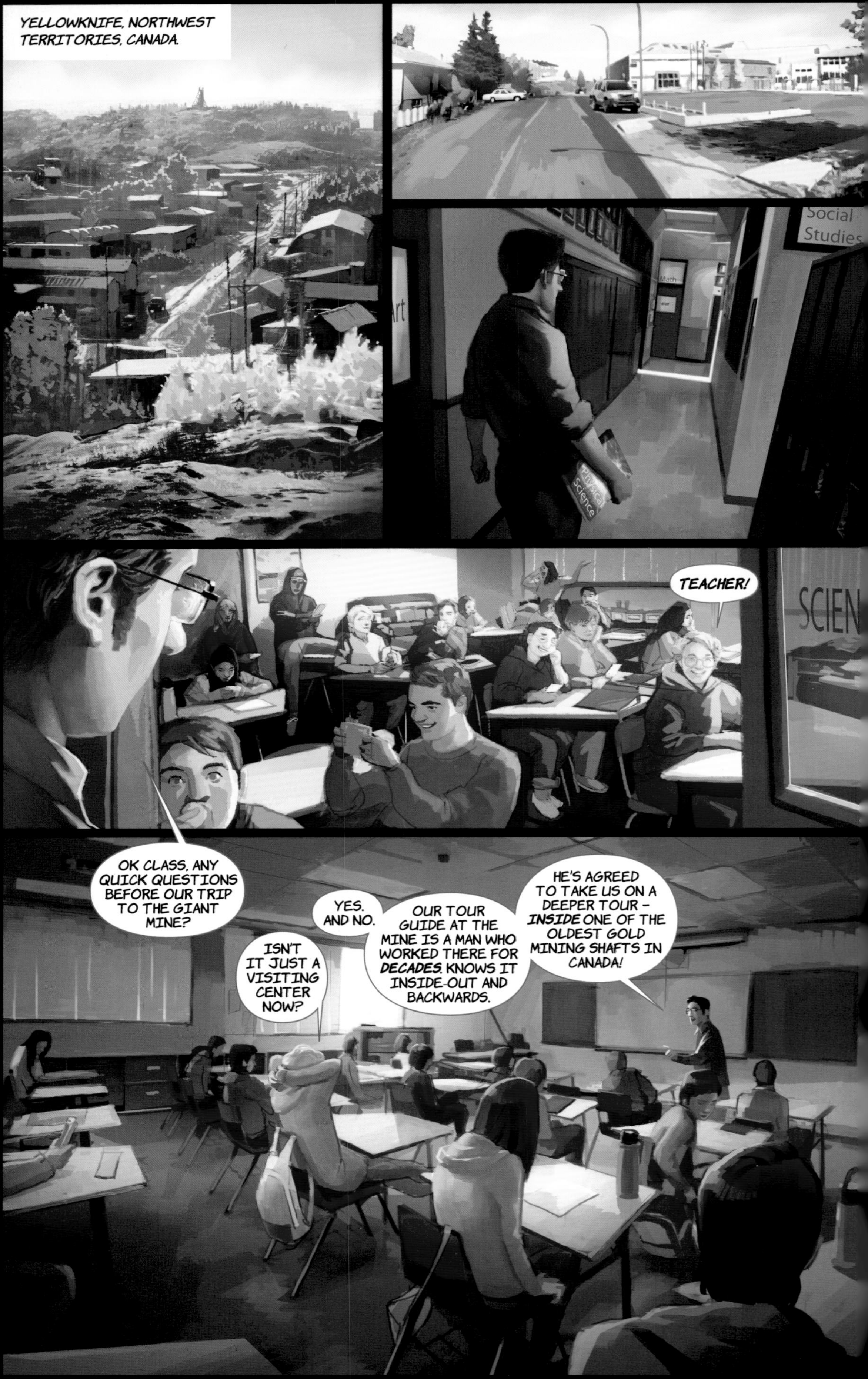
YELLOWKNIFE, NORTHWEST TERRITORIES, CANADA.
Social Studies
Math
Art
Physical Science
TEACHER!
SCIEN
OK CLASS, ANY QUICK QUESTIONS BEFORE OUR TRIP TO THE GIANT MINE?
ISN'T IT JUST A VISITING CENTER NOW?
YES. AND NO.
OUR TOUR GUIDE AT THE MINE IS A MAN WHO WORKED THERE FOR *DECADES*. KNOWS IT INSIDE-OUT AND BACKWARDS.
HE'S AGREED TO TAKE US ON A DEEPER TOUR – *INSIDE* ONE OF THE OLDEST GOLD MINING SHAFTS IN CANADA!

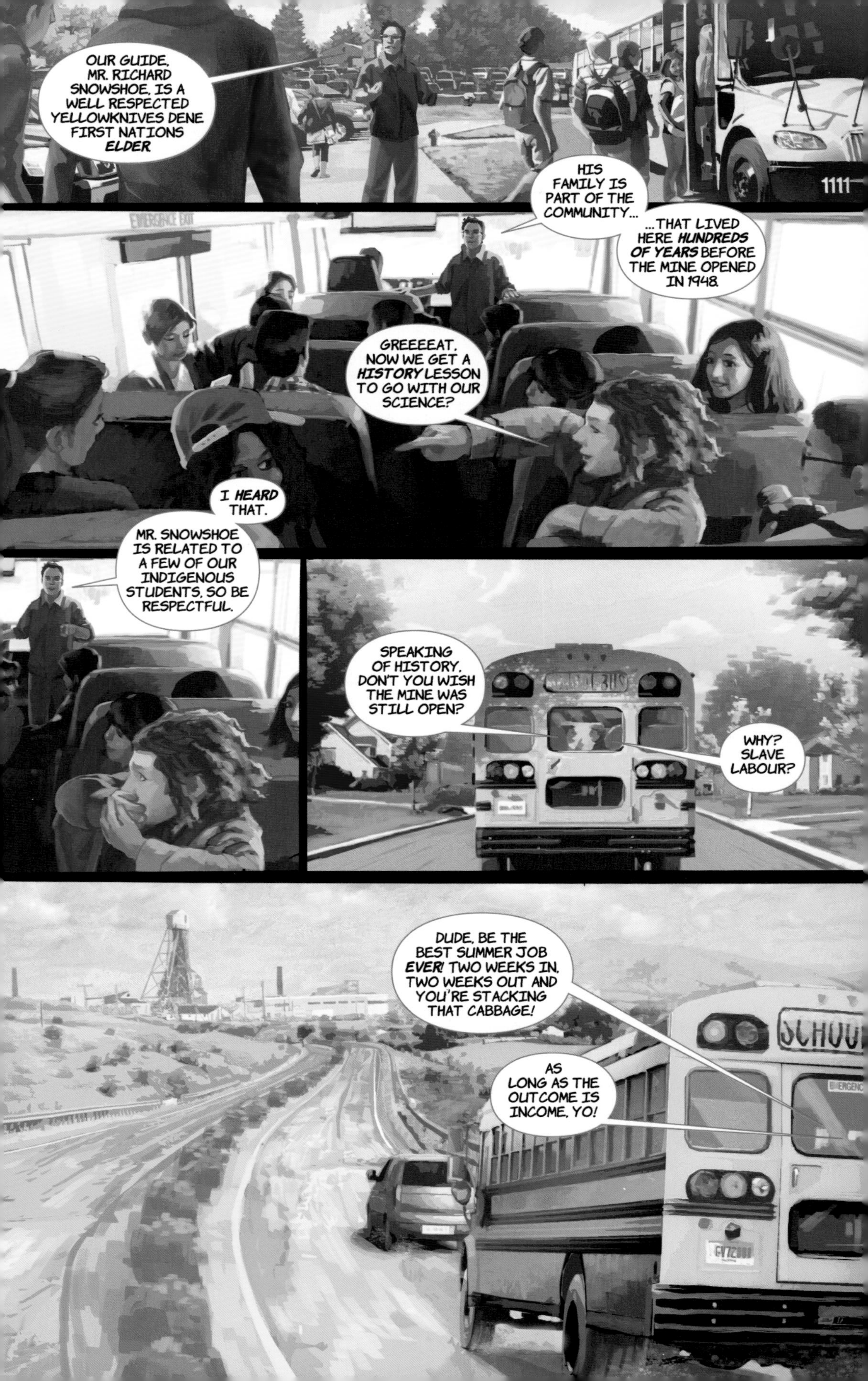
OUR GUIDE, MR. RICHARD SNOWSHOE, IS A WELL RESPECTED YELLOWKNIVES DENE FIRST NATIONS ELDER.
HIS FAMILY IS PART OF THE COMMUNITY...
...THAT LIVED HERE HUNDREDS OF YEARS BEFORE THE MINE OPENED IN 1948.
GREEEEAT, NOW WE GET A HISTORY LESSON TO GO WITH OUR SCIENCE?
I HEARD THAT.
MR. SNOWSHOE IS RELATED TO A FEW OF OUR INDIGENOUS STUDENTS, SO BE RESPECTFUL.
SPEAKING OF HISTORY, DON'T YOU WISH THE MINE WAS STILL OPEN?
WHY? SLAVE LABOUR?
DUDE, BE THE BEST SUMMER JOB EVER! TWO WEEKS IN, TWO WEEKS OUT AND YOU'RE STACKING THAT CABBAGE!
AS LONG AS THE OUTCOME IS INCOME, YO!

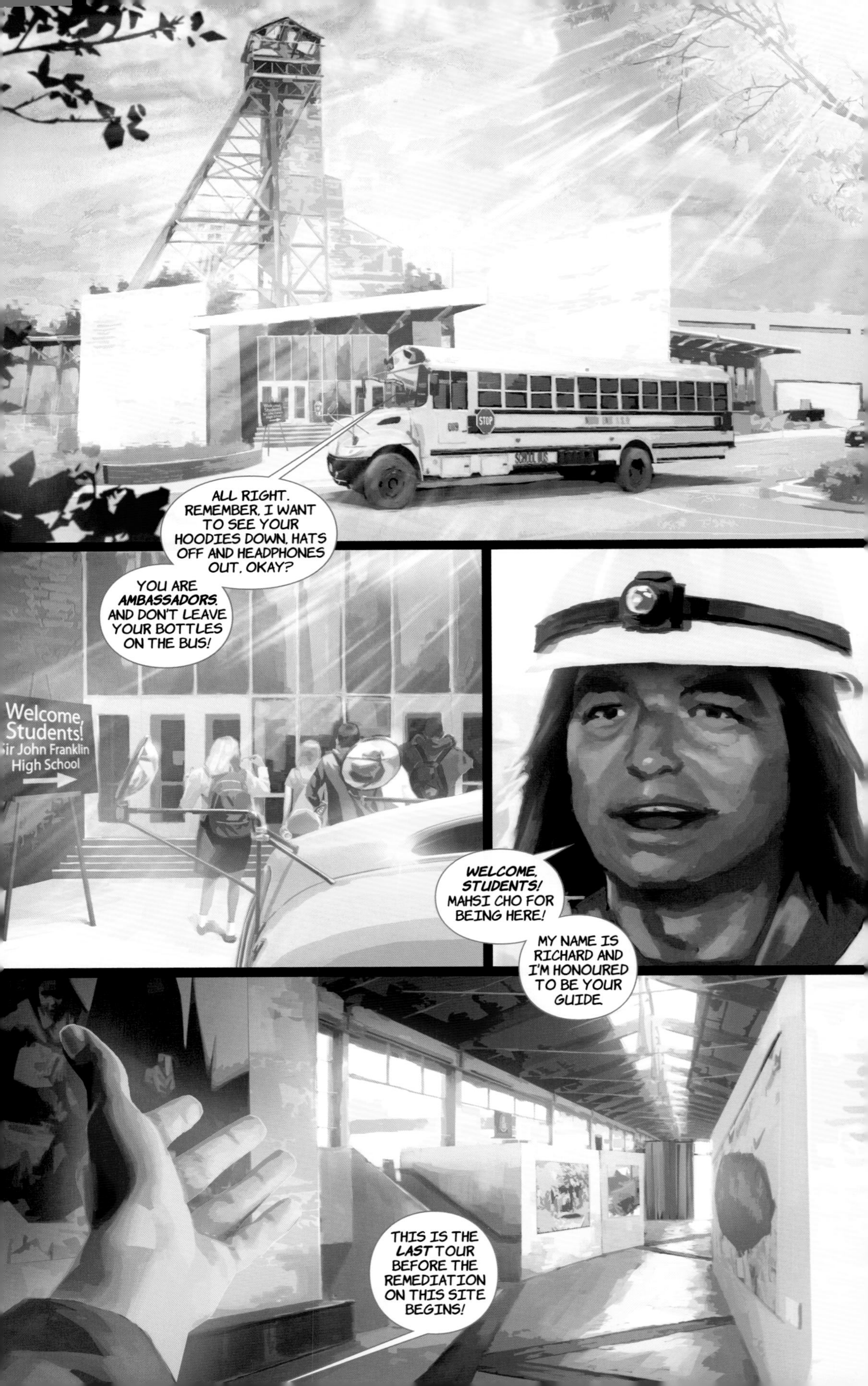
ALL RIGHT. REMEMBER, I WANT TO SEE YOUR HOODIES DOWN, HATS OFF AND HEADPHONES OUT, OKAY?
YOU ARE AMBASSADORS. AND DON'T LEAVE YOUR BOTTLES ON THE BUS!
Welcome, Students! Sir John Franklin High School
WELCOME, STUDENTS! MAHSI CHO FOR BEING HERE!
MY NAME IS RICHARD AND I'M HONOURED TO BE YOUR GUIDE.
THIS IS THE LAST TOUR BEFORE THE REMEDIATION ON THIS SITE BEGINS!

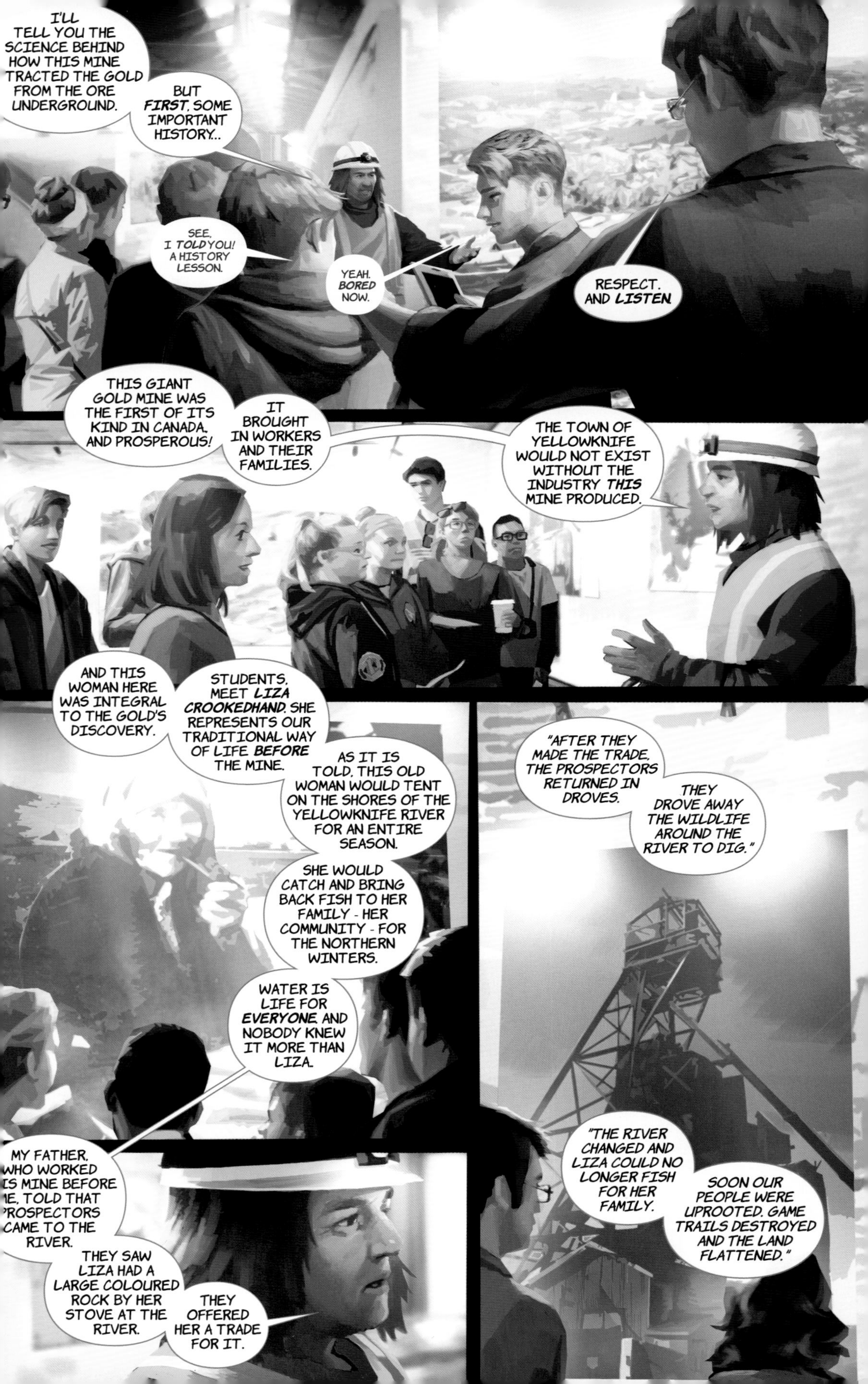
I'LL TELL YOU THE SCIENCE BEHIND HOW THIS MINE TRACTED THE GOLD FROM THE ORE UNDERGROUND.
BUT FIRST, SOME IMPORTANT HISTORY...
SEE, I TOLD YOU! A HISTORY LESSON.
YEAH. BORED NOW.
RESPECT. AND LISTEN.
THIS GIANT GOLD MINE WAS THE FIRST OF ITS KIND IN CANADA, AND PROSPEROUS!
IT BROUGHT IN WORKERS AND THEIR FAMILIES.
THE TOWN OF YELLOWKNIFE WOULD NOT EXIST WITHOUT THE INDUSTRY THIS MINE PRODUCED.
AND THIS WOMAN HERE WAS INTEGRAL TO THE GOLD'S DISCOVERY.
STUDENTS, MEET LIZA CROOKEDHAND. SHE REPRESENTS OUR TRADITIONAL WAY OF LIFE BEFORE THE MINE.
AS IT IS TOLD, THIS OLD WOMAN WOULD TENT ON THE SHORES OF THE YELLOWKNIFE RIVER FOR AN ENTIRE SEASON.
SHE WOULD CATCH AND BRING BACK FISH TO HER FAMILY - HER COMMUNITY - FOR THE NORTHERN WINTERS.
WATER IS LIFE FOR EVERYONE, AND NOBODY KNEW IT MORE THAN LIZA.
MY FATHER, WHO WORKED IS MINE BEFORE IE, TOLD THAT PROSPECTORS CAME TO THE RIVER.
THEY SAW LIZA HAD A LARGE COLOURED ROCK BY HER STOVE AT THE RIVER.
THEY OFFERED HER A TRADE FOR IT.
"AFTER THEY MADE THE TRADE, THE PROSPECTORS RETURNED IN DROVES.
THEY DROVE AWAY THE WILDLIFE AROUND THE RIVER TO DIG."
"THE RIVER CHANGED AND LIZA COULD NO LONGER FISH FOR HER FAMILY.
SOON OUR PEOPLE WERE UPROOTED. GAME TRAILS DESTROYED AND THE LAND FLATTENED."

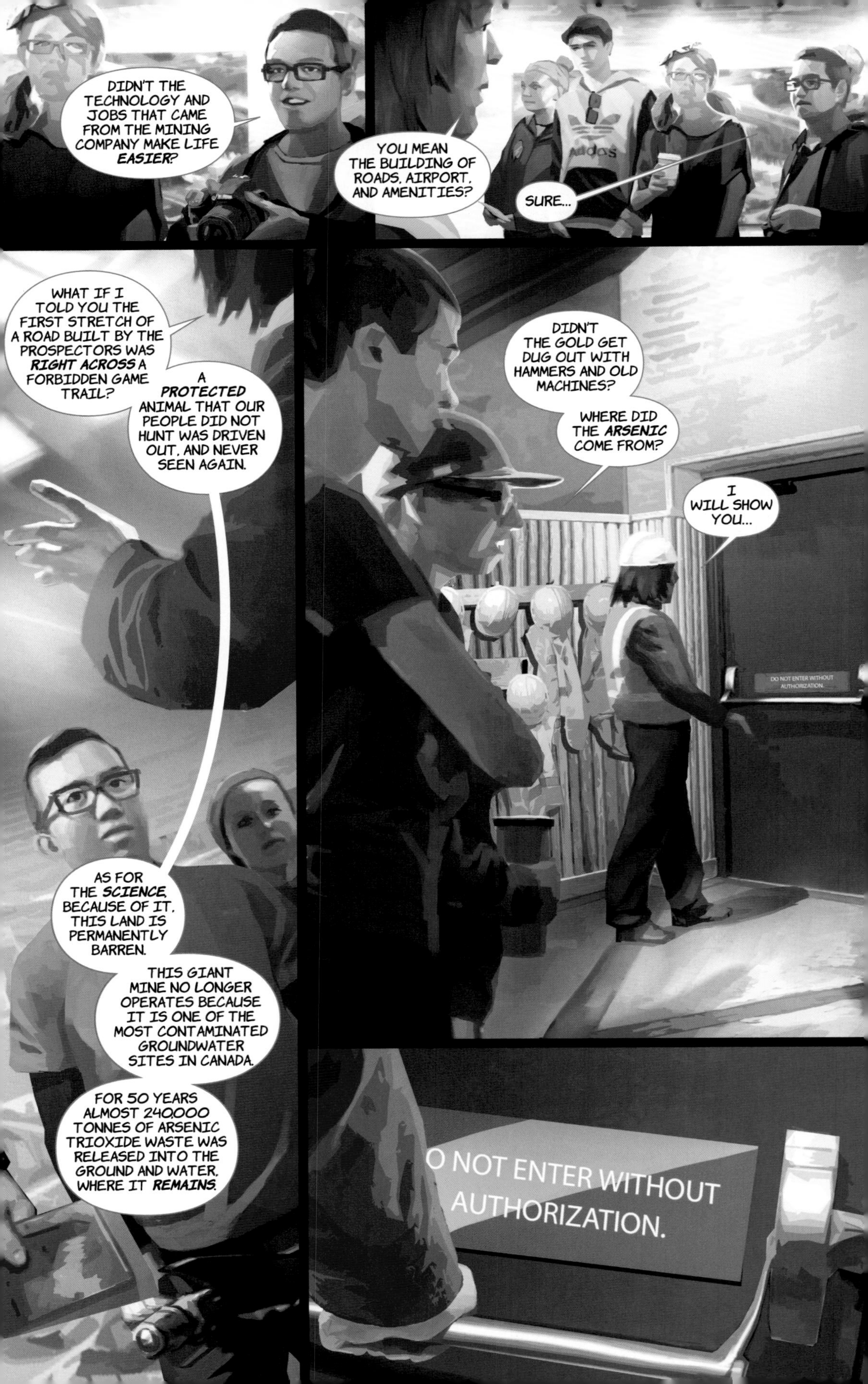
DIDN'T THE TECHNOLOGY AND JOBS THAT CAME FROM THE MINING COMPANY MAKE LIFE **EASIER**?
YOU MEAN THE BUILDING OF ROADS, AIRPORT, AND AMENITIES?
SURE...
WHAT IF I TOLD YOU THE FIRST STRETCH OF A ROAD BUILT BY THE PROSPECTORS WAS **RIGHT ACROSS** A FORBIDDEN GAME TRAIL?
A **PROTECTED** ANIMAL THAT OUR PEOPLE DID NOT HUNT WAS DRIVEN OUT, AND NEVER SEEN AGAIN.
DIDN'T THE GOLD GET DUG OUT WITH HAMMERS AND OLD MACHINES?
WHERE DID THE **ARSENIC** COME FROM?
I WILL SHOW YOU...
DO NOT ENTER WITHOUT AUTHORIZATION.
AS FOR THE **SCIENCE**, BECAUSE OF IT, THIS LAND IS PERMANENTLY BARREN.
THIS GIANT MINE NO LONGER OPERATES BECAUSE IT IS ONE OF THE MOST CONTAMINATED GROUNDWATER SITES IN CANADA.
FOR 50 YEARS ALMOST 240,000 TONNES OF ARSENIC TRIOXIDE WASTE WAS RELEASED INTO THE GROUND AND WATER, WHERE IT **REMAINS**.
O NOT ENTER WITHOUT AUTHORIZATION.

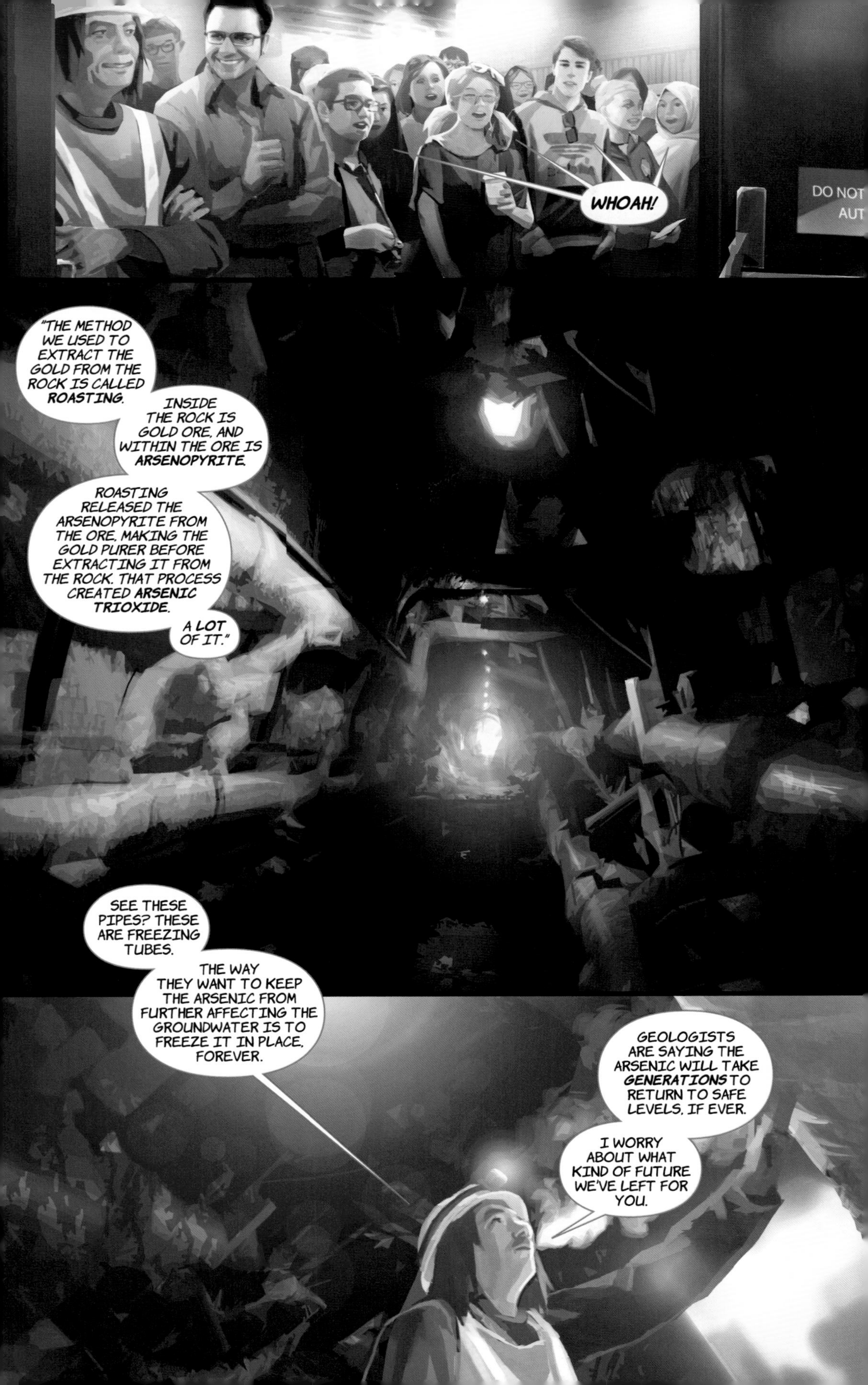
WHOAH!
DO NOT
AUT
"THE METHOD WE USED TO EXTRACT THE GOLD FROM THE ROCK IS CALLED **ROASTING**.
INSIDE THE ROCK IS GOLD ORE, AND WITHIN THE ORE IS **ARSENOPYRITE**.
ROASTING RELEASED THE ARSENOPYRITE FROM THE ORE, MAKING THE GOLD PURER BEFORE EXTRACTING IT FROM THE ROCK. THAT PROCESS CREATED **ARSENIC TRIOXIDE**.
A **LOT** OF IT."
SEE THESE PIPES? THESE ARE FREEZING TUBES.
THE WAY THEY WANT TO KEEP THE ARSENIC FROM FURTHER AFFECTING THE GROUNDWATER IS TO FREEZE IT IN PLACE, FOREVER.
GEOLOGISTS ARE SAYING THE ARSENIC WILL TAKE ***GENERATIONS*** TO RETURN TO SAFE LEVELS, IF EVER.
I WORRY ABOUT WHAT KIND OF FUTURE WE'VE LEFT FOR YOU.

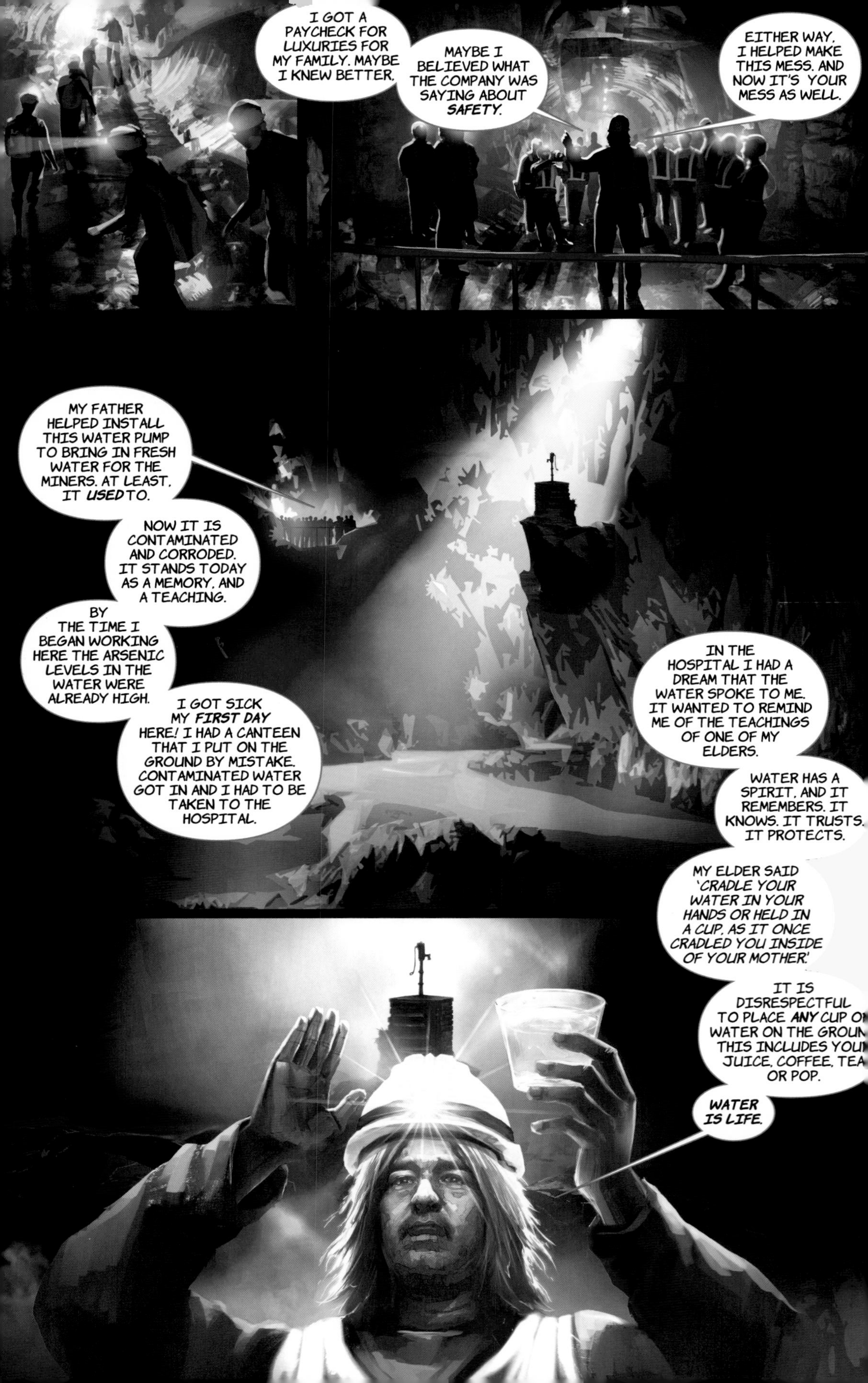
I GOT A PAYCHECK FOR LUXURIES FOR MY FAMILY. MAYBE I KNEW BETTER.
MAYBE I BELIEVED WHAT THE COMPANY WAS SAYING ABOUT SAFETY.
EITHER WAY, I HELPED MAKE THIS MESS. AND NOW IT'S YOUR MESS AS WELL.
MY FATHER HELPED INSTALL THIS WATER PUMP TO BRING IN FRESH WATER FOR THE MINERS. AT LEAST, IT USED TO.
NOW IT IS CONTAMINATED AND CORRODED. IT STANDS TODAY AS A MEMORY, AND A TEACHING.
BY THE TIME I BEGAN WORKING HERE THE ARSENIC LEVELS IN THE WATER WERE ALREADY HIGH.
I GOT SICK MY FIRST DAY HERE! I HAD A CANTEEN THAT I PUT ON THE GROUND BY MISTAKE. CONTAMINATED WATER GOT IN AND I HAD TO BE TAKEN TO THE HOSPITAL.
IN THE HOSPITAL I HAD A DREAM THAT THE WATER SPOKE TO ME. IT WANTED TO REMIND ME OF THE TEACHINGS OF ONE OF MY ELDERS.
WATER HAS A SPIRIT, AND IT REMEMBERS. IT KNOWS. IT TRUSTS. IT PROTECTS.
MY ELDER SAID 'CRADLE YOUR WATER IN YOUR HANDS OR HELD IN A CUP, AS IT ONCE CRADLED YOU INSIDE OF YOUR MOTHER.'
IT IS DISRESPECTFUL TO PLACE ANY CUP O WATER ON THE GROUN THIS INCLUDES YOU JUICE, COFFEE, TEA OR POP.
WATER IS LIFE.

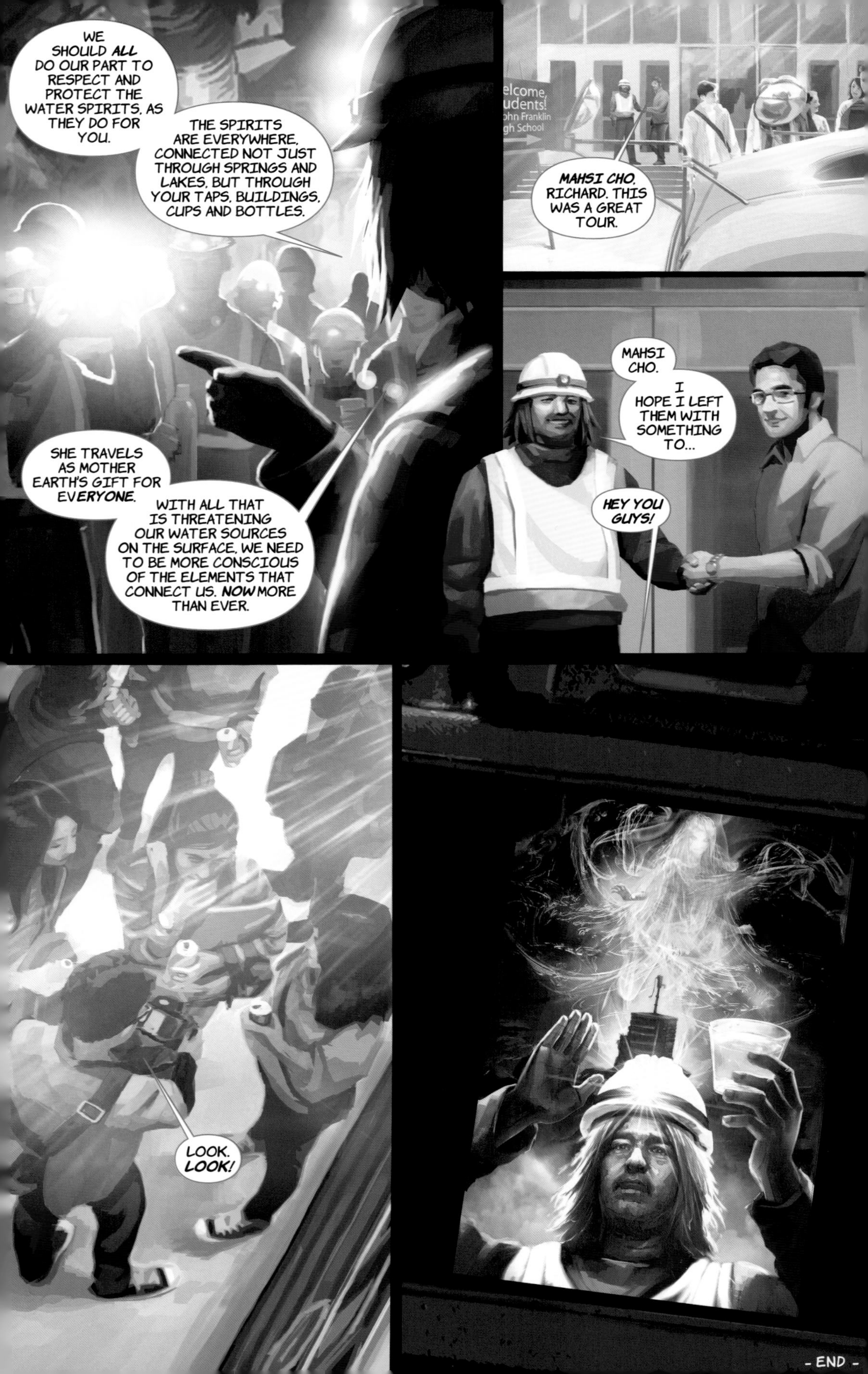
WE SHOULD ALL DO OUR PART TO RESPECT AND PROTECT THE WATER SPIRITS, AS THEY DO FOR YOU.
THE SPIRITS ARE EVERYWHERE, CONNECTED NOT JUST THROUGH SPRINGS AND LAKES, BUT THROUGH YOUR TAPS, BUILDINGS, CUPS AND BOTTLES.
SHE TRAVELS AS MOTHER EARTH'S GIFT FOR EVERYONE.
WITH ALL THAT IS THREATENING OUR WATER SOURCES ON THE SURFACE, WE NEED TO BE MORE CONSCIOUS OF THE ELEMENTS THAT CONNECT US. NOW MORE THAN EVER.
elcome, udents! ohn Franklin gh School
MAHSI CHO, RICHARD. THIS WAS A GREAT TOUR.
MAHSI CHO.
I HOPE I LEFT THEM WITH SOMETHING TO...
HEY YOU GUYS!
LOOK. LOOK!
- END -

Gerard and Peta-Gay Roberts'

THE CREATOR TAMOSI

Illustrated by Nicholas Burns

BACKGROUND

The Creation story that forms the centre of this piece has been handed down through the Haudenosaunee from generation to generation in the oral tradition. It is not typically written or ever seen in print, making this an extremely unique experience. There are many variations of the Creation story in Iroquoian culture, as there are names for the Creator – Tamosi (as this story uses), as well as Son Gwayadiso ("Holder of the Heavens") and Rahketniha ("Father of All"). This autobiographic account also involves the popular Strawberry Ceremony in Six Nations. The strawberry is the first of the fruits that can be picked, and represents the heart and circulatory system. It is symbolic of the circle of life, which is a gift from the Creator to all walks of life.

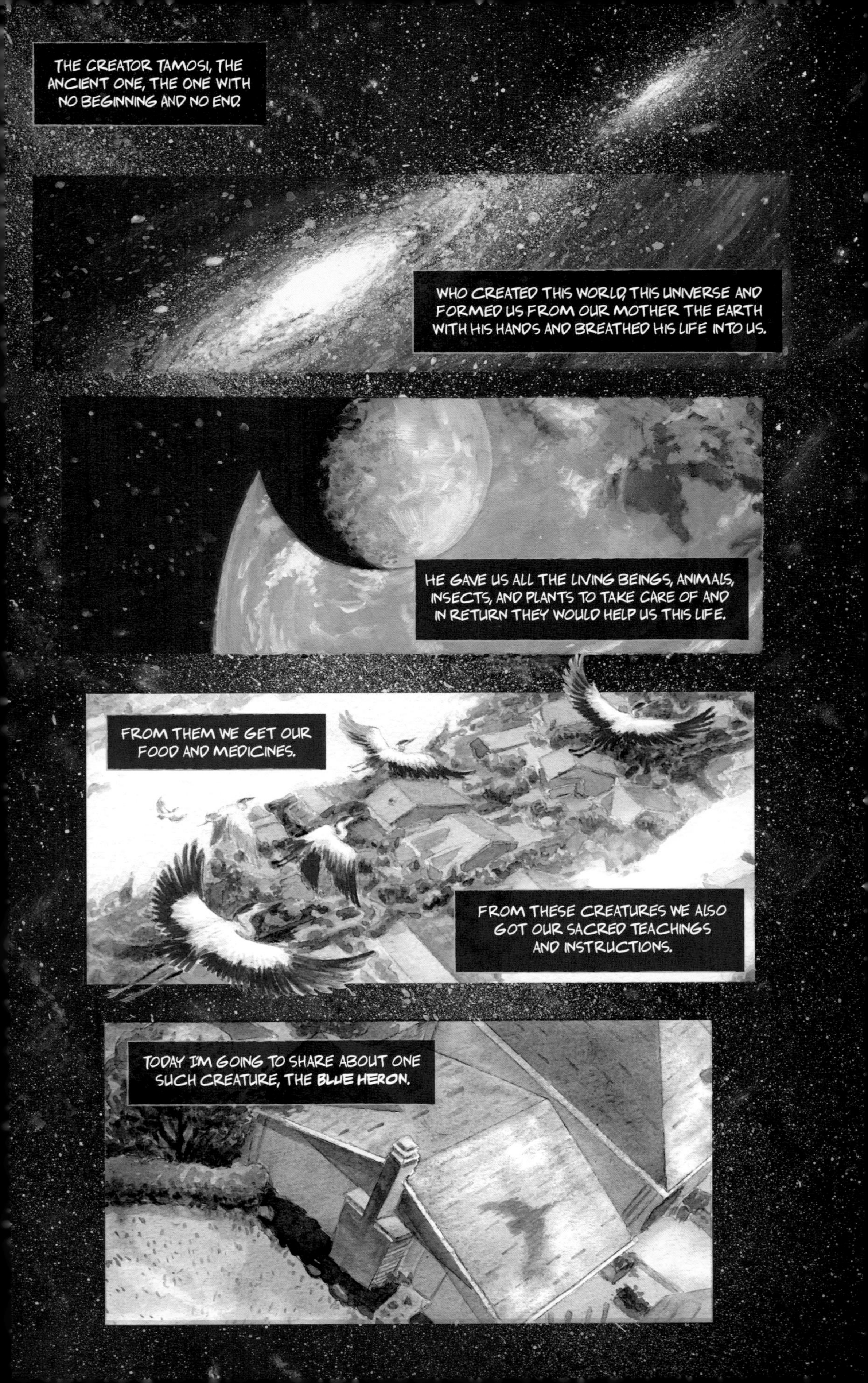
THE CREATOR TAMOSI, THE ANCIENT ONE, THE ONE WITH NO BEGINNING AND NO END.
WHO CREATED THIS WORLD, THIS UNIVERSE AND FORMED US FROM OUR MOTHER THE EARTH WITH HIS HANDS AND BREATHED HIS LIFE INTO US.
HE GAVE US ALL THE LIVING BEINGS, ANIMALS, INSECTS, AND PLANTS TO TAKE CARE OF AND IN RETURN THEY WOULD HELP US THIS LIFE.
FROM THEM WE GET OUR FOOD AND MEDICINES.
FROM THESE CREATURES WE ALSO GOT OUR SACRED TEACHINGS AND INSTRUCTIONS.
TODAY I'M GOING TO SHARE ABOUT ONE SUCH CREATURE, THE **BLUE HERON**.

WE AS A FAMILY WERE GOING THROUGH A DIFFICULT TIME EMOTIONALLY, AND FINANCIALLY.

TRYING TO STRETCH THAT DOLLAR AS FAR AS WE CAN.

IT WAS A TIME OF SAYING "NO" TO MY WIFE AND CHILDREN.

WHICH HURT SO DEEP THAT YOU MISS THE BEAUTY THAT'S AROUND YOU.

BUT HE WILL ALWAYS MAKE A WAY WHEN THERE SEEMS TO BE NO WAY.

RING!
RING!

IT WAS DURING THIS TIME OF DEPRESSION THAT WE GOT AN INVITATION...

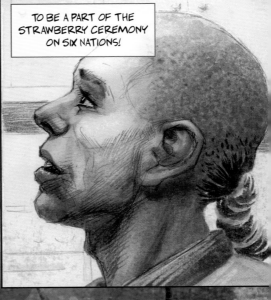

TO BE A PART OF THE STRAWBERRY CEREMONY ON SIX NATIONS!

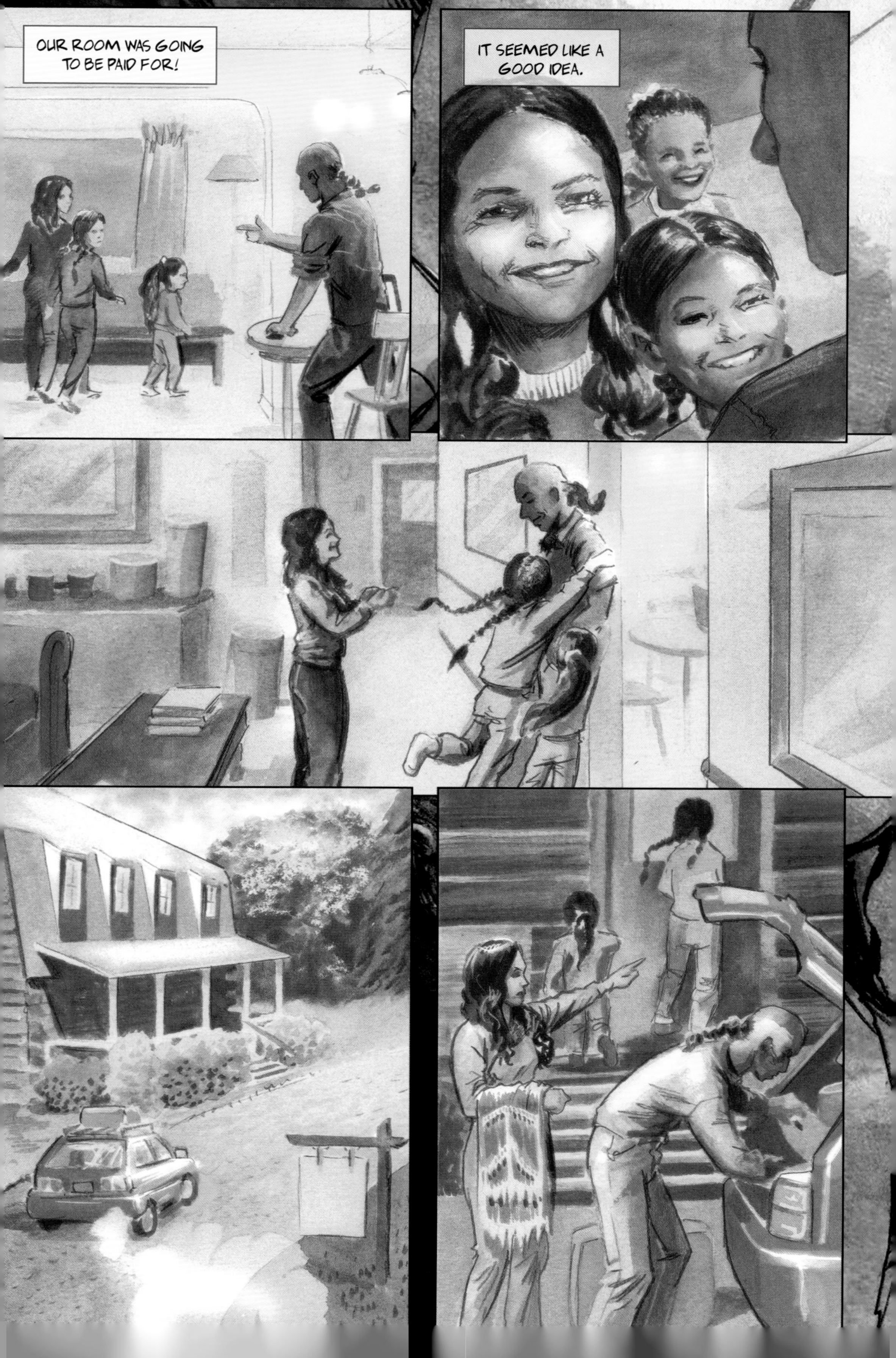
OUR ROOM WAS GOING TO BE PAID FOR!
IT SEEMED LIKE A GOOD IDEA.

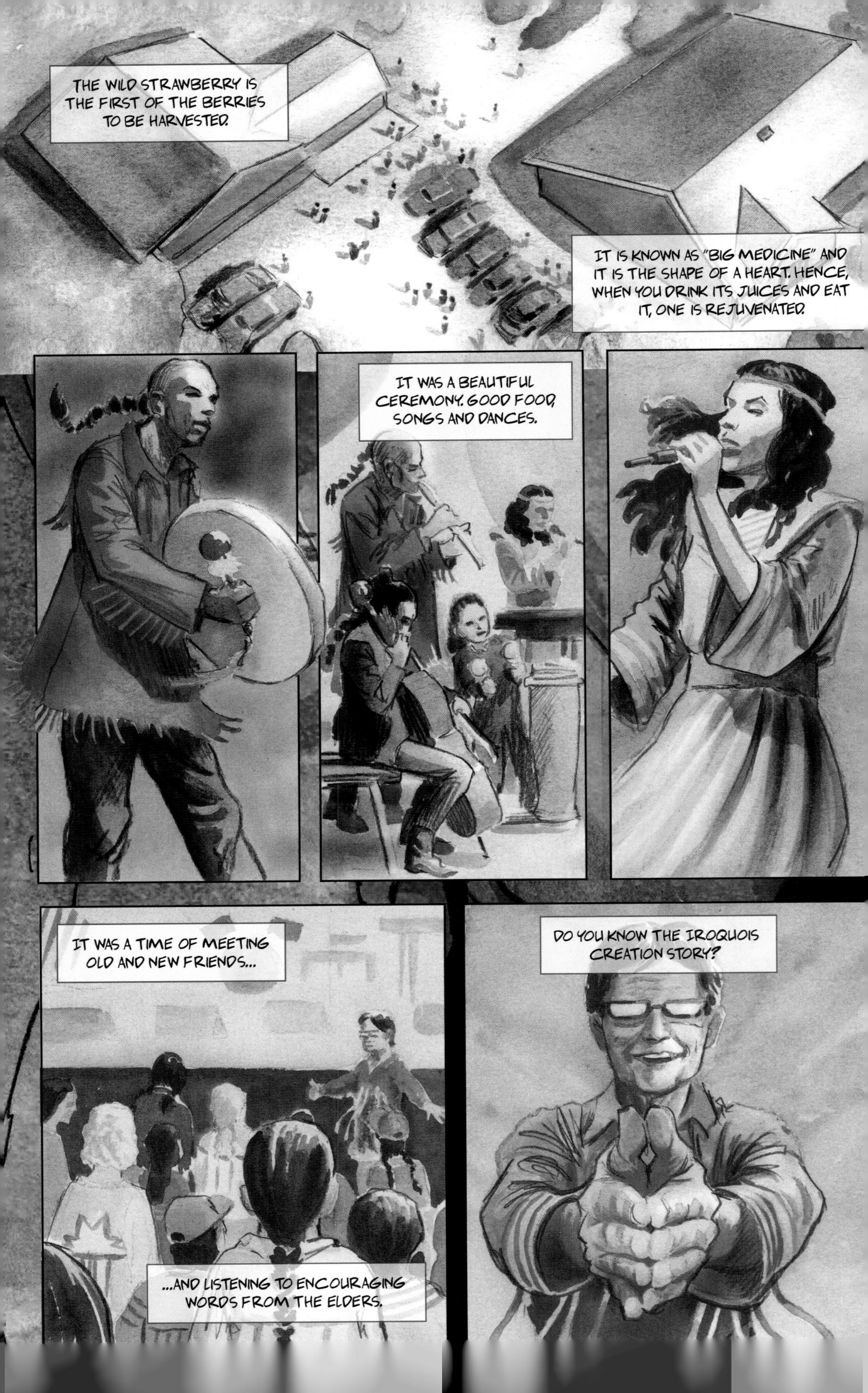
THE WILD STRAWBERRY IS THE FIRST OF THE BERRIES TO BE HARVESTED.
IT IS KNOWN AS "BIG MEDICINE" AND IT IS THE SHAPE OF A HEART. HENCE, WHEN YOU DRINK ITS JUICES AND EAT IT, ONE IS REJUVENATED.
IT WAS A BEAUTIFUL CEREMONY. GOOD FOOD, SONGS AND DANCES.
IT WAS A TIME OF MEETING OLD AND NEW FRIENDS...
...AND LISTENING TO ENCOURAGING WORDS FROM THE ELDERS.
DO YOU KNOW THE IROQUOIS CREATION STORY?

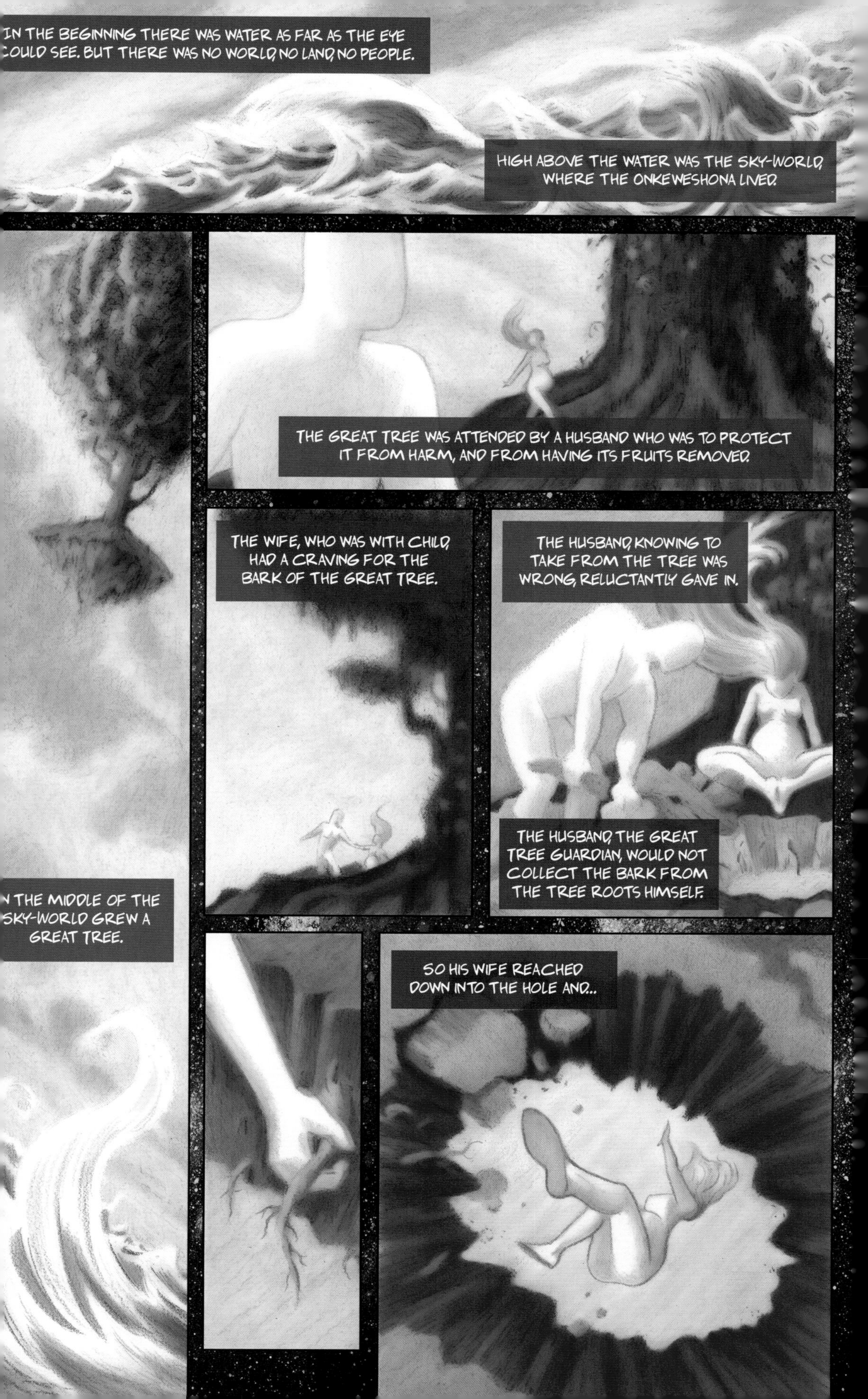
IN THE BEGINNING THERE WAS WATER AS FAR AS THE EYE COULD SEE. BUT THERE WAS NO WORLD, NO LAND, NO PEOPLE.
HIGH ABOVE THE WATER WAS THE SKY-WORLD, WHERE THE ONKEWESHONA LIVED.
IN THE MIDDLE OF THE SKY-WORLD GREW A GREAT TREE.
THE GREAT TREE WAS ATTENDED BY A HUSBAND WHO WAS TO PROTECT IT FROM HARM, AND FROM HAVING ITS FRUITS REMOVED.
THE WIFE, WHO WAS WITH CHILD, HAD A CRAVING FOR THE BARK OF THE GREAT TREE.
THE HUSBAND, KNOWING TO TAKE FROM THE TREE WAS WRONG, RELUCTANTLY GAVE IN.
THE HUSBAND, THE GREAT TREE GUARDIAN, WOULD NOT COLLECT THE BARK FROM THE TREE ROOTS HIMSELF.
SO HIS WIFE REACHED DOWN INTO THE HOLE AND...

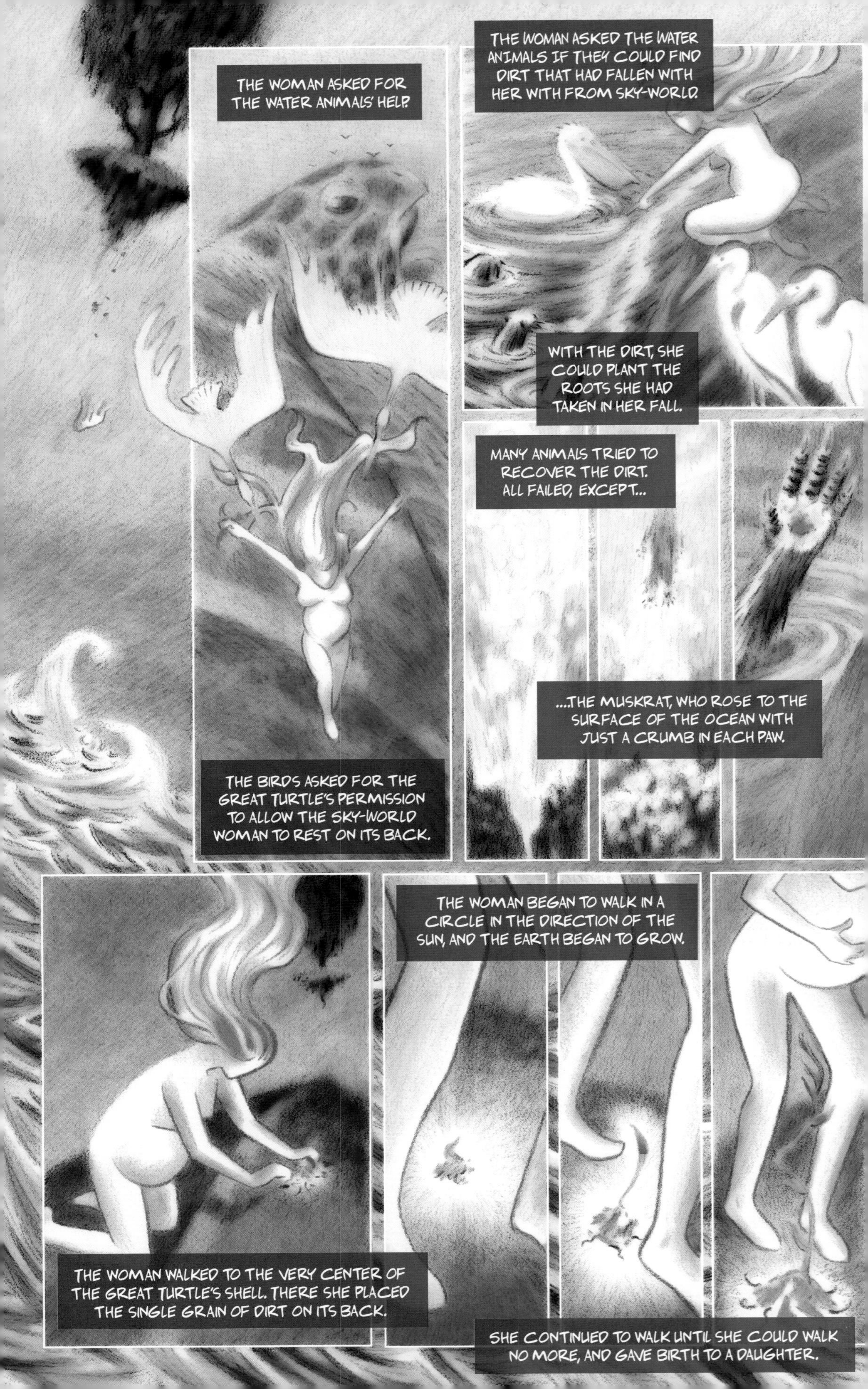
THE WOMAN ASKED FOR THE WATER ANIMALS' HELP.
THE BIRDS ASKED FOR THE GREAT TURTLE'S PERMISSION TO ALLOW THE SKY-WORLD WOMAN TO REST ON ITS BACK.
THE WOMAN ASKED THE WATER ANIMALS IF THEY COULD FIND DIRT THAT HAD FALLEN WITH HER WITH FROM SKY-WORLD.
WITH THE DIRT, SHE COULD PLANT THE ROOTS SHE HAD TAKEN IN HER FALL.
MANY ANIMALS TRIED TO RECOVER THE DIRT. ALL FAILED, EXCEPT...
...THE MUSKRAT, WHO ROSE TO THE SURFACE OF THE OCEAN WITH JUST A CRUMB IN EACH PAW.
THE WOMAN WALKED TO THE VERY CENTER OF THE GREAT TURTLE'S SHELL. THERE SHE PLACED THE SINGLE GRAIN OF DIRT ON ITS BACK.
THE WOMAN BEGAN TO WALK IN A CIRCLE IN THE DIRECTION OF THE SUN, AND THE EARTH BEGAN TO GROW.
SHE CONTINUED TO WALK UNTIL SHE COULD WALK NO MORE, AND GAVE BIRTH TO A DAUGHTER.

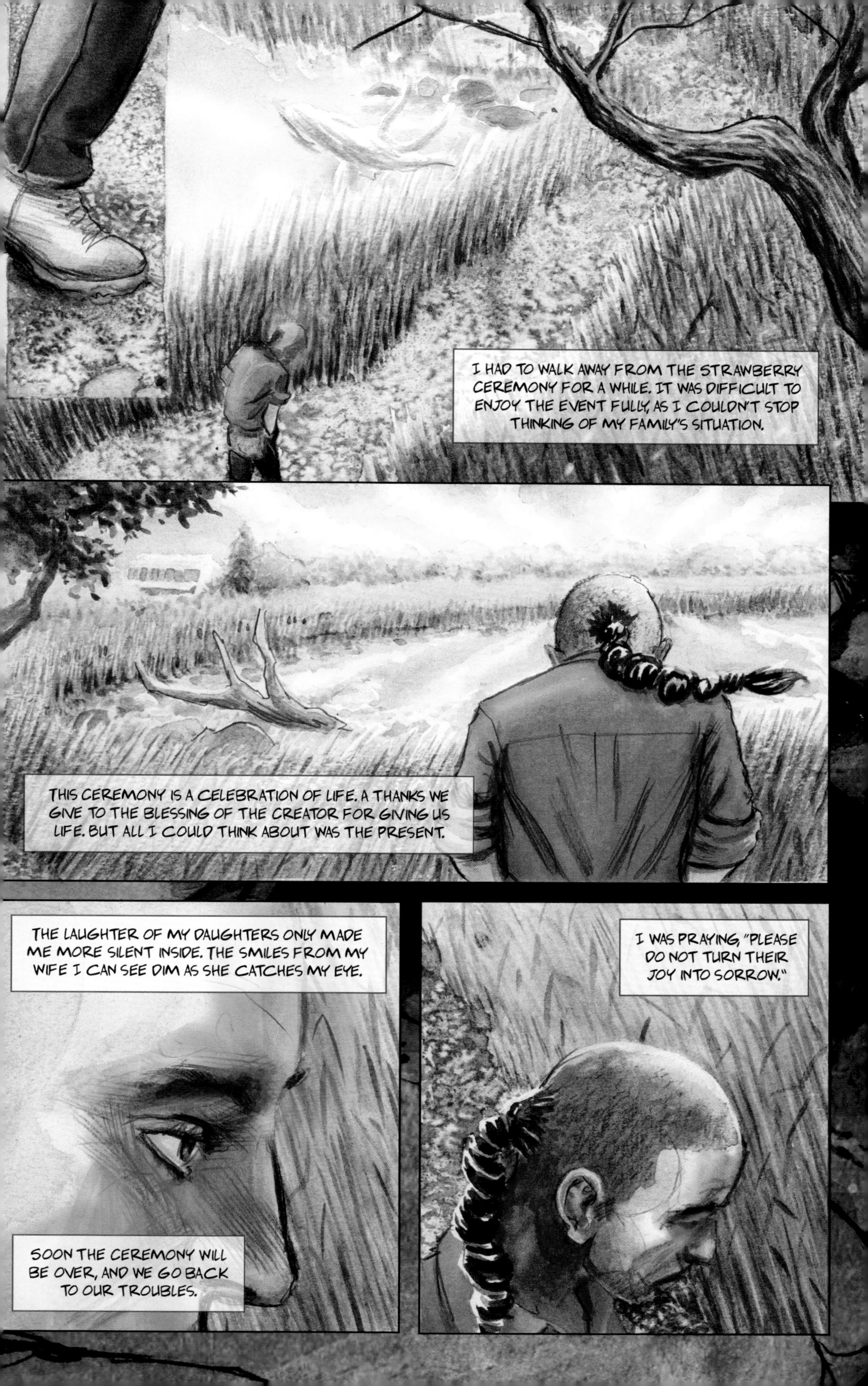
I HAD TO WALK AWAY FROM THE STRAWBERRY CEREMONY FOR A WHILE. IT WAS DIFFICULT TO ENJOY THE EVENT FULLY, AS I COULDN'T STOP THINKING OF MY FAMILY'S SITUATION.
THIS CEREMONY IS A CELEBRATION OF LIFE. A THANKS WE GIVE TO THE BLESSING OF THE CREATOR FOR GIVING US LIFE. BUT ALL I COULD THINK ABOUT WAS THE PRESENT.
THE LAUGHTER OF MY DAUGHTERS ONLY MADE ME MORE SILENT INSIDE. THE SMILES FROM MY WIFE I CAN SEE DIM AS SHE CATCHES MY EYE.
SOON THE CEREMONY WILL BE OVER, AND WE GO BACK TO OUR TROUBLES.
I WAS PRAYING, "PLEASE DO NOT TURN THEIR JOY INTO SORROW."

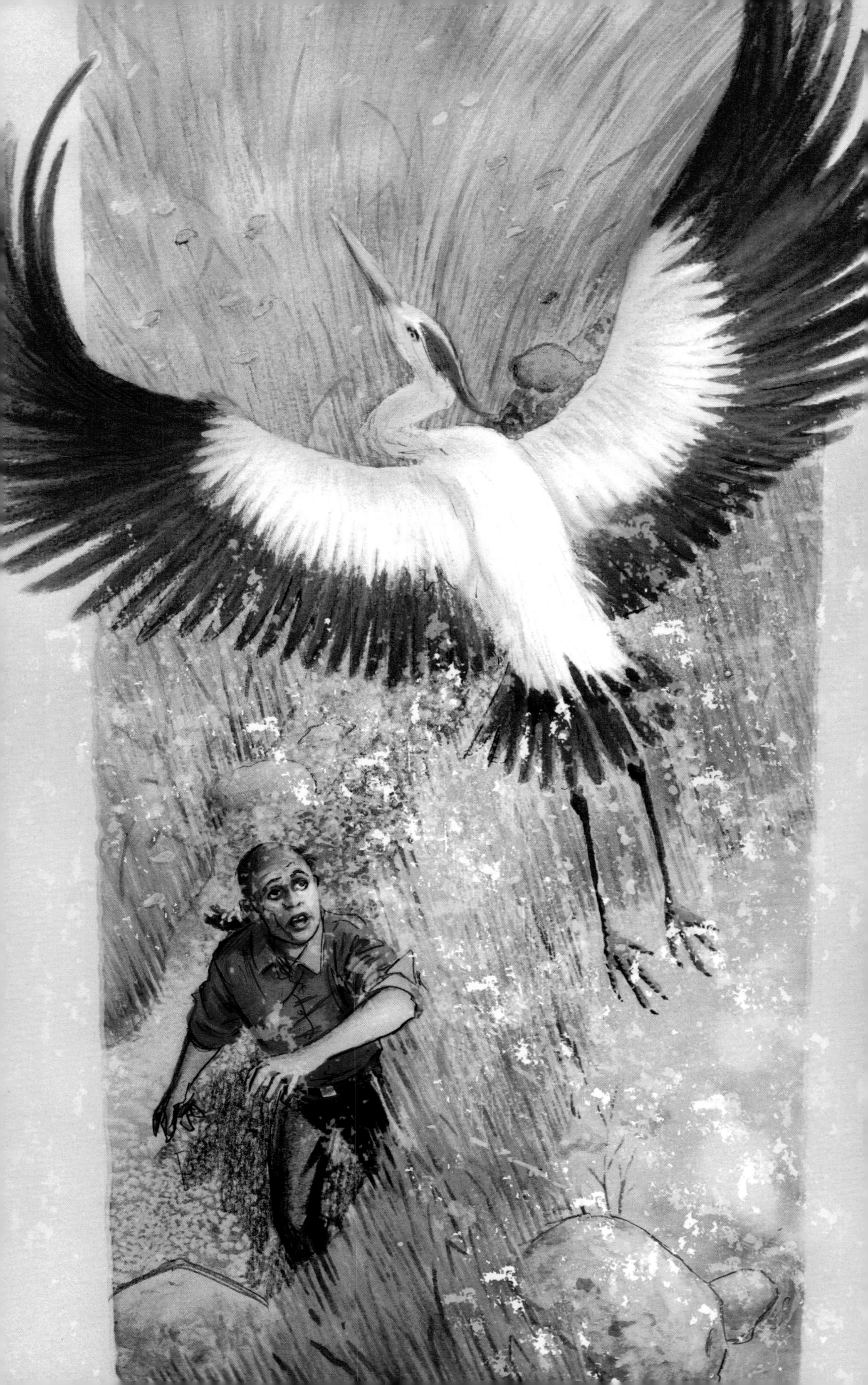

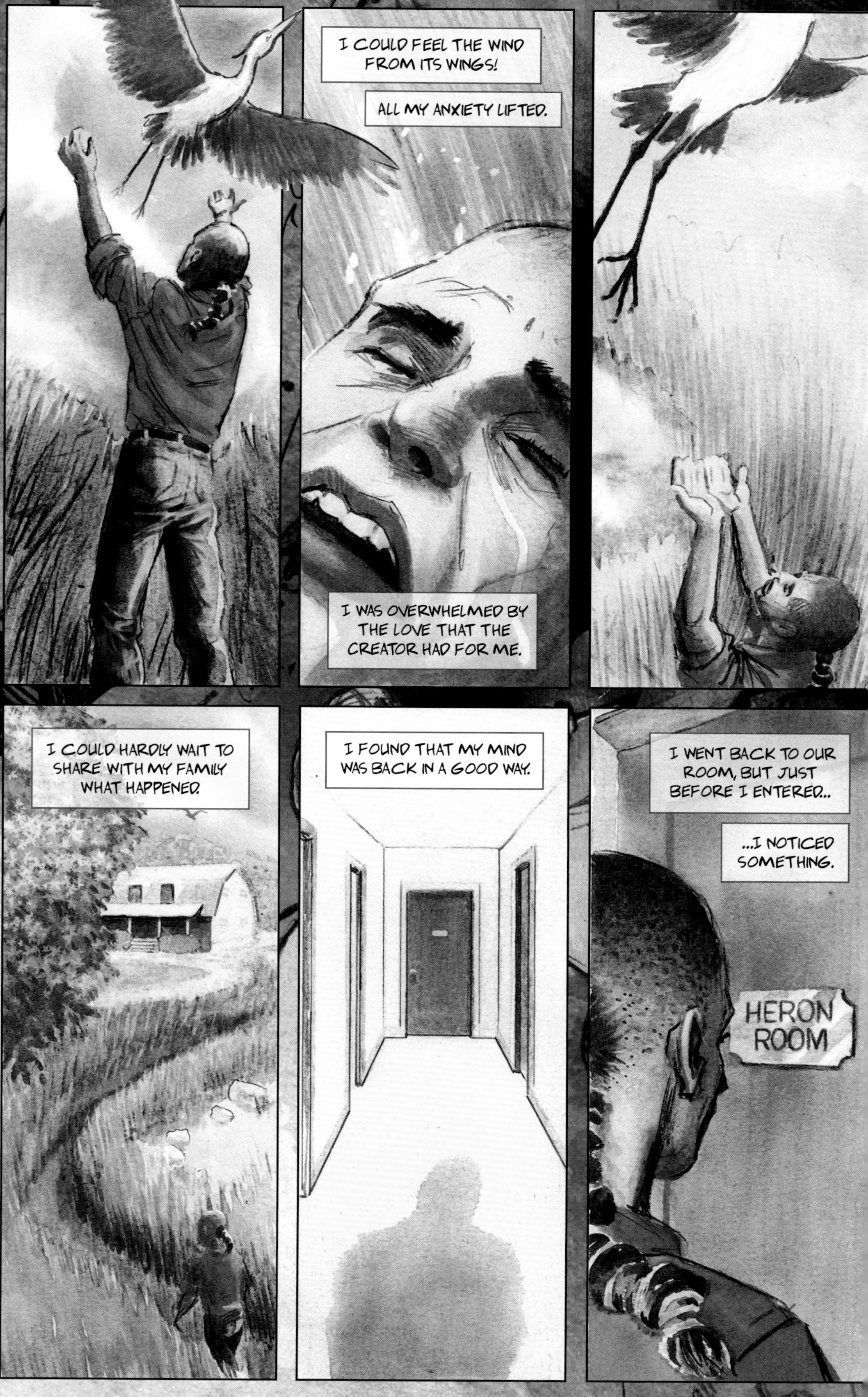
I COULD FEEL THE WIND FROM ITS WINGS!
ALL MY ANXIETY LIFTED.
I WAS OVERWHELMED BY THE LOVE THAT THE CREATOR HAD FOR ME.
I COULD HARDLY WAIT TO SHARE WITH MY FAMILY WHAT HAPPENED.
I FOUND THAT MY MIND WAS BACK IN A GOOD WAY.
I WENT BACK TO OUR ROOM, BUT JUST BEFORE I ENTERED...
...I NOTICED SOMETHING.
HERON ROOM

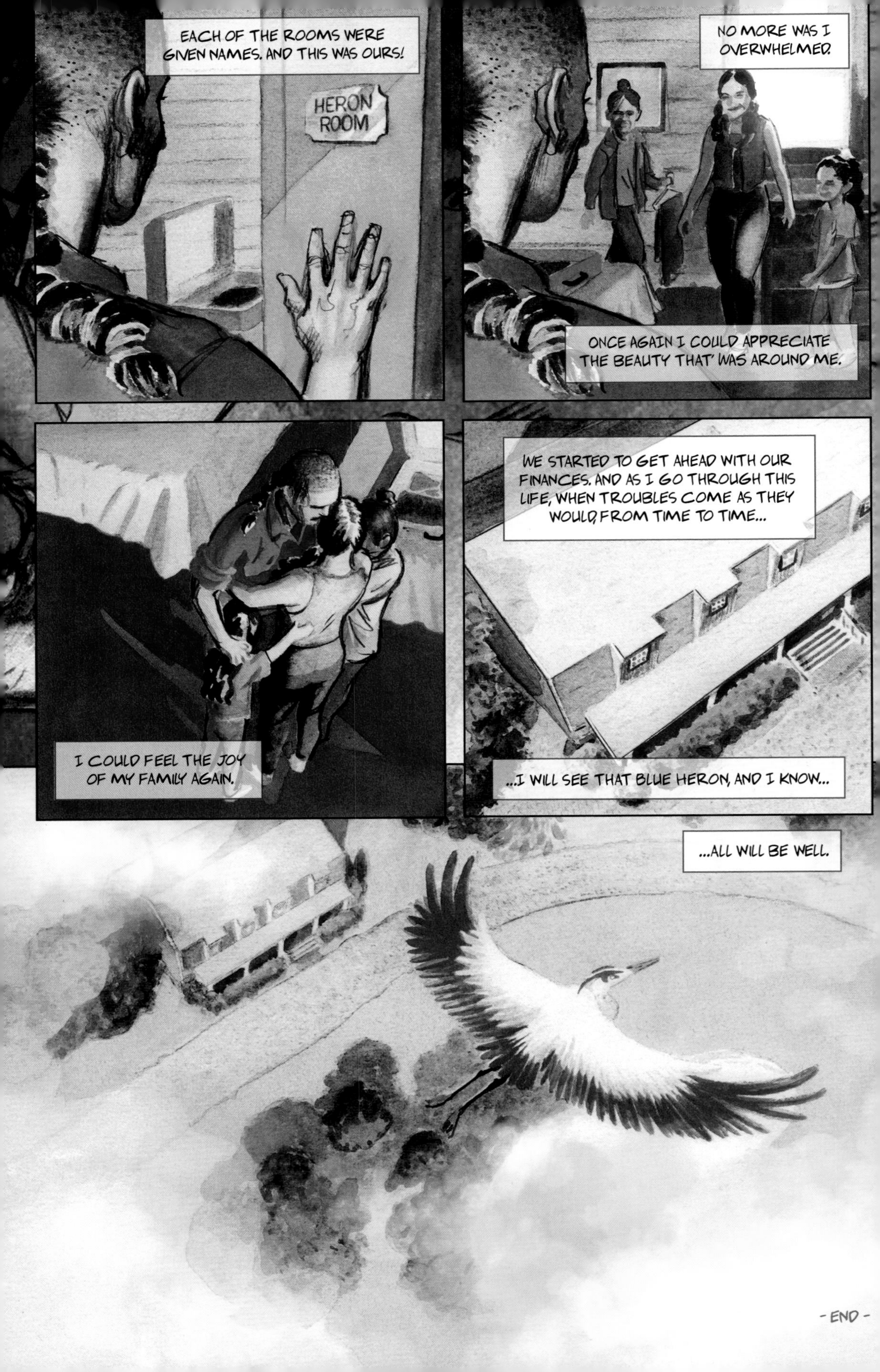
EACH OF THE ROOMS WERE GIVEN NAMES. AND THIS WAS OURS!
HERON ROOM
NO MORE WAS I OVERWHELMED.
ONCE AGAIN I COULD APPRECIATE THE BEAUTY THAT WAS AROUND ME.
I COULD FEEL THE JOY OF MY FAMILY AGAIN.
WE STARTED TO GET AHEAD WITH OUR FINANCES. AND AS I GO THROUGH THIS LIFE, WHEN TROUBLES COME AS THEY WOULD, FROM TIME TO TIME...
...I WILL SEE THAT BLUE HERON, AND I KNOW...
...ALL WILL BE WELL.
- END -

Steve Keewatin Sanderson's

WHERE WE LEFT OFF

Art by Steve Keewatin Sanderson
Colours by Peter Dawes

BACKGROUND

Set in a post-apocalyptic world, the author has created a story based on his Plains Cree heritage, acknowledging the lessons passed down from his father, and his father's ancestors. In what appears to be an Earth fast-forwarded into disaster, the preservation of knowledge and tradition is not something to be seen as an "ancient" way of being. It is an important way of life that brings communities together, and helps create strength for an uncertain future. This story highlights the tradition of honouring the ancestors by living and preserving the here and now. The lessons passed down through generations are considered gifts, being part of a proud and beautiful culture that the people who came before fought to protect.

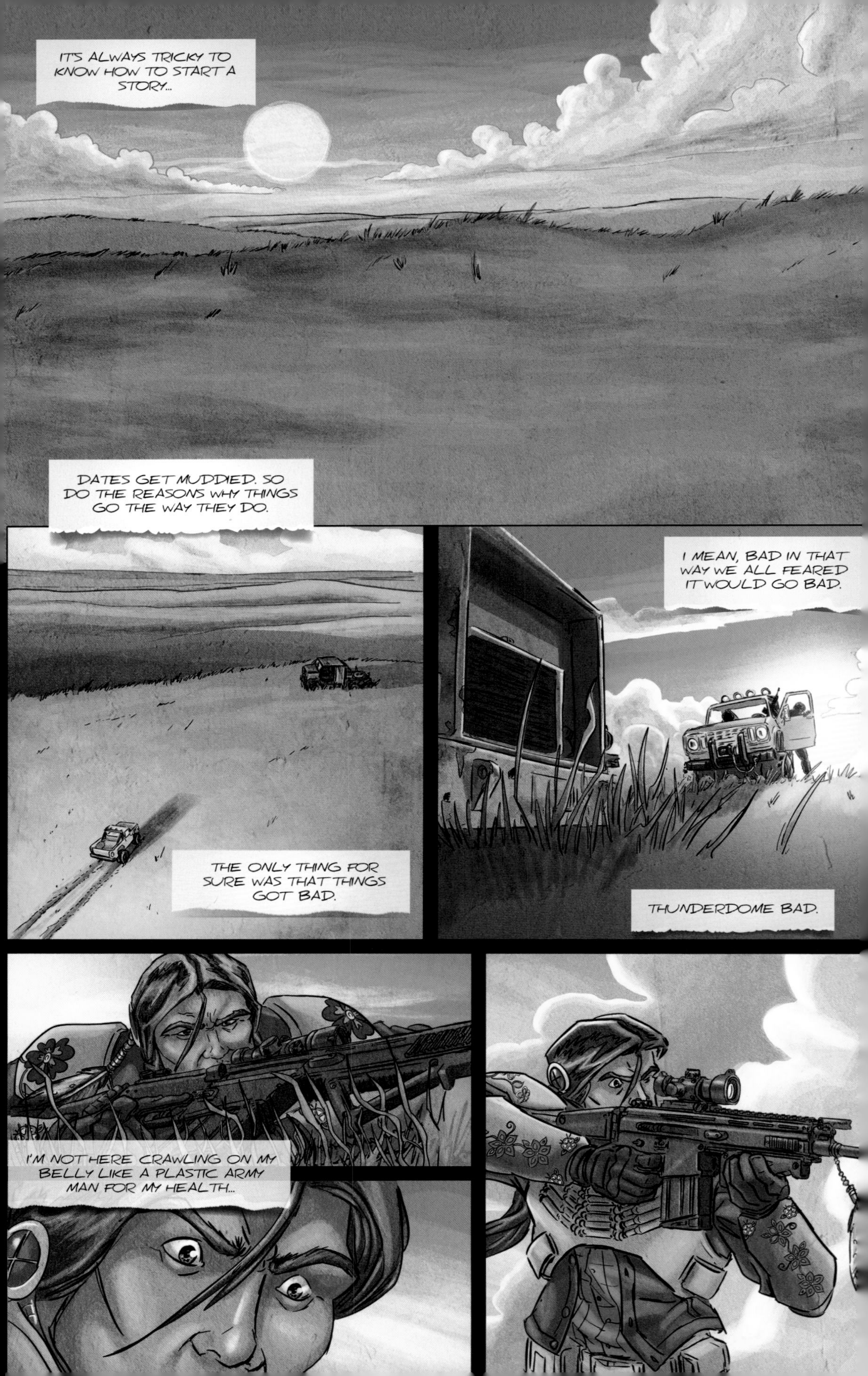
IT'S ALWAYS TRICKY TO KNOW HOW TO START A STORY...
DATES GET MUDDIED. SO DO THE REASONS WHY THINGS GO THE WAY THEY DO.
THE ONLY THING FOR SURE WAS THAT THINGS GOT BAD.
I MEAN, BAD IN THAT WAY WE ALL FEARED IT WOULD GO BAD.
THUNDERDOME BAD.
I'M NOT HERE CRAWLING ON MY BELLY LIKE A PLASTIC ARMY MAN FOR MY HEALTH...

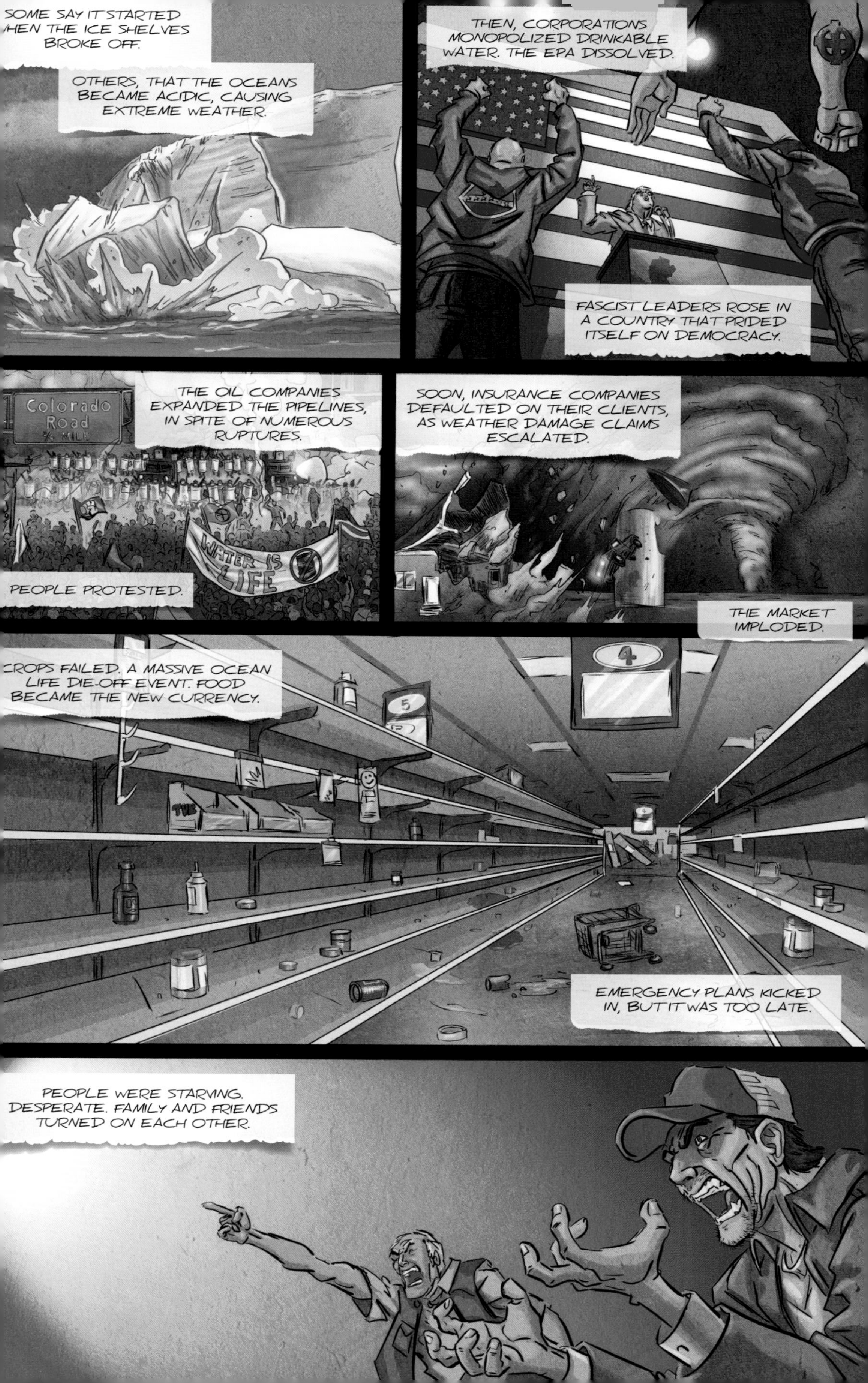

SOME SAY IT STARTED WHEN THE ICE SHELVES BROKE OFF.
OTHERS, THAT THE OCEANS BECAME ACIDIC, CAUSING EXTREME WEATHER.
THEN, CORPORATIONS MONOPOLIZED DRINKABLE WATER. THE EPA DISSOLVED.
FASCIST LEADERS ROSE IN A COUNTRY THAT PRIDED ITSELF ON DEMOCRACY.
Colorado Road
THE OIL COMPANIES EXPANDED THE PIPELINES, IN SPITE OF NUMEROUS RUPTURES.
WATER IS LIFE
PEOPLE PROTESTED.
SOON, INSURANCE COMPANIES DEFAULTED ON THEIR CLIENTS, AS WEATHER DAMAGE CLAIMS ESCALATED.
THE MARKET IMPLODED.
CROPS FAILED. A MASSIVE OCEAN LIFE DIE-OFF EVENT. FOOD BECAME THE NEW CURRENCY.
4
5
EMERGENCY PLANS KICKED IN, BUT IT WAS TOO LATE.
PEOPLE WERE STARVING. DESPERATE. FAMILY AND FRIENDS TURNED ON EACH OTHER.

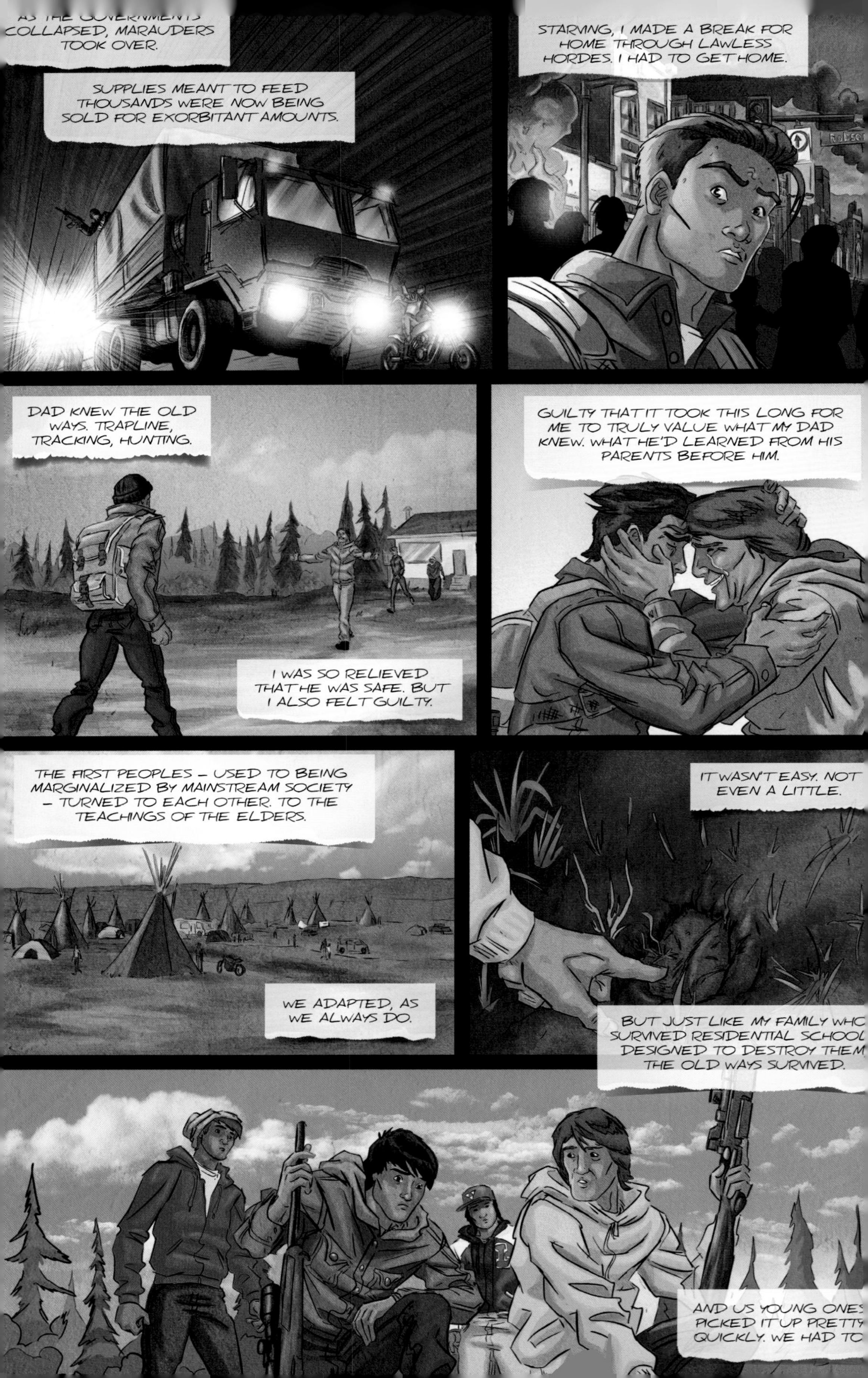
AS THE GOVERNMENTS COLLAPSED, MARAUDERS TOOK OVER.
SUPPLIES MEANT TO FEED THOUSANDS WERE NOW BEING SOLD FOR EXORBITANT AMOUNTS.
STARVING, I MADE A BREAK FOR HOME THROUGH LAWLESS HORDES. I HAD TO GET HOME.
DAD KNEW THE OLD WAYS. TRAPLINE, TRACKING, HUNTING.
I WAS SO RELIEVED THAT HE WAS SAFE. BUT I ALSO FELT GUILTY.
GUILTY THAT IT TOOK THIS LONG FOR ME TO TRULY VALUE WHAT MY DAD KNEW. WHAT HE'D LEARNED FROM HIS PARENTS BEFORE HIM.
THE FIRST PEOPLES – USED TO BEING MARGINALIZED BY MAINSTREAM SOCIETY – TURNED TO EACH OTHER. TO THE TEACHINGS OF THE ELDERS.
WE ADAPTED, AS WE ALWAYS DO.
IT WASN'T EASY. NOT EVEN A LITTLE.
BUT JUST LIKE MY FAMILY WHO SURVIVED RESIDENTIAL SCHOOL DESIGNED TO DESTROY THEM THE OLD WAYS SURVIVED.
AND US YOUNG ONES PICKED IT UP PRETTY QUICKLY. WE HAD TO

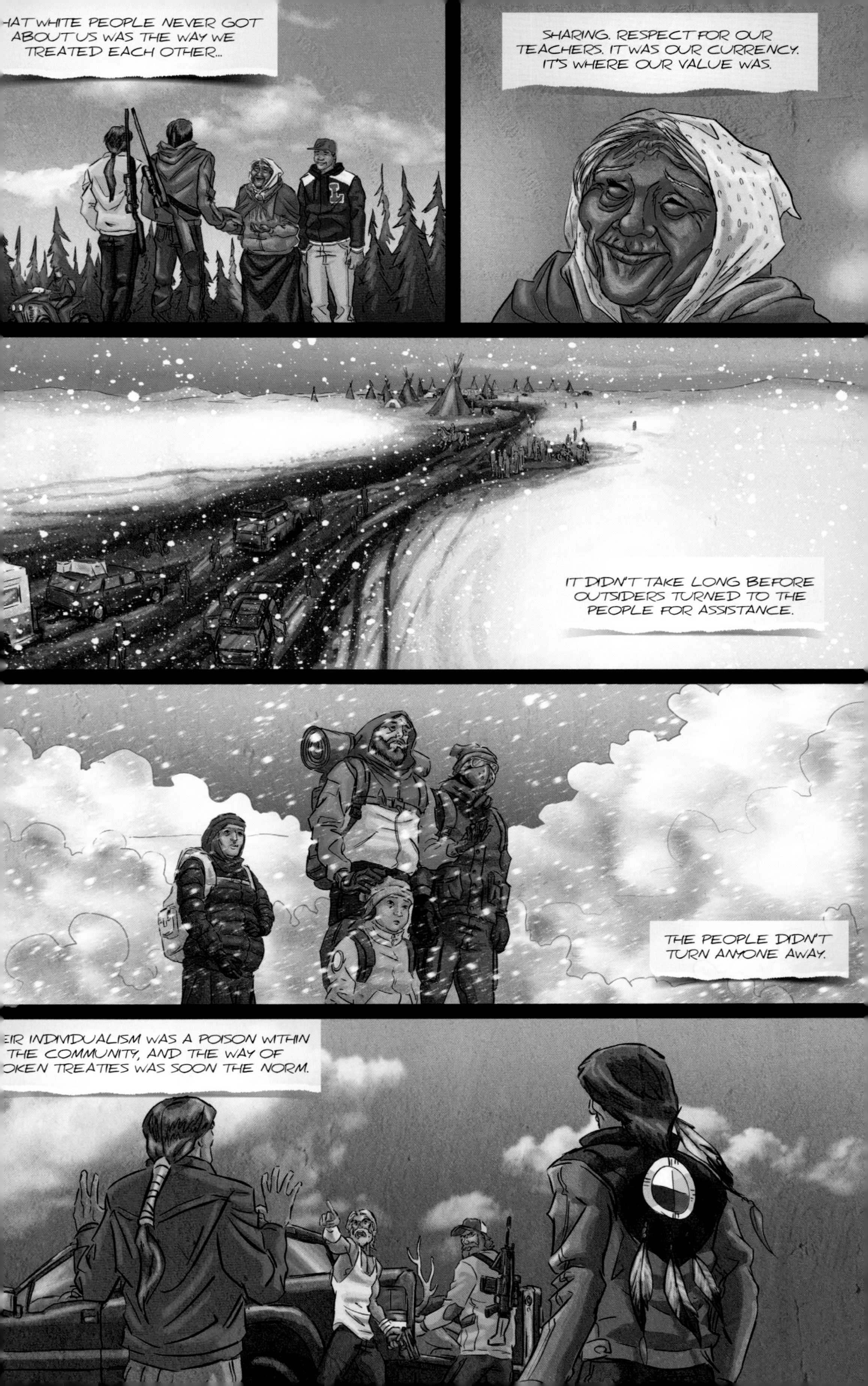
HAT WHITE PEOPLE NEVER GOT ABOUT US WAS THE WAY WE TREATED EACH OTHER...
SHARING. RESPECT FOR OUR TEACHERS. IT WAS OUR CURRENCY. IT'S WHERE OUR VALUE WAS.
IT DIDN'T TAKE LONG BEFORE OUTSIDERS TURNED TO THE PEOPLE FOR ASSISTANCE.
THE PEOPLE DIDN'T TURN ANYONE AWAY.
EIR INDIVIDUALISM WAS A POISON WITHIN THE COMMUNITY, AND THE WAY OF OKEN TREATIES WAS SOON THE NORM.

GREED LEADS TO
DISTRUST, FEAR,
RESENTMENT.

THESE ARE
POWERFUL
POISONS.

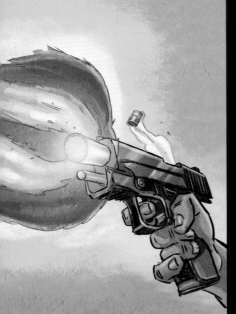

THE OLD ONES SAY THAT GREED IS A
DISEASE. IT TAKES YOU OVER AND YOU
BECOME LOST TO A MONSTER.

YOU BECOME A WIHTIKÔW.

A WIHTIKÔW IS AN INSATIABLE
BEAST. IT CAN NEVER GET
ENOUGH TO EAT. IT HAS
GREEDY GUTS.

IT IS A
MALEVOLENT
DISEASE.

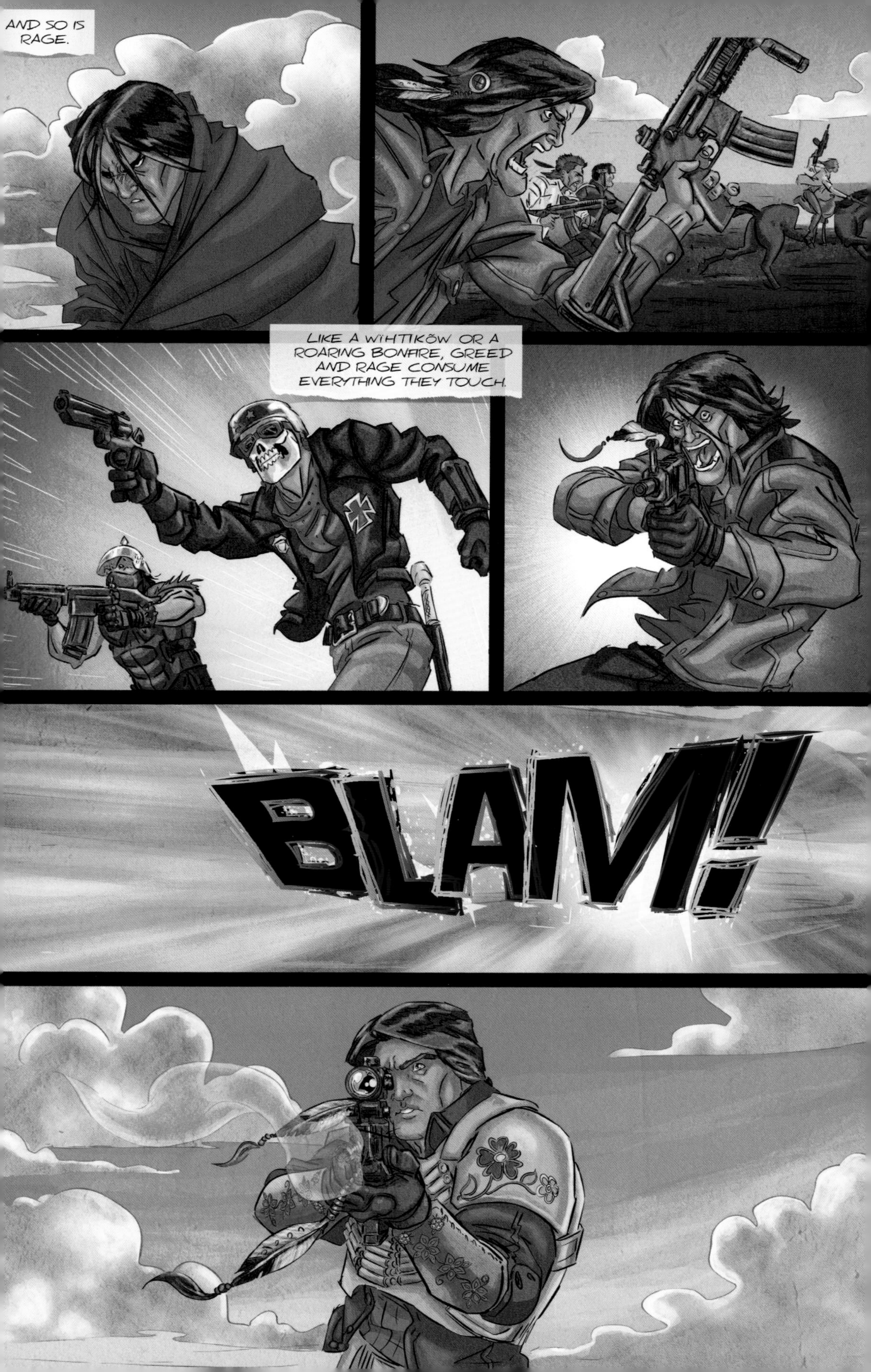
AND SO IS RAGE.
LIKE A WÎHTIKÔW OR A ROARING BONFIRE, GREED AND RAGE CONSUME EVERYTHING THEY TOUCH.
BLAM!

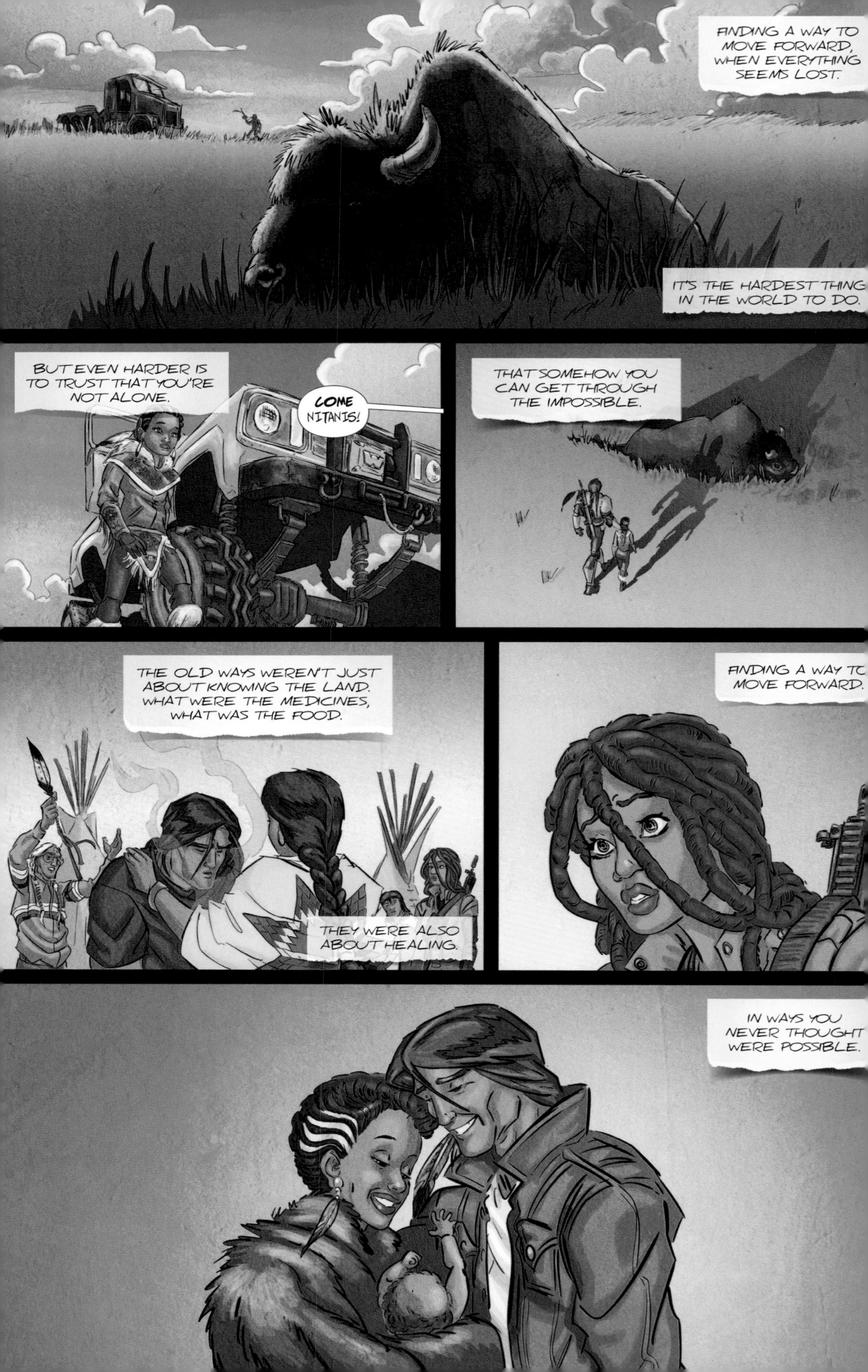
FINDING A WAY TO MOVE FORWARD, WHEN EVERYTHING SEEMS LOST.
IT'S THE HARDEST THING IN THE WORLD TO DO.
BUT EVEN HARDER IS TO TRUST THAT YOU'RE NOT ALONE.
COME NITANIS!
THAT SOMEHOW YOU CAN GET THROUGH THE IMPOSSIBLE.
THE OLD WAYS WEREN'T JUST ABOUT KNOWING THE LAND. WHAT WERE THE MEDICINES, WHAT WAS THE FOOD.
THEY WERE ALSO ABOUT HEALING.
FINDING A WAY TO MOVE FORWARD.
IN WAYS YOU NEVER THOUGHT WERE POSSIBLE.

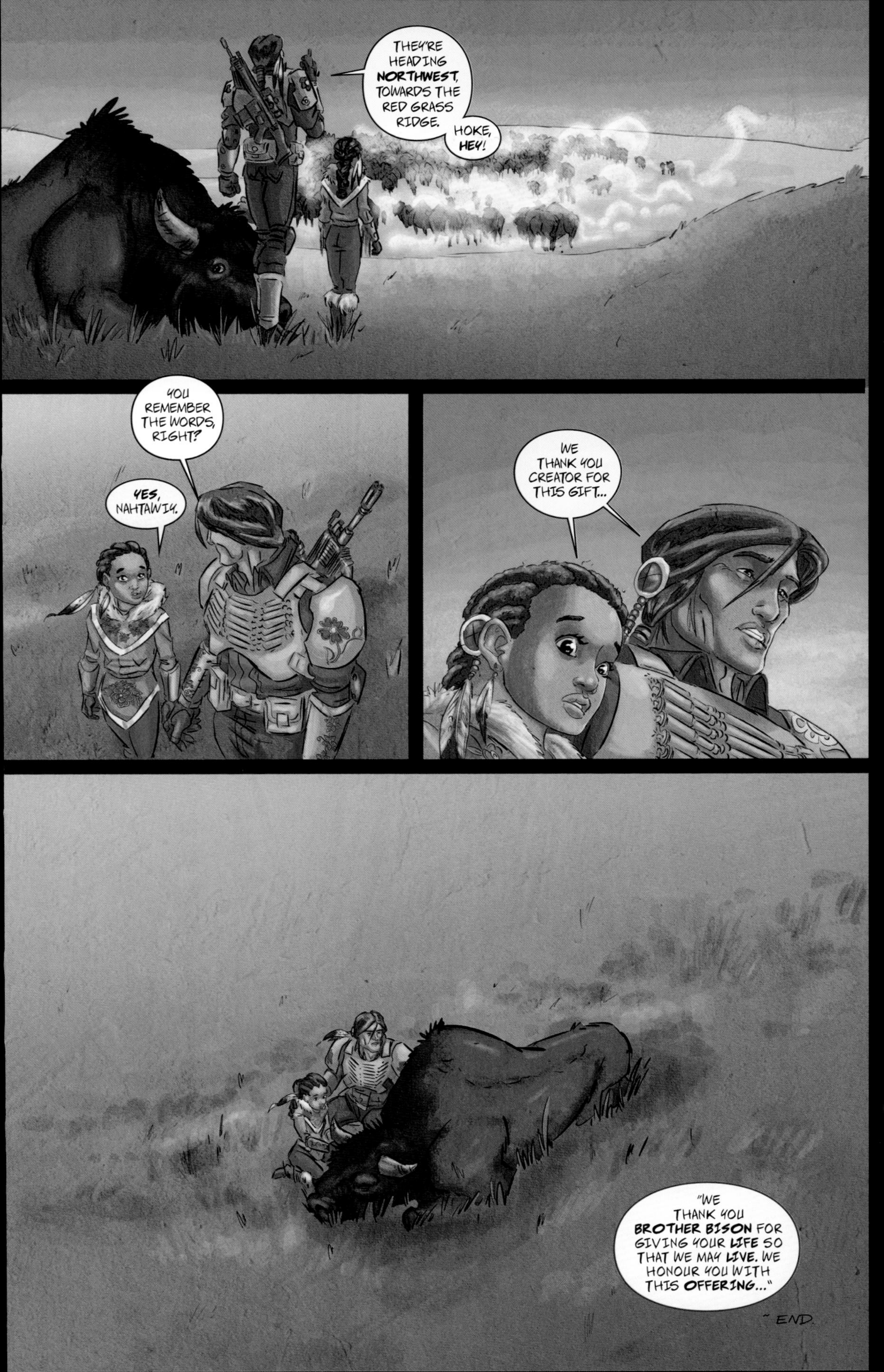
THEY'RE HEADING **NORTHWEST**, TOWARDS THE RED GRASS RIDGE.
HOKE, **HEY**!
YOU REMEMBER THE WORDS, RIGHT?
YES, NAHTAWIY.
WE THANK YOU CREATOR FOR THIS GIFT...
"WE THANK YOU **BROTHER BISON** FOR GIVING YOUR **LIFE** SO THAT WE MAY **LIVE**. WE HONOUR YOU WITH THIS **OFFERING**..."
~ END.

Michael Sheyahshe's

DO WILD TURKEYS DREAM OF ELECTRIC DRUMS

Illustrated by Kim Hunter

BACKGROUND

While this story is presented in an entertaining and humorous fashion, the *Núh Ka͡ꞌáwshan* – "Turkey Dance" – is arguably one of the most recognizable and important present-day traditions in Caddo (Hasinai) culture. These beautiful dances are performed by women, with the dance steps themselves similar in form to turkeys stepping in time to music. Although the tradition is called the "Turkey Dance" (singular), there is not just one song or dance. Today, there are over 50 songs, performed in specific phases, with each one representing and recalling important events in Caddo history. Building on this visual aspect of the turkeys dancing, the author retells a modernized version of a traditional Caddo predator versus prey story.

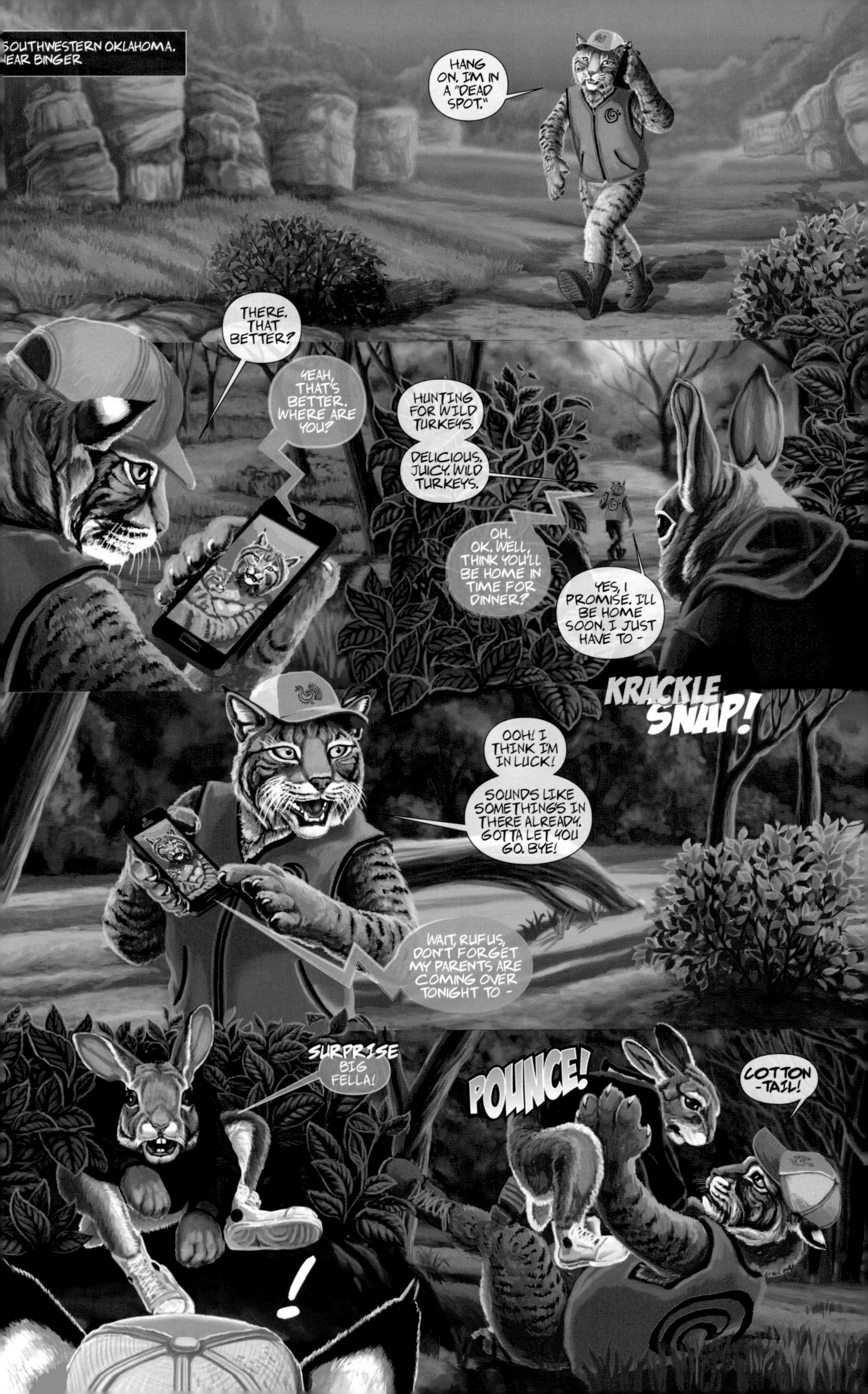
SOUTHWESTERN OKLAHOMA. NEAR BINGER
HANG ON. I'M IN A "DEAD SPOT."
THERE. THAT BETTER?
YEAH, THAT'S BETTER. WHERE ARE YOU?
HUNTING FOR WILD TURKEYS.
DELICIOUS. JUICY. WILD TURKEYS.
OH. OK. WELL, THINK YOU'LL BE HOME IN TIME FOR DINNER?
YES, I PROMISE. I'LL BE HOME SOON. I JUST HAVE TO -
KRACKLE SNAP!
OOH! I THINK I'M IN LUCK!
SOUNDS LIKE SOMETHING'S IN THERE ALREADY. GOTTA LET YOU GO. BYE!
WAIT, RUFUS, DON'T FORGET MY PARENTS ARE COMING OVER TONIGHT TO -
SURPRISE BIG FELLA!
!
POUNCE!
COTTON-TAIL!

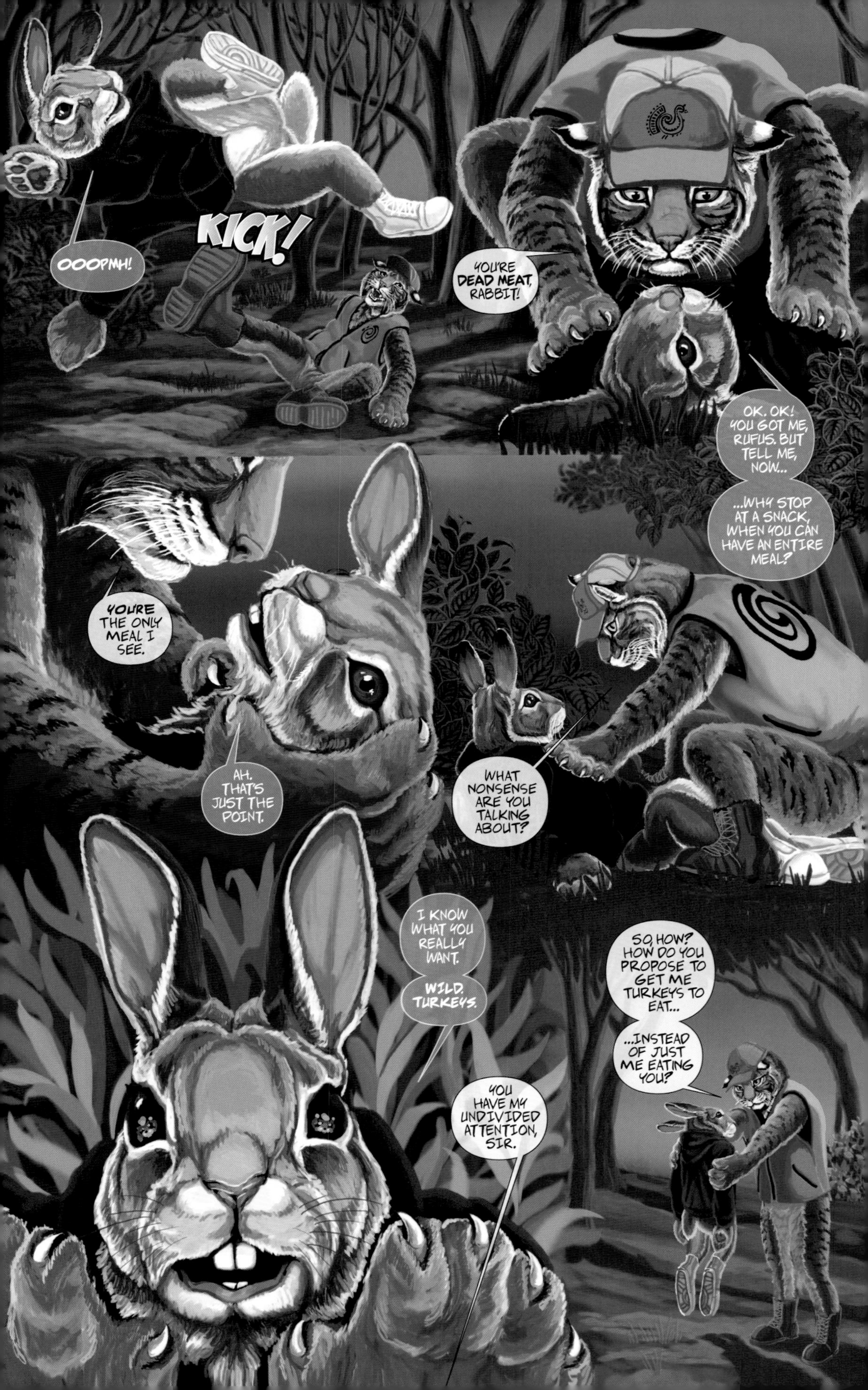
OOOPMH!
KICK!
YOU'RE DEAD MEAT, RABBIT!
OK. OK! YOU GOT ME, RUFUS. BUT TELL ME, NOW...
...WHY STOP AT A SNACK, WHEN YOU CAN HAVE AN ENTIRE MEAL?
YOU'RE THE ONLY MEAL I SEE.
AH. THAT'S JUST THE POINT.
WHAT NONSENSE ARE YOU TALKING ABOUT?
I KNOW WHAT YOU REALLY WANT.
WILD. TURKEYS.
YOU HAVE MY UNDIVIDED ATTENTION, SIR.
SO, HOW? HOW DO YOU PROPOSE TO GET ME TURKEYS TO EAT...
...INSTEAD OF JUST ME EATING YOU?

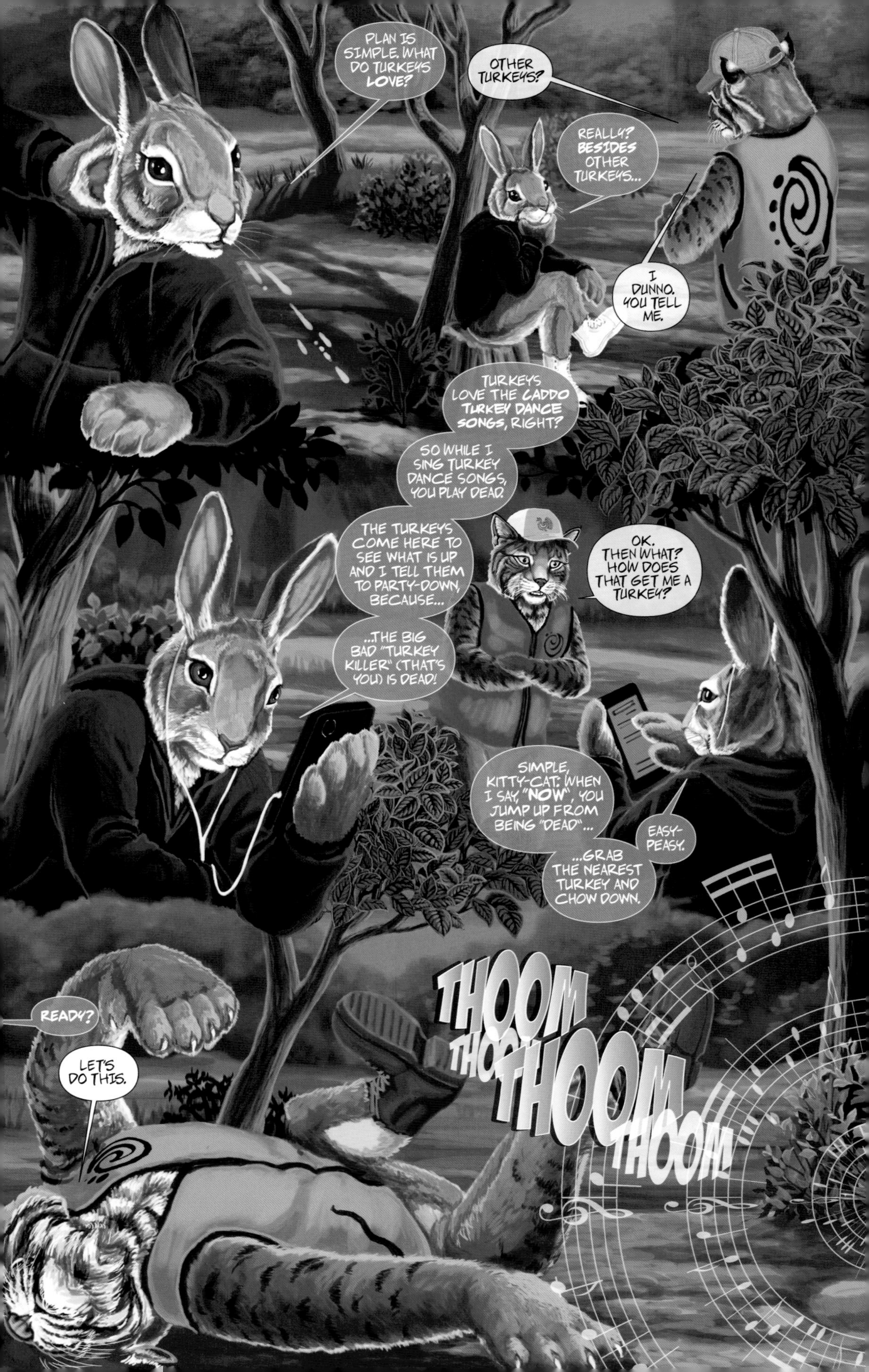
PLAN IS SIMPLE. WHAT DO TURKEYS **LOVE**?
OTHER TURKEYS?
REALLY? **BESIDES** OTHER TURKEYS...
I DUNNO. YOU TELL ME.
TURKEYS LOVE THE **CADDO TURKEY DANCE SONGS**, RIGHT?
SO WHILE I SING TURKEY DANCE SONGS, YOU PLAY DEAD.
THE TURKEYS COME HERE TO SEE WHAT IS UP AND I TELL THEM TO PARTY-DOWN, BECAUSE...
...THE BIG BAD "TURKEY KILLER" (THAT'S YOU) IS DEAD!
OK. THEN WHAT? HOW DOES THAT GET ME A TURKEY?
SIMPLE, KITTY-CAT: WHEN I SAY, "**NOW**", YOU JUMP UP FROM BEING "DEAD"...
...GRAB THE NEAREST TURKEY AND CHOW DOWN.
EASY-PEASY.
READY?
LET'S DO THIS.
THOOM
THOOM
THOOM
THOOM

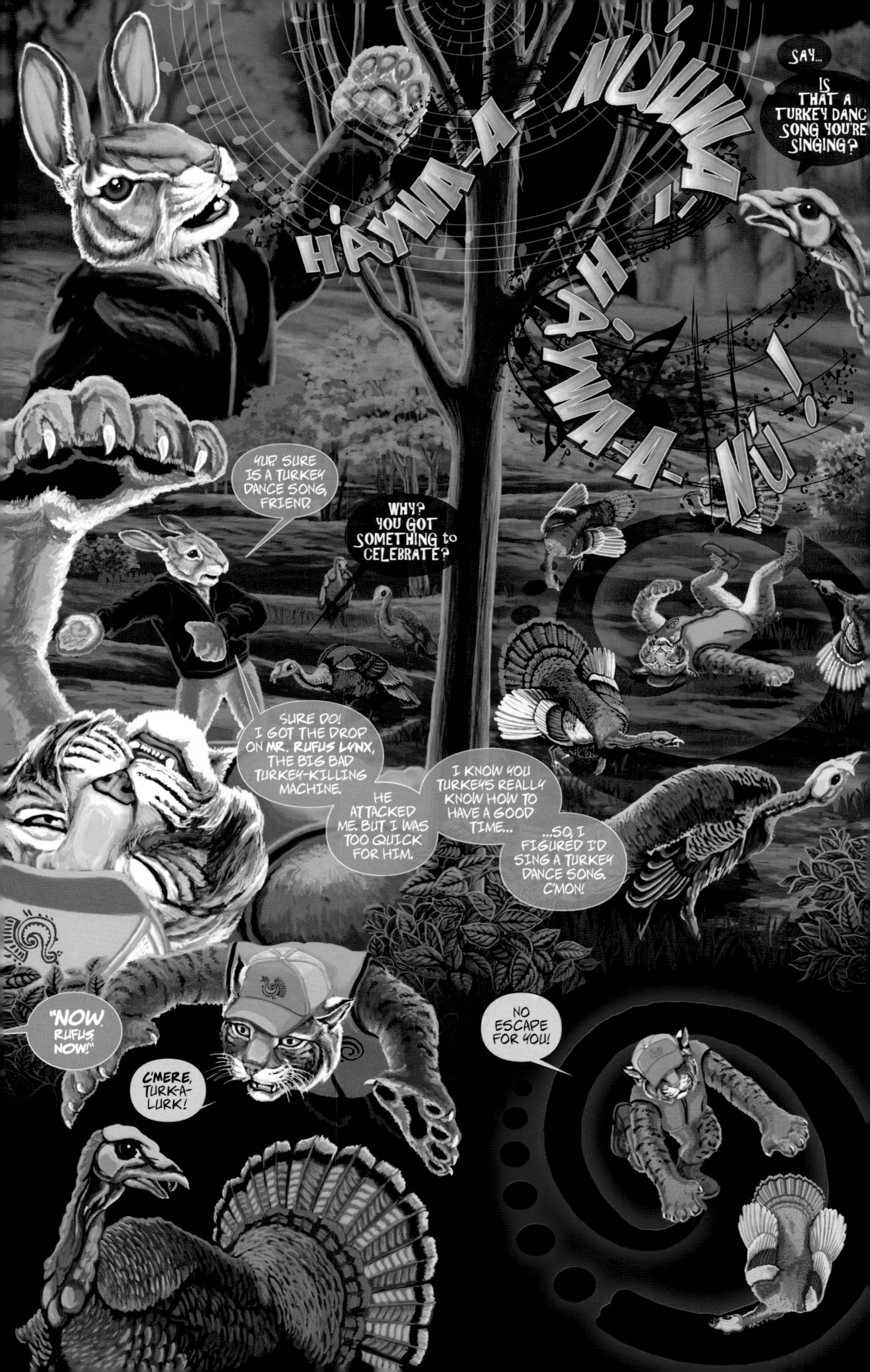
SAY...
IS THAT A TURKEY DANC SONG YOU'RE SINGING?
HÁYWA-A-NÚWA-Í, HÁYWA-A-NÚ!
YUP. SURE IS A TURKEY DANCE SONG, FRIEND.
WHY? YOU GOT SOMETHING to CELEBRATE?
SURE DO! I GOT THE DROP ON MR. RUFUS LYNX, THE BIG BAD TURKEY-KILLING MACHINE.
HE ATTACKED ME. BUT I WAS TOO QUICK FOR HIM.
I KNOW YOU TURKEYS REALLY KNOW HOW TO HAVE A GOOD TIME...
...SO, I FIGURED I'D SING A TURKEY DANCE SONG. C'MON!
"NOW. RUFUS. NOW!"
C'MERE, TURK-A-LURK!
NO ESCAPE FOR YOU!

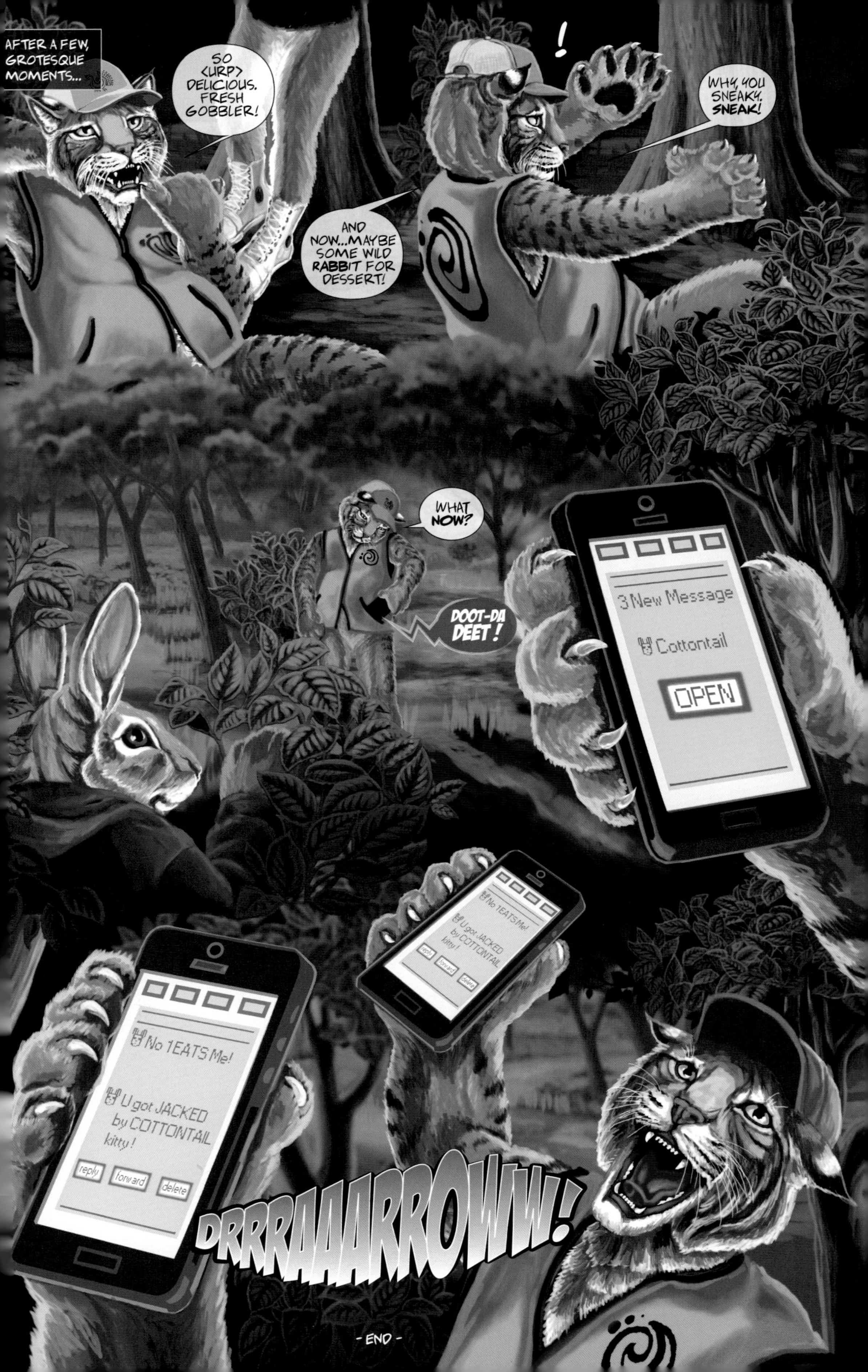
AFTER A FEW, GROTESQUE MOMENTS...
SO <URP> DELICIOUS. FRESH GOBBLER!
!
WHY, YOU SNEAKY, SNEAK!
AND NOW...MAYBE SOME WILD RABBIT FOR DESSERT!
WHAT NOW?
DOOT-DA DEET!
3 New Message
Cottontail
OPEN
No 1EATS Me!
U got JACKED by COTTONTAIL kitty!
reply
forward
delete
No 1EATS Me!
U got JACKED by COTTONTAIL kitty!
reply
forward
delete
DRRRAAARROWW!
- END -

JOURNEYS

Written and Illustrated by Jeffrey Veregge

BACKGROUND

The canoe journey that is a part of this story illustrates one of the traditional practices of the author's community as they visit neighbouring tribal lands. Travellers through the rivers would bring their own culture to the lands they visit, in an act of sharing and respect. This is a current ritual practised today and is an important part of maintaining the teachings and beliefs of the Suquamish community. The Native words overlaid throughout the story are written in the Suquamish language, and are lyrics from a traditional canoe journey song that is sung by travellers. The story created here by the author is one of the first times ever these lyrics have been written down. In this way, this brings the existing tradition into a contemporary medium. Just like the Janus ship from the story. Janus was the Greek god of beginnings, passageways, and endings. He was one who could look to both the past and the future. With this, the author has created a piece that is truly representative of the message behind the canoe journey – in the present day, it is important to remember that we are sharing lands, and should welcome new travellers with the spirit of sharing and respect.

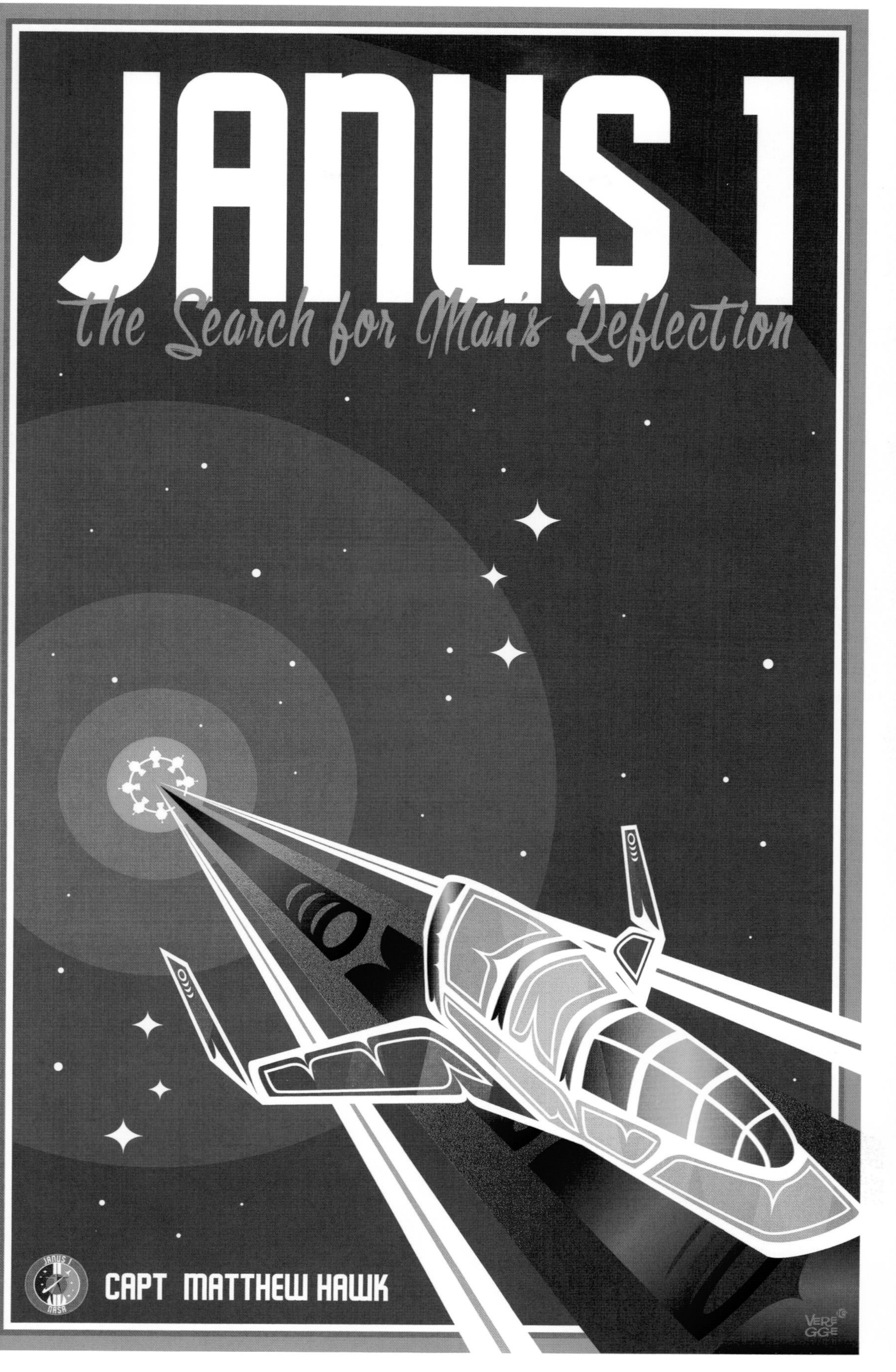
JANUS 1
the Search for Man's Reflection
JANUS 1
NASA
CAPT MATTHEW HAWK
VEREGGE

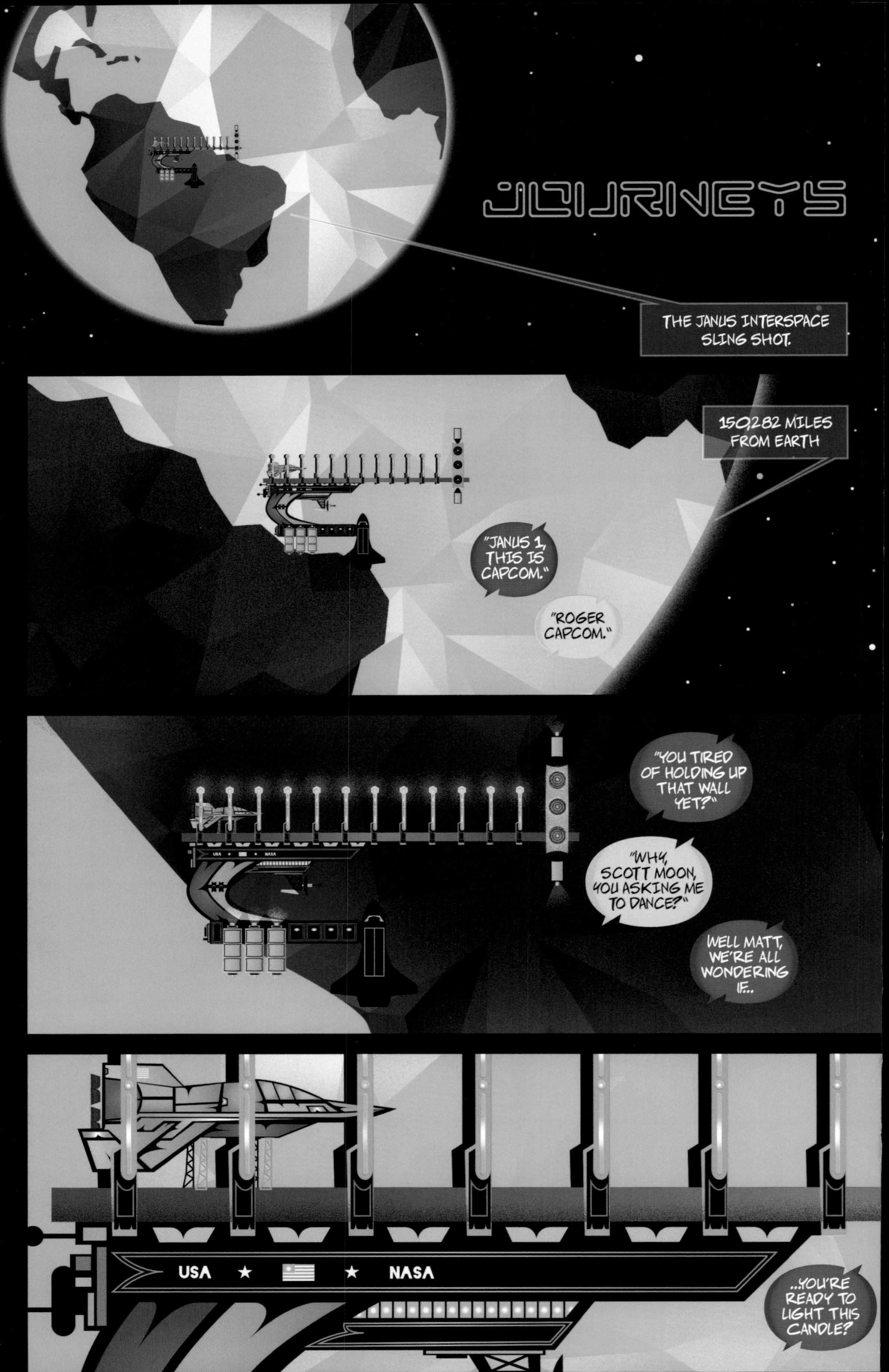
JOURNEYS
THE JANUS INTERSPACE SLING SHOT.
150,282 MILES FROM EARTH
"JANUS 1, THIS IS CAPCOM."
"ROGER CAPCOM."
"YOU TIRED OF HOLDING UP THAT WALL YET?"
"WHY, SCOTT MOON, YOU ASKING ME TO DANCE?"
WELL MATT, WE'RE ALL WONDERING IF...
USA NASA
...YOU'RE READY TO LIGHT THIS CANDLE?

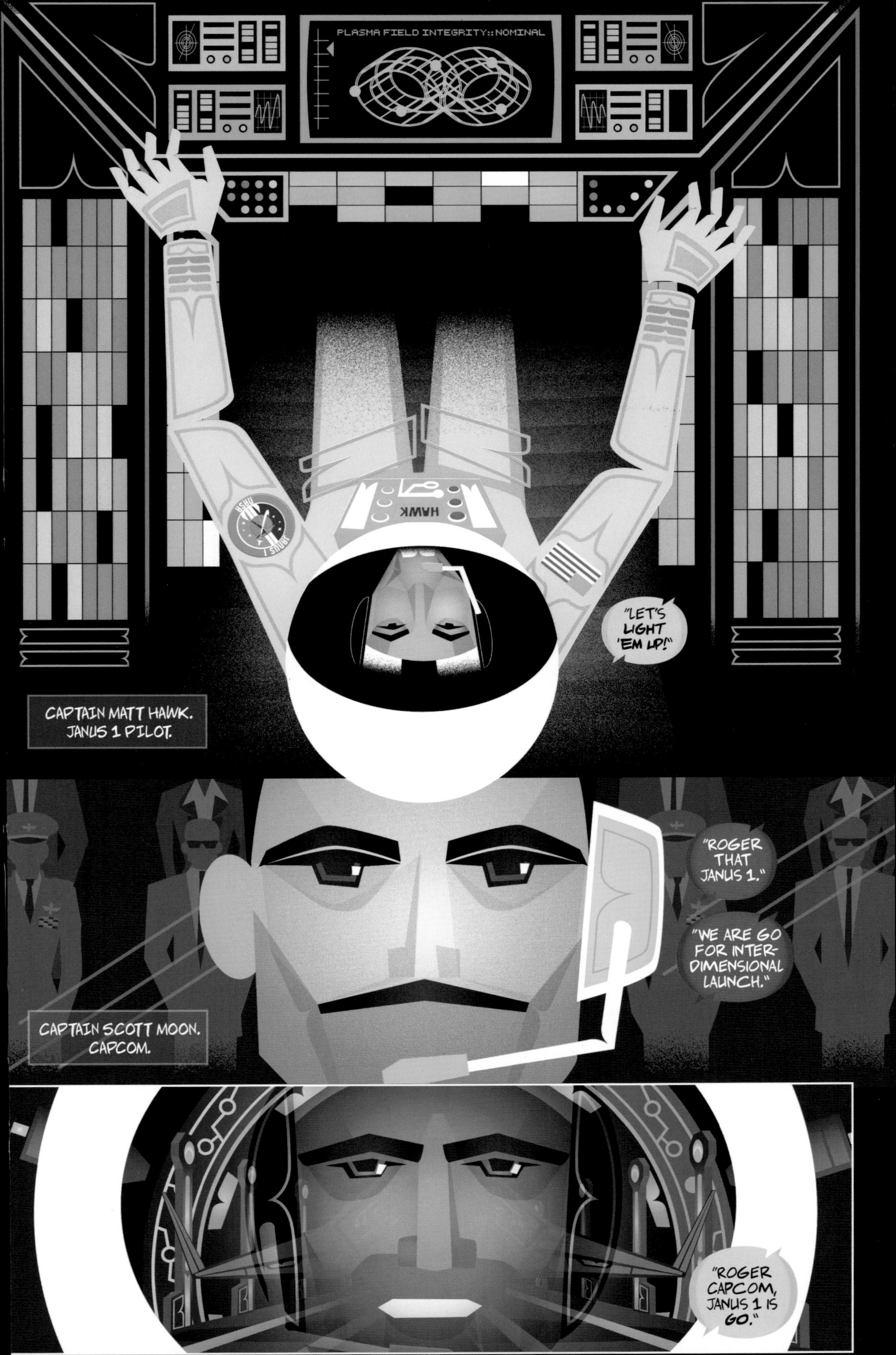

PLASMA FIELD INTEGRITY:: NOMINAL
HAWK
JANUS 1
"LET'S LIGHT 'EM UP!"
CAPTAIN MATT HAWK. JANUS 1 PILOT.
"ROGER THAT JANUS 1."
"WE ARE GO FOR INTER-DIMENSIONAL LAUNCH."
CAPTAIN SCOTT MOON. CAPCOM.
"ROGER CAPCOM, JANUS 1 IS GO."

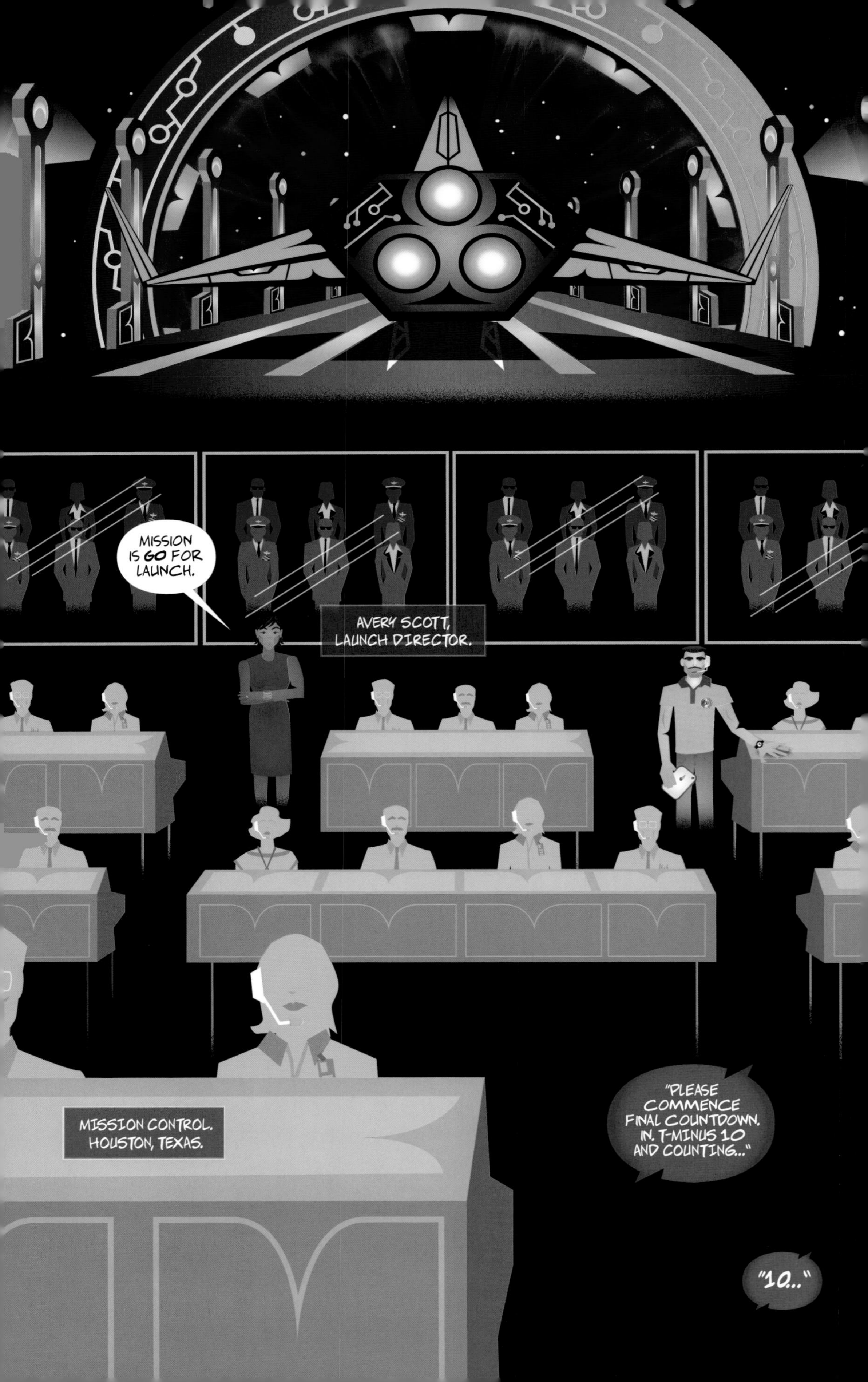
MISSION IS GO FOR LAUNCH.
AVERY SCOTT, LAUNCH DIRECTOR.
MISSION CONTROL. HOUSTON, TEXAS.
"PLEASE COMMENCE FINAL COUNTDOWN. IN. T-MINUS 10 AND COUNTING..."
"10..."

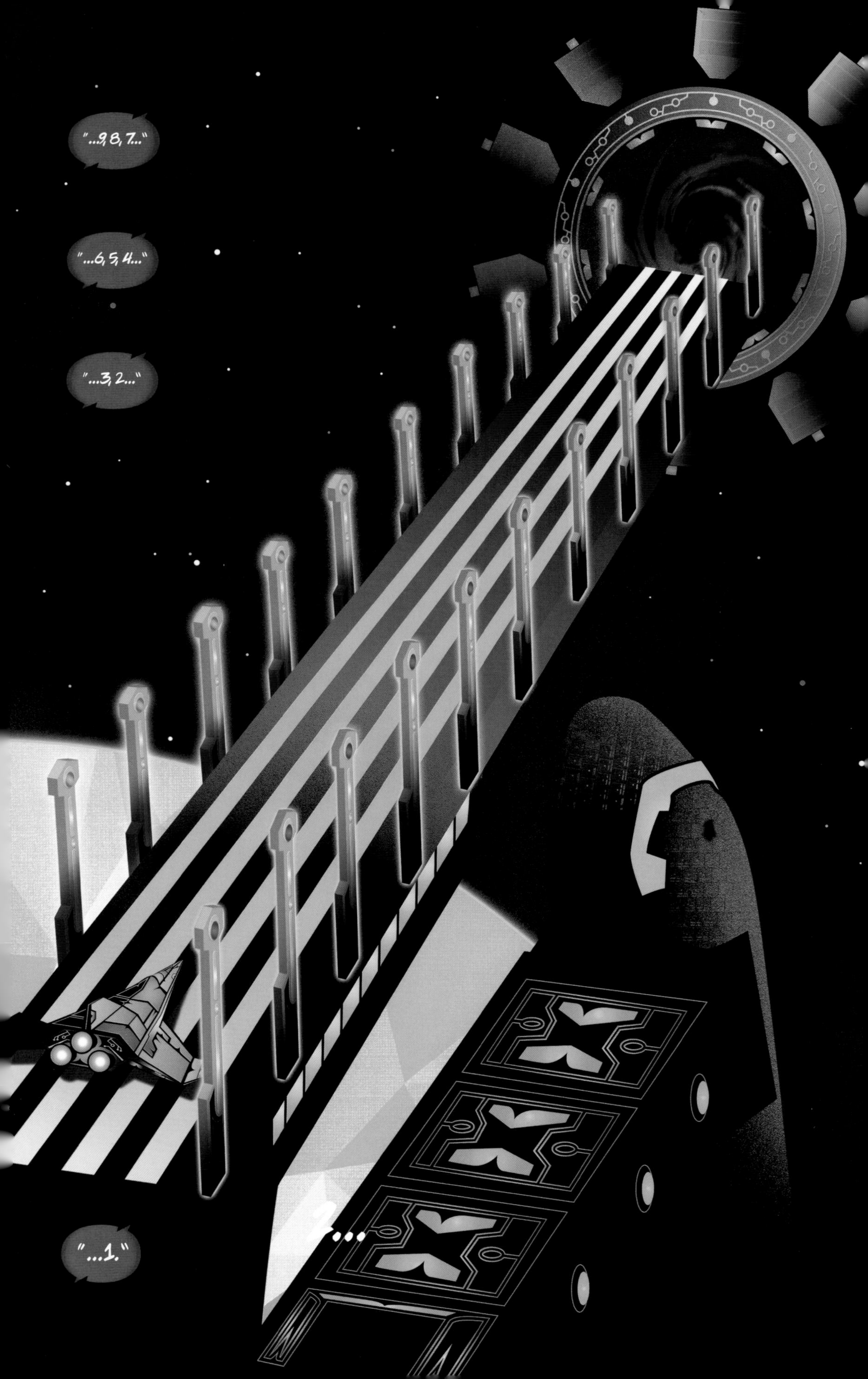
"...9, 8, 7..."
"...6, 5, 4..."
"...3, 2..."
"...1."

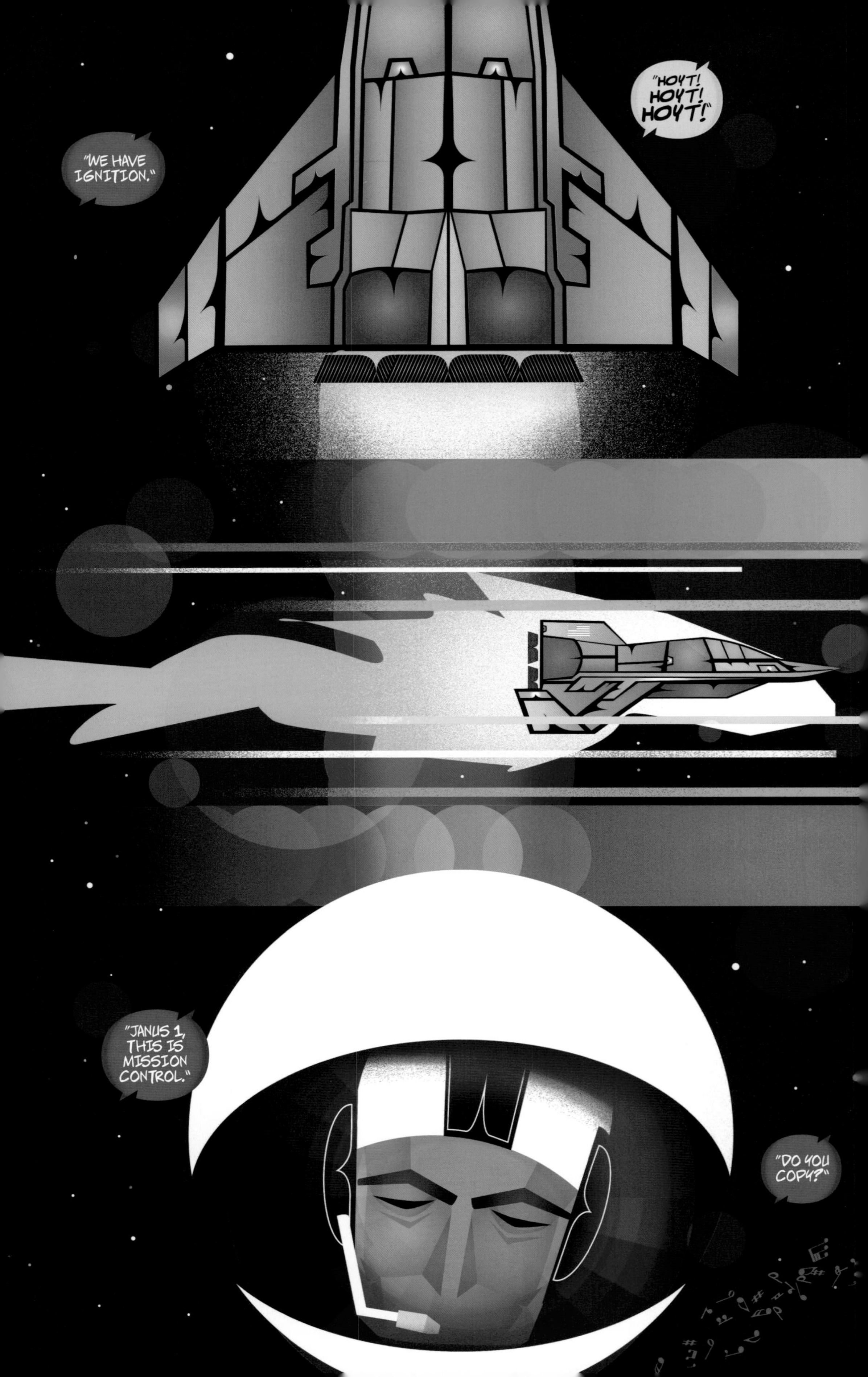
"WE HAVE IGNITION."
"HOYT! HOYT! HOYT!"
"JANUS 1, THIS IS MISSION CONTROL."
"DO YOU COPY?"

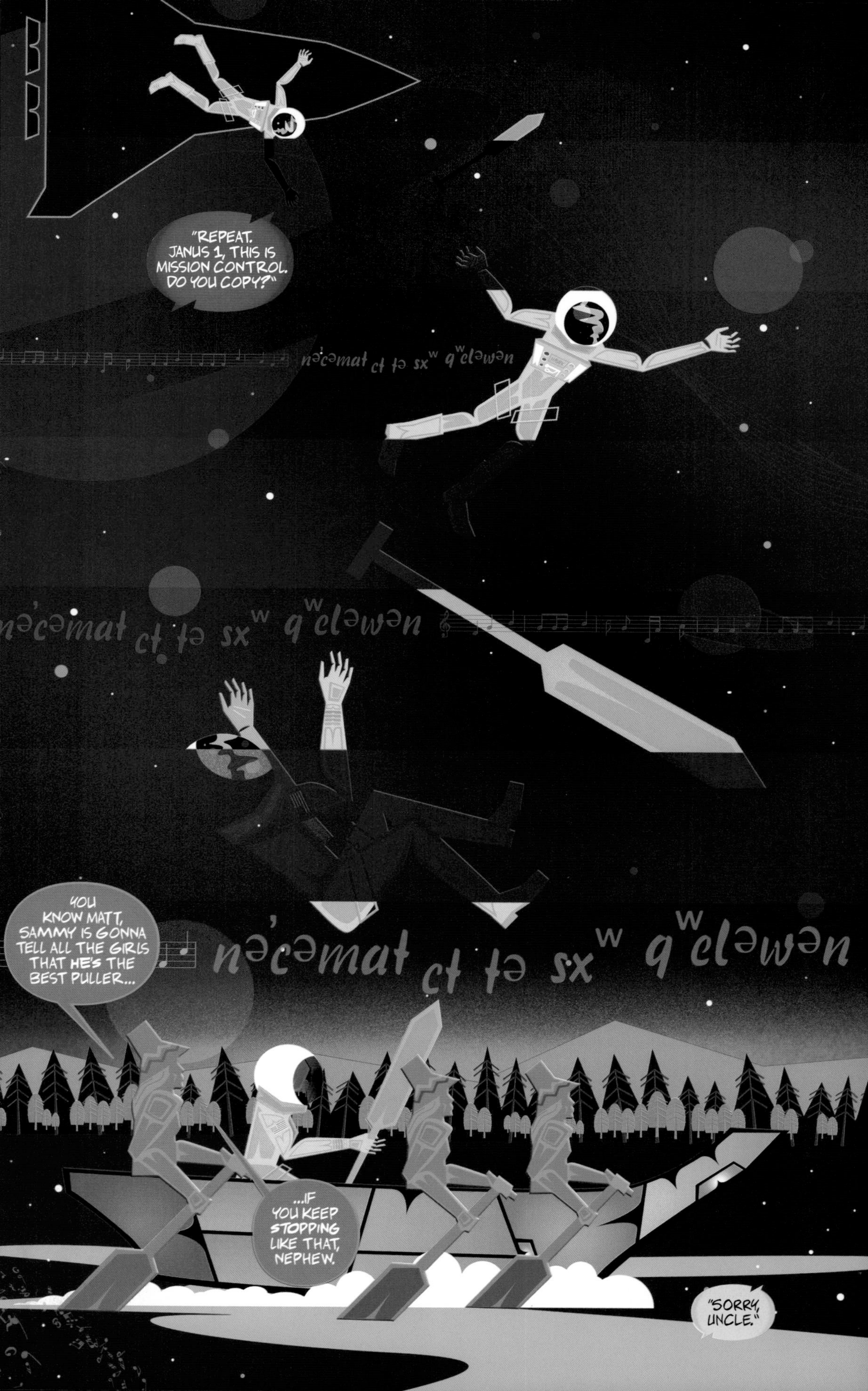
"REPEAT. JANUS 1, THIS IS MISSION CONTROL. DO YOU COPY?"
nəc̓əmat ct tə sxʷ qʷcləwən
nəc̓əmat ct tə sxʷ qʷcləwən
YOU KNOW MATT, SAMMY IS GONNA TELL ALL THE GIRLS THAT **HE'S** THE BEST PULLER...
nəc̓əmat ct tə sxʷ qʷcləwən
...IF YOU KEEP **STOPPING** LIKE THAT, NEPHEW.
"SORRY, UNCLE."

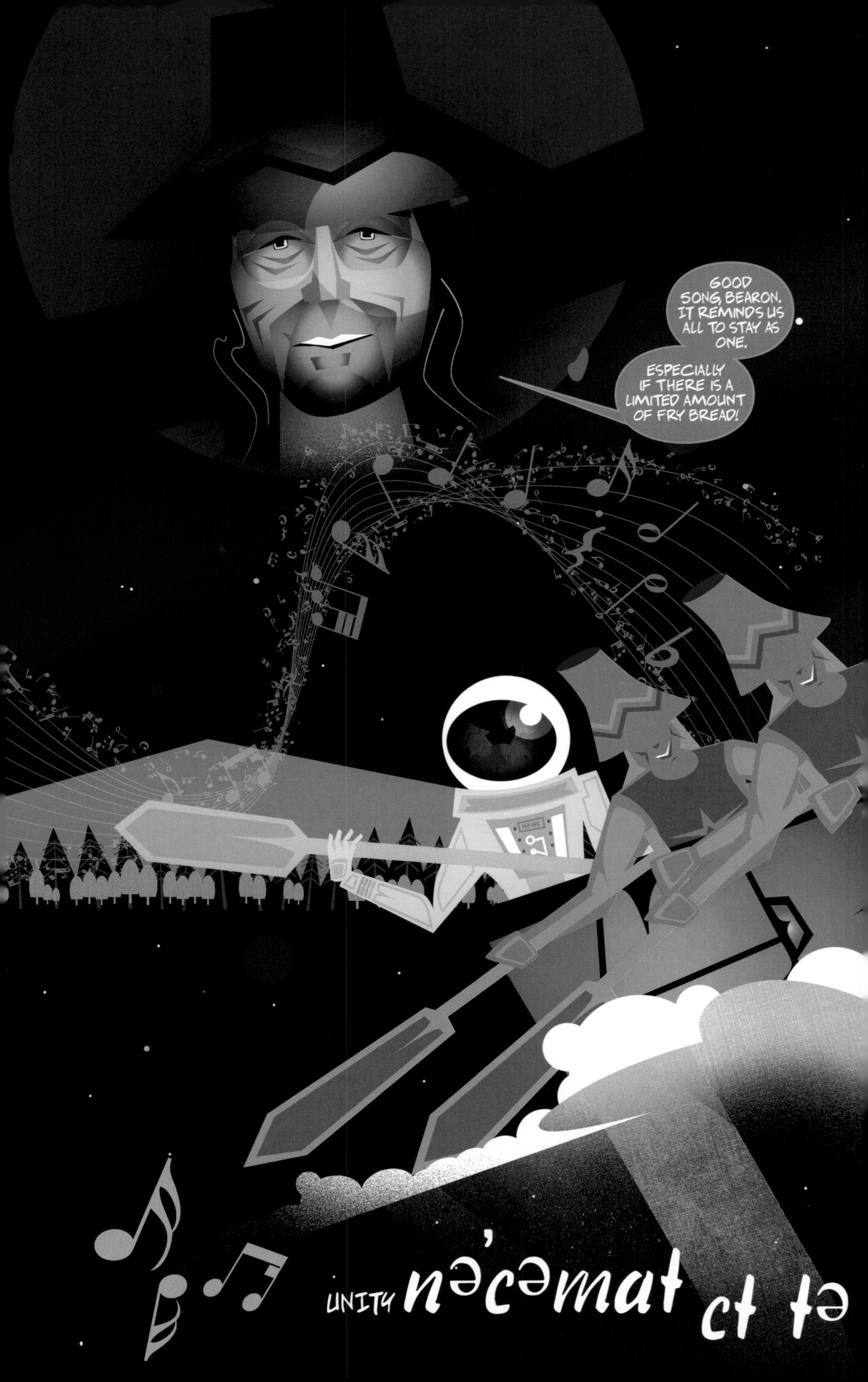
GOOD SONG, BEARON. IT REMINDS US ALL TO STAY AS ONE.
ESPECIALLY IF THERE IS A LIMITED AMOUNT OF FRY BREAD!
UNITY nəc̓əmat ct tə

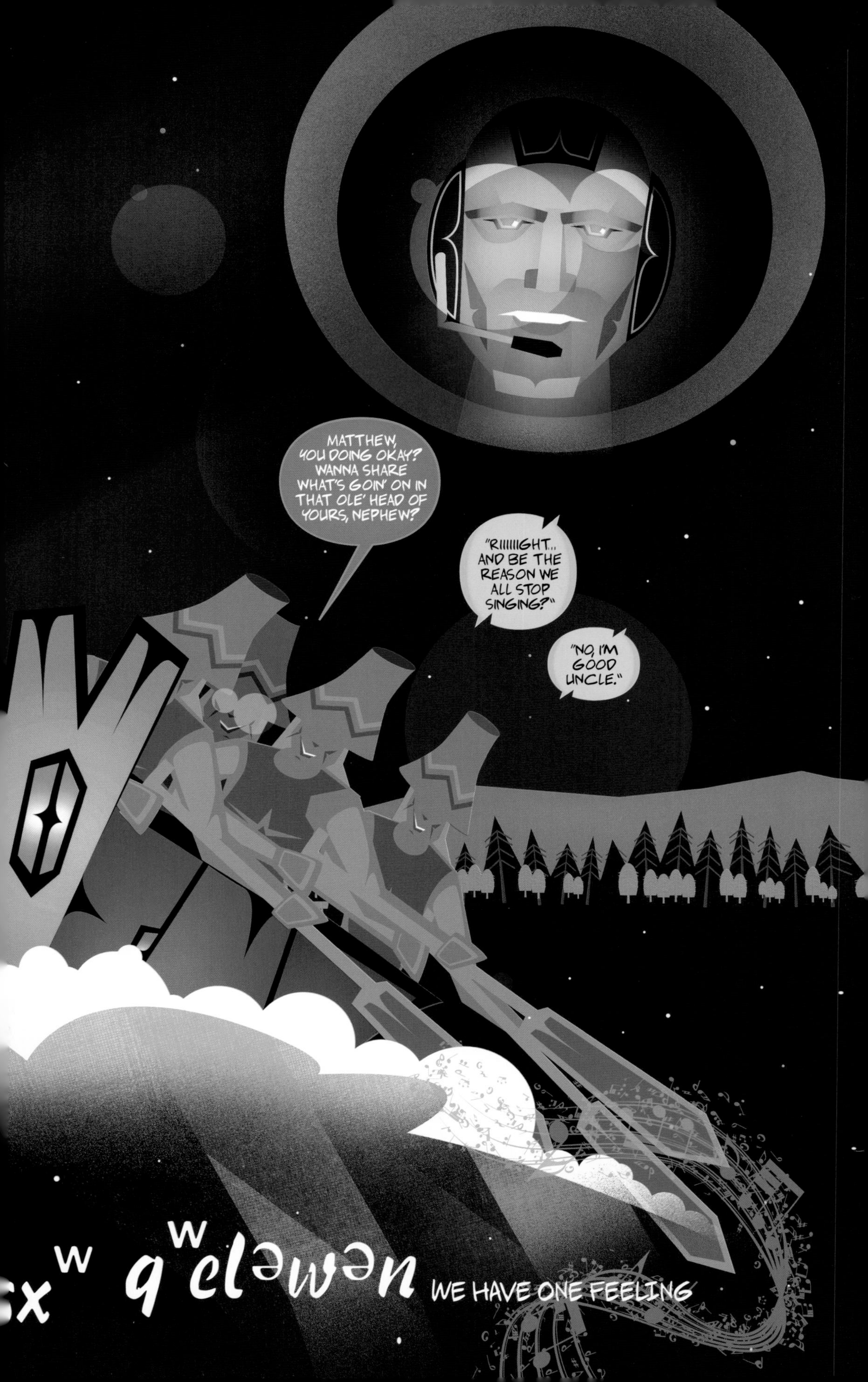

MATTHEW, YOU DOING OKAY? WANNA SHARE WHAT'S GOIN' ON IN THAT OLE' HEAD OF YOURS, NEPHEW?
"RIIIIIGHT... AND BE THE REASON WE ALL STOP SINGING?"
"NO, I'M GOOD UNCLE."
sxʷ qʷeləwən WE HAVE ONE FEELING

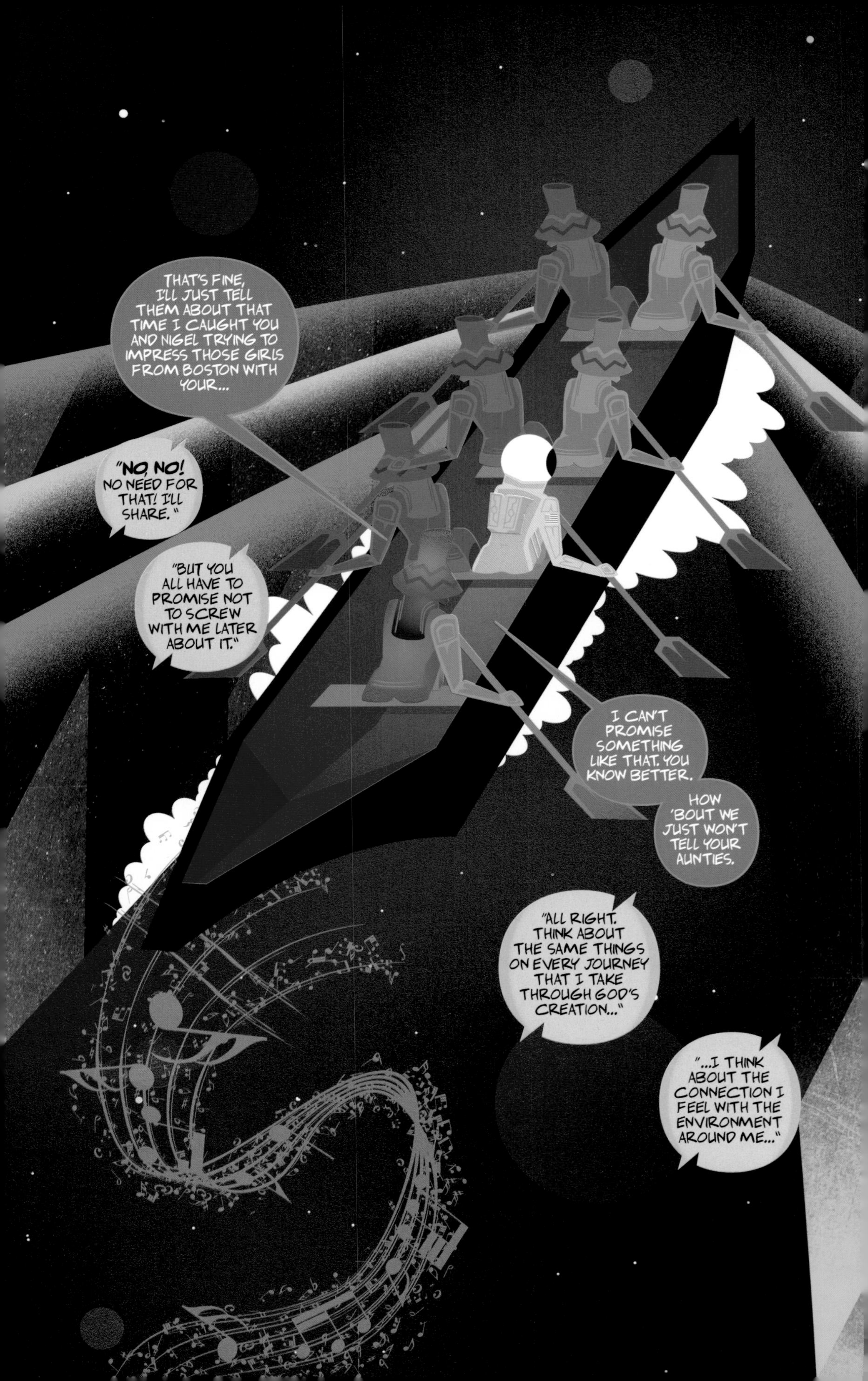
THAT'S FINE, I'LL JUST TELL THEM ABOUT THAT TIME I CAUGHT YOU AND NIGEL TRYING TO IMPRESS THOSE GIRLS FROM BOSTON WITH YOUR...
"NO, NO! NO NEED FOR THAT! I'LL SHARE."
"BUT YOU ALL HAVE TO PROMISE NOT TO SCREW WITH ME LATER ABOUT IT."
I CAN'T PROMISE SOMETHING LIKE THAT. YOU KNOW BETTER.
HOW 'BOUT WE JUST WON'T TELL YOUR AUNTIES.
"ALL RIGHT. THINK ABOUT THE SAME THINGS ON EVERY JOURNEY THAT I TAKE THROUGH GOD'S CREATION..."
"...I THINK ABOUT THE CONNECTION I FEEL WITH THE ENVIRONMENT AROUND ME..."

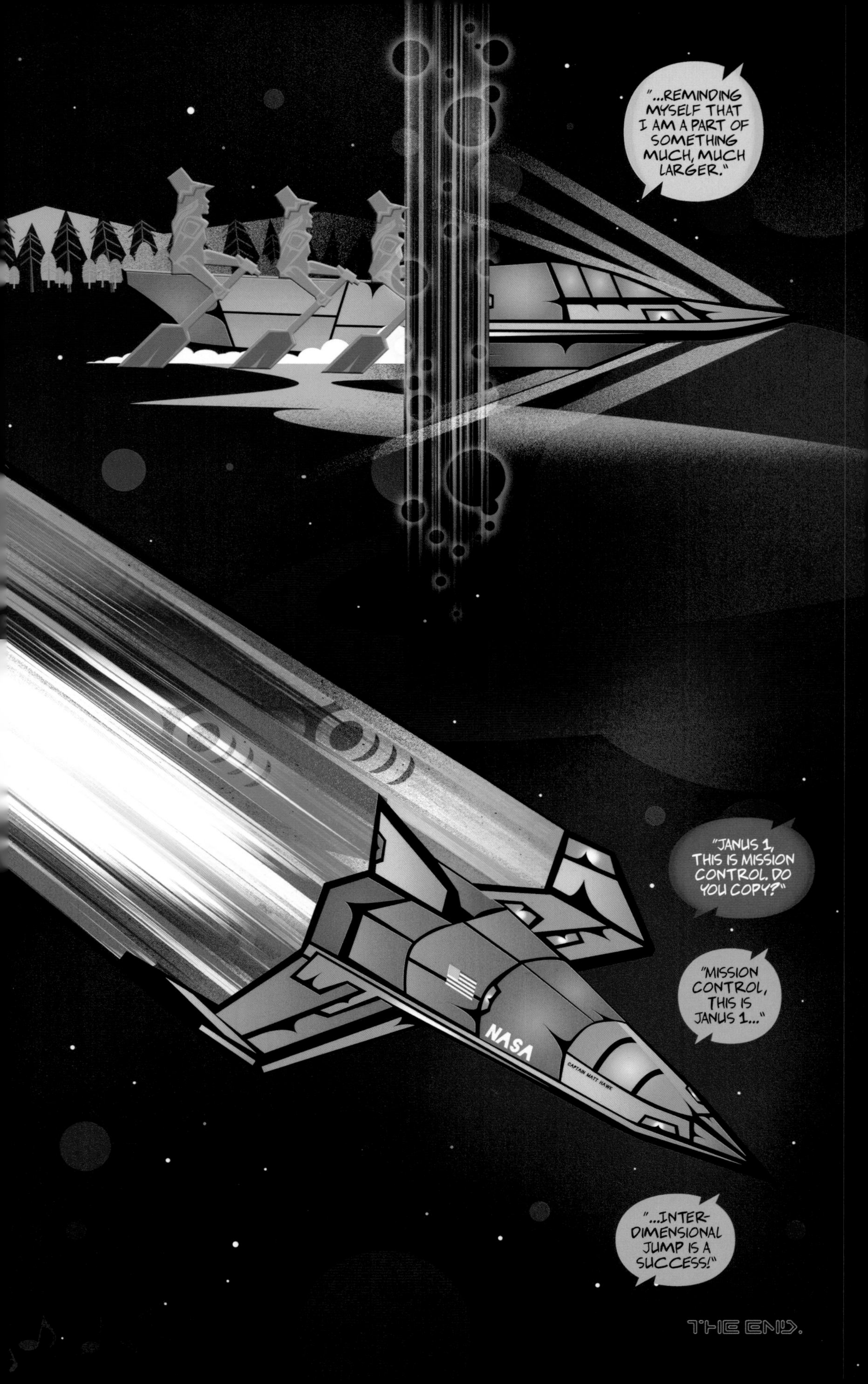
"...REMINDING MYSELF THAT I AM A PART OF SOMETHING MUCH, MUCH LARGER."
"JANUS 1, THIS IS MISSION CONTROL. DO YOU COPY?"
NASA
CAPTAIN MATT HAWK
"MISSION CONTROL, THIS IS JANUS 1..."
"...INTER-DIMENSIONAL JUMP IS A SUCCESS!"
THE END.

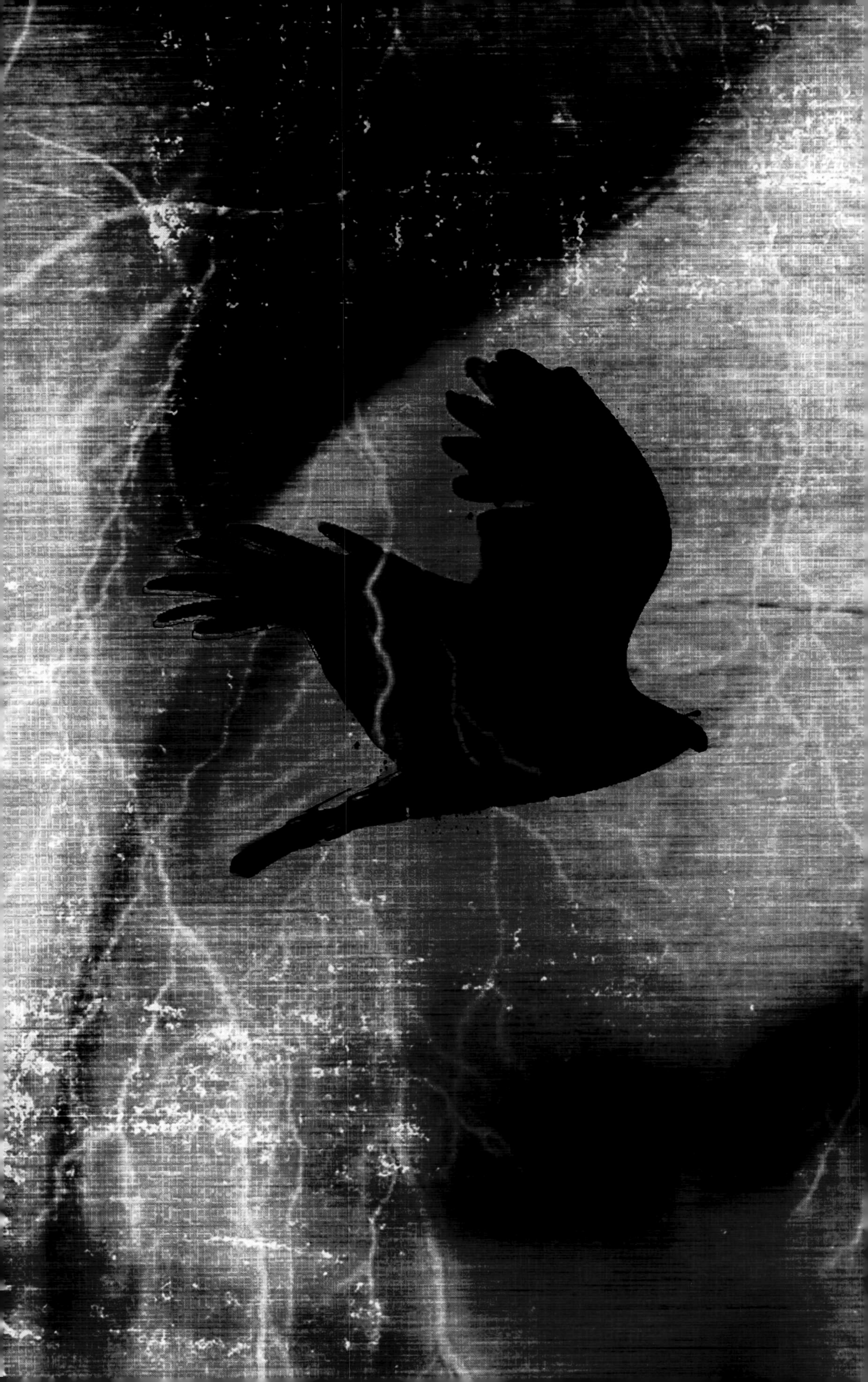

When I was asked by *MOONSHOT* publisher AH Comics to offer up a Thunderbird story, I was like, sure, so long as I can tell people about chemical spills that are messing up Aamjiwnaang, where Thunderbird stories are told!

Just as our stories are very much living, they are also responsive to the changing needs of every moment. What is evoked reflects what needs to be heard and seen.

Through and through, *MOONSHOT: The Indigenous Comics Collection, Volume 2* brings ongoing issues in Indigenous communities to the forefront through comics. From Richard Van Camp's reflection on a damaging mine disaster, to youth struggling to connect with teachings, to the day-to-day ramifications of toxicity, to imagining transformative futures, this collection addresses present concerns and celebrates our continuance through self-determined representations.

Until recently, most conversations about Native representations in comic books were focused on stereotypes and tropes. In fact, comic books are often thought of negatively in Indigenous communities, such as my own, due to the damage they perpetuate against us. Michael Sheyahshe's book *Native Americans in Comic Books: A Critical Study* contributed to connecting a community of aspiring and established comic book creatives who wanted instead to see self-determined representations. We would dream about days of shelves filled with Indigenous comic books. From light print runs of independent comic books to the launch of Indigenous-owned and -operated comic book publisher Native Realities Press, we have been working towards self-determination.

Now there is a huge demand, thanks to awareness created through the *MOONSHOT* collection, alongside events such as the Indigenous Comic Con. The Central Canada Comic Con even hosted an Indigenous comics panel! It's incredibly exciting to see so many voices present.

However, the work can't just be on us. You are vital as a reader. By supporting this collection, you are encouraging the mass comic book market to turn their attention to better representations. When you make an effort to be better informed about accurate representations as well as read comic books such as *MOONSHOT*, you are making a direct contribution to better work that benefits everyone. It takes interest and action to hold publishers accountable for content so that we can continue the momentum of this transition. Look for who was involved in a comic book, especially whether or not they included the people who are represented in roles as consultants, or better yet, as creatives who have a direct hand in bringing the comic book into form. Also look for the response to a representation from that particular community. If there are issues, bring them forward, because the more voices there are in support of self-determination, the more we will see robust, meaningful representations.

Importantly, this collection is a place of self-determination for Indigenous writers and comic book artists. Here's a great irony: a few years ago, there wasn't enough comic book work for someone like me to exclusively develop my skills in inks and colours for comics, so I took on balancing

◀ **"Animikiig"** *by Elizabeth LaPensée*

several contracts at once and spread my focus across design, writing, and art in games and animations. So many stories were dreams and notes until *MOONSHOT Volume 1*, which uplifted me as a comic writer thanks to the editor who tracked down my award-winning comics from years earlier.

With the ongoing interest in comic books with Indigenous themes and projects such as *MOONSHOT Volume 2* comes the need for more creatives who specialize in sequential storytelling, ranging from writing to pencils to inks to colours to lettering to editing.

If you're interested in contributing to comic books, awesome! Thankfully, there are many pathways to working in sequential storytelling. Jeffrey Veregge started as a graphic designer whose remix of popular comic book characters in coastal style reflecting his Port Gamble S'Klallam community caught the attention of Marvel. He was given work making comic book covers, but notably still had limited creative say over the content within. *MOONSHOT Volume 2* gives him well-deserved space to take his work a step further as both a writer and illustrator. His approach is unique to him, and just as there is space now for his voice, there is space for many more voices from many different communities.

Whatever your skills or interests may be, always be true to yourself. Just as Jeffrey Veregge's success shows, this work is about answering to your community and reflecting yourself and those who come before you. Of course, it's also about reflecting your own life experiences, such as seen in the writing of Darcie Little Badger. Wherever your inspiration comes from,

just get started and build yourself a portfolio of work.

Personally, I dig small vignettes with characters I never stick with. Mostly I write stories as first-person narrations that end up as voiceovers in comic book form. In contrast, Jay Odjick, whose work is highlighted in *MOONSHOT Volume 1*, went the route of passionately acting as both a writer and artist on his character Kagagi and built him up over time through a comic that grew into an animated series on the Aboriginal Peoples Television Network. I admire his dedication, which garnered him opportunities to contribute to other projects.

For those who are all about writing, Richard Van Camp is an amazing role model, because he moves fluidly between stories, poems, and comic books, which has led to film adaptations of his work. It all comes down to how your perseverance to develop your skills forms your life journey and where your greatest hopes lead you.

Just as we have always been, we are here, and our futures are unfolding. *MOONSHOT: The Indigenous Comics Collection, Volume 2* is a signifier of expanding interest in meaningful representations in comic books and empowers an ever-expanding wider body of work.

With hope for self-determination and with gratitude to all those who help in this path.

Miigwech,

Elizabeth LaPensée, *Ph.D*

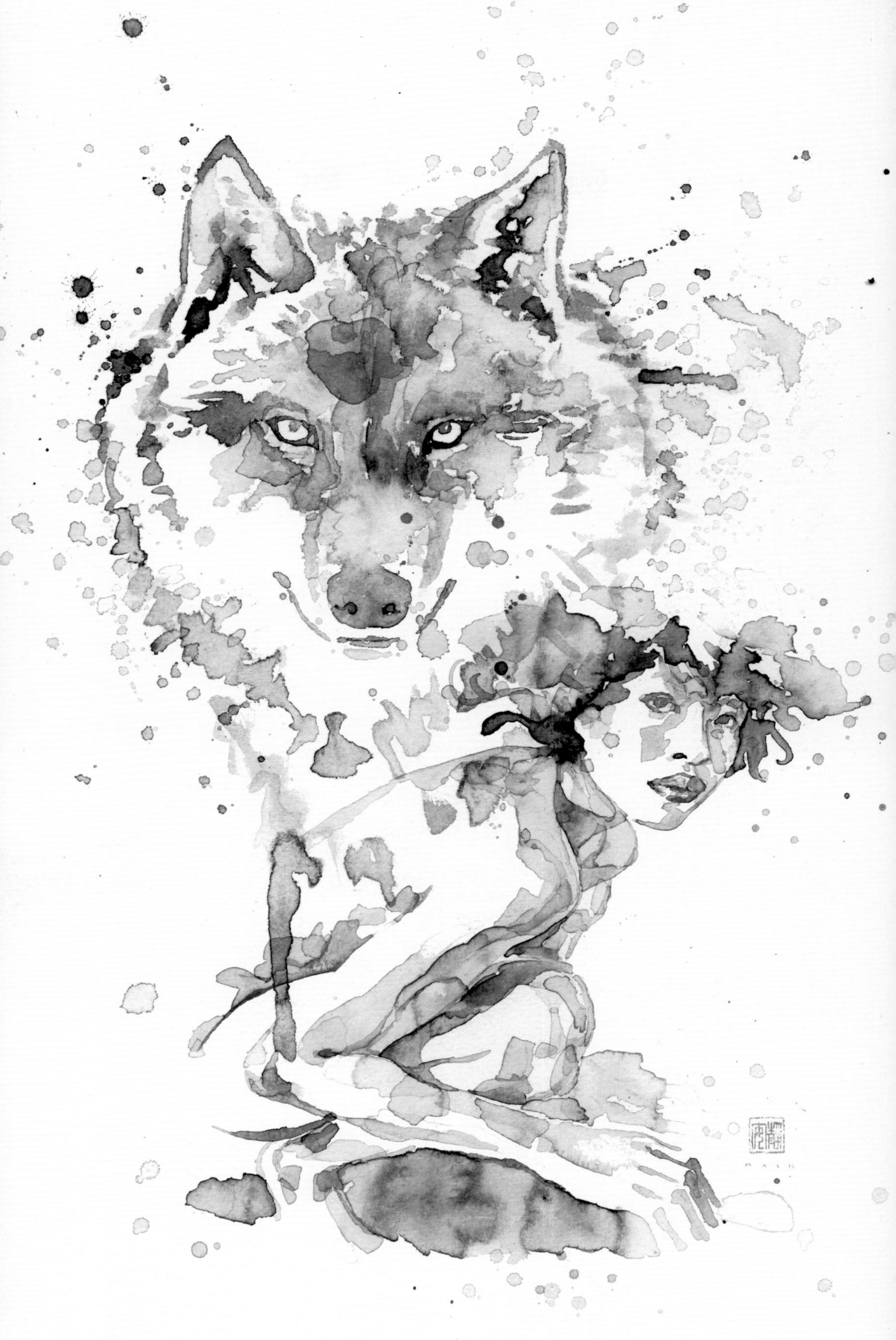
MACK

MOONSHOT The Indigenous Comics Collection

BIOGRAPHIES

Volume 2

BACKGROUND

Over 30 creators brought this work to life, including award-winning Indigenous authors and comic book industry veterans. Each story was written by a different Indigenous author, bringing their own community's traditions into each piece. Read here about where our creators are from, and the incredible bodies of work they have produced that led them to the *MOONSHOT Volume 2* collection. The biographies are listed alphabetically by first name.

ALEXANDRIA NEONAKIS

Alexandria Neonakis is an award-winning illustrator and UI designer from Dartmouth, Nova Scotia. Her work is seen in the popular games *Uncharted 4*, *The Last of Us*, and its DLC, *Left Behind*. She illustrated the award-winning book *Sweetest Kulu*, written by acclaimed Inuit throat singer Celina Kalluk, which won the Wordcraft Circle Award in the Picture Book category, presented by the Wordcraft Circle of Native Writers and Storytellers.

ALINA PETE

Alina is a Cree artist and writer from Little Pine First Nation in western Saskatchewan. She writes popular short stories, poems, and RPG (role playing game) supplements. Her stories and artwork have been featured in several commercial comic book anthologies, and she also works in animation and digital effects. Her work can be seen in the Gemini Award–winning children's animated series *Wapos Bay*. Alina is best known as the creator of the Aurora Award–winning webcomic *Weregeek*.

ARMAND GARNET RUFFO

Armand's writing is strongly influenced by his Ojibway heritage. His publications include *Water Lily Woman*, *Introduction to Indigenous Literary Criticism*, *The Thunderbird Poems,* and more. He writes for a variety of genres and his work has won several awards, including the 2016 Best Canadian Poetry Award. His award-winning film *A Windigo Tale* was honoured with Best Picture at the Dreamspeakers Film Festival. He is also a Professor at Queen's University, Ontario, teaching a course in the literature of incarceration.

DANIEL HEATH JUSTICE

Daniel Heath Justice is a Colorado-born Canadian citizen of the Cherokee Nation. He holds the Canada Research Chair in Indigenous Literature and Expressive Culture in First Nations and Indigenous Studies at the University of British Columbia, on the unceded territories of the Musqueam people. Widely published in the field of Indigenous literary studies, his critical and creative work engages issues of Indigenous being, belonging, and other-than-human kinship in literature and the expressive arts.

DARCIE LITTLE BADGER

Darcie Little Badger is a Lipan Apache scientist and writer. After studying gene expression in toxin-producing phytoplankton, she received a Ph.D. from Texas A&M University. Her short fiction has appeared in several publications, including *Strange Horizons*, *Lightspeed Magazine*, *Mythic Delirium*, and *Love Beyond Body, Space, and Time*, an anthology of LGBT speculative fiction by Indigenous writers. Darcie is a Ford Fellow and serves as an environmental science consultant for her tribe.

DAVID ALEXANDER ROBERTSON

David, of Irish, Scottish, and Cree heritage, is a graphic novelist and writer. He has created several bestselling publications, including the *7 Generations* series, the *Tales from Big Spirit* series, as well as *Betty: The Helen Betty Osborne Story*. He has been featured in *CV2* and *Prairie Fire*, and he has made appearances on APTN, CTV, and CBC. David's work has been reviewed in many national publications, and he is a four-time 2015 Manitoba Book Awards nominee.

DAVID CUTLER

David is a Newfoundland-born artist based in Toronto, Canada. He is a member of the Qalipu Mi'kmaq First Nation and studied illustration for sequential art at Max the Mutt Animation School. Working in comics for almost a decade, David is a special guest artist at national shows and events. His comic book work has appeared in various publications, magazines, and series, including *Wonderland*, *Robyn Hood vs Red Riding Hood*, *Snow White vs Snow White*, *The Secret World of Glacier Thorne*, *Hacktivist*, *Northern Guard,* and *Adventure Time*.

DAVID MACK

David is the New York Times bestselling author of the *Kabuki* graphic novels, as well as a writer and cover artist for Marvel's *Daredevil* – one of the ten bestselling comics in the US today. His painted work also appears on the covers of *Fight Club 2* and Marvel's *Jessica Jones*. David has worked on *Alias*, *New Avengers*, *Green Arrow*, *Justice League of America*, *Swamp Thing*, *Ms. Marvel,* and more. He has been nominated and won multiple awards, including International Eagle Awards, the Eisner Award (America's most prestigious in the industry), Harvey and Kirby Awards, and many more.

ELIZABETH LAPENSÉE, Ph.D

Elizabeth is an Anishinaabe, Métis, and Irish designer, writer, and researcher whose focus is Indigenous game development, comics, and animation. Her work is informed by cultural values and teachings. She has written several popular comic book titles, including *The West Was Lost* – an Aboriginal Peoples Television Network's Comic Creation Nation Contest winner. She is an Assistant Professor of Media & Information and Writing, Rhetoric & American Cultures at Michigan State University. She is co-editor of *Sequential Survivance* and editor of *Relational Constellation: An Indigenous Love Comics Collection*.

FRED PASHE

Fred is an illustrator, painter, and 3D artist from Long Plain/Dakota Tipi First Nation bands, Canada. His artwork can be seen in the original graphic novel *SpiritWolf: Birth of a Legend,* and he has done character modelling and artwork for popular games, books, and animation such as *Lord of the Rings: WITN*, *Spiderman*, *Ascend: Hand of Kul,* and *Project Spark*. Fred is also the winner of the 1995 Peace Hills Trust Aboriginal Art Award.

GERARD AND PETA-GAY ROBERTS

Gerard and Peta are Karina and Taino/Arawak First Nations storytellers, songwriters, musicians, and performing artists. They are ordained with Indigenous Messengers International, and are wampum carriers of the Grand River Six Nations. With their band, Okama, they have performed across the world, sharing traditional and spiritual music, dance, and art. The word *okama* is a Taino First Nation word meaning "listen" or "hear."

HAIWEI HOU

Haiwei is an internationally renowned illustrator, animator, character artist, and conceptual artist. She has worked all over the world, from California to China, and her work can be seen in magazines, television, film, books, and games. Haiwei has worked on high-profile projects for Nelvana Animation, Nickelodeon, EA Games, and Sideshow Collectibles, designing figures of Iron Man, the Dark Knight, The Hulk, and more. Her animated film, *Vernal Equinox*, has been screened across the globe, winning numerous selections and awards.

JAMES LEASK

James Leask is a Métis writer, critic, and researcher from Edmonton, Alberta, interested in multimedia representations of Indigenous peoples. His writing has appeared at outlets such as *ComicsAlliance*, *Comics! The Blog* and *Jay & Miles X-Plain the X-Men*. He is also the recipient of a Harpy Agenda Microgrant for Comics Journalism, awarded to select authors of colour in the field of comic criticism and journalism. James was given this award grant for his published review of *MOONSHOT: The Indigenous Comics Collection, Volume 1* in 2015.

JEFFREY VEREGGE

Jeffrey is an award-winning artist and illustrator of the Port Gamble S'Klallam Tribe, also with both Suquamish and Duwamish tribal ancestry. He is an award-winning artist and designer working in mainstream comics, with titles such as *Transformers*, *G.I. Joe*, *Captain America*, *Judge Dredd*, *New Avengers* and *Red Wolf*. He consciously blends a Native perspective with his visual art, which has led him to being named one of the Top 60 Masters of Contemporary Art of 2013 from ArtTour International, New York, as well as creating one of The Top 100 Comic Book Covers of 2014 as recognized by IGN.

KIM HUNTER

Kim is a contemporary Canadian artist of Métis heritage, and grew up in the sub-Arctic climate of Churchill, Manitoba, in northern Canada. Working in a variety of styles, disciplines, and mediums, her work is displayed and sold in art galleries across Canada, and she has won numerous awards in her career.

MENTON3

As an award-winning American painter, illustrator, and comic book artist currently living in Chicago, menton3 (Menton J. Matthews III) has created work for Image Comics and IDW, most notably on the hugely successful *MONOCYTE* series, as well as *Memory Collector*s, *X-Files*, *Zombies vs. Robots*, *Crawl to Me*, *Silent Hill,* and *Three Feathers*. His fine art paintings have been shown in prominent galleries, including La Luz De Jesus, Strychnin Gallery, COPRO Gallery, and Last Rites Gallery in New York.

MICHAEL SHEYAHSHE

Michael is an enrolled member of the Caddo Nation of Oklahoma, and has been published in *Illusions*, *Native Peoples Magazine*, *Games for Windows: The Official Magazine*, *New Plains Review*, and *First American Art Magazine*. He is a Gates Millennium Scholar, a Ronald E. McNair Scholar, and a recipient of the Smithsonian Institution's Native American Award. He has taken readers on an in-depth look into the world of comics through *Native Americans in Comic Books*, and one of his comic book character creations, Dark Owl, was featured in the Indigenous Narratives Collective (INC)'s popular INC Universe Issue #0.

NATASHA ALTERICI

Natasha is an artist and writer from Oklahoma. She earned her Bachelor's in Art from Northeastern State University, and has been working commercially in illustration and comics for almost a decade. Her work includes the popular titles *Heathen*, *Dinosaur Project*, *Gotham Academy: Yearbook*, *Grayson Annual*, *The Lez Film Review*, and more.

NICHOLAS BURNS

Nicholas is an author, storyboard artist, award-winning fine artist, and filmmaker. In the 1980s, while in Rankin Inlet, Northwest Territories (now Nunavut), he wrote and drew *Arctic Comics*, *Super Shamou*, *True North*, and several other educational comics for federal and territorial agencies. He also helped form, and chaired, the community's first library board. In the 1990s he contributed comic art to *Sunburn*, has written for Kitchen Sink, Metal Hurlant, and DC Comics, and storyboarded a long list of feature films, including *Curse of Chucky* and *The Lookout*.

PETER DAWES

Peter is an artist and expert colourist who has been in the industry for over 25 years. He has coloured for all of the major publishers, including Marvel, DC, Dark Horse, Image, Topps, and IDW. His work adorns the pages of many comic books, including *Superman*, *Batman*, *Avengers*, *G.I. Joe*, *Conan*, and *Star Wars,* and he had the honour of authoring and designing a story for *Captain Canuck*. Along with colouring, his skills include digital inking and archival restoration on popular commercial projects like *Will Eisner's The Spirit*.

RICHARD PACE

Richard is a multiple award-winning illustrator and author, with French and Métis ancestry. In his early career, his art and design work drew acclaim working with Tree House Press, creating award-winning educational and poetry books for children and schools. With over 20 years in the industry, he is now an author, illustrator, and cover artist for many popular titles in the market today, including *Batman*, *Doctor Strange*, *X-Men*, *Captain Marvel*, *Pitt*, and more.

RICHARD VAN CAMP

Richard is a proud Tlicho Dene from Fort Smith, Northwest Territories, Canada. Richard is an international bestselling author, winning over a dozen awards in several countries, including the Canadian Authors Association Air Canada Award and the Jugendiliteraturpreis Award – the highest award for a translation awarded by the German government. His graphic novel *A Blanket of Butterflies,* illustrated by fellow *MOONSHOT* creator Scott Henderson, was nominated for the prestigious Eisner Award in 2016.

ROSSI GIFFORD

Rossi is a Scottish graphic novelist, animator, concept artist, and editorial illustrator based in Toronto, Canada. A graduate of the Duncan of Jordanstone College of Art and Design, she is the creator, author, and illustrator of the immensely popular *Spirit Leaves* comic book series, which is now published in countries across the globe. Rossi was also the designer for the short animated film *Curse of Clara: A Holiday Tale*, aired by CBC in Canada, and lead character designer for Nickolodeon's *Welcome to the Wayne*.

SCOTT HENDERSON

Scott is a comic book artist and illustrator from Manitoba, Canada. He has worked on many book titles across Canada, including selected works from the *Tales from Big Spirit* Indigenous publication series. He illustrated the bestselling graphic novel series *7 Generations: a Plains Cree Saga* with fellow *MOONSHOT* creator David Robertson, and the Eisner award–nominated graphic novel *A Blanket of Butterflies*, written by fellow *MOONSHOT* creator Richard Van Camp.

SEAN AND RACHEL QITSUALIK-TINSLEY

Rachel Qitsualik-Tinsley is an Inuit-Cree mix, born at the northernmost edge of Baffin Island in Canada's Arctic. Sean is of Scottish-Mohawk ancestry, born in the southernmost region of Ontario. They were brought together by a mutual love of nature, and each other. Together they write award-winning Arctic fantasy and have published hundreds of articles on Inuit culture and folklore. Their young adult novel *Skraelings* won the Burt Award for First Nations, Métis and Inuit Literature.

STEPHEN GLADUE

Originally from the Fishing Lake Métis Settlement in Alberta, Canada, Stephen is a Métis illustrator, painter, and animator working in Vancouver, Canada. His work has been displayed in print, television, fashion, and film. He was a special guest filmmaker at the inaugural Vancouver Indigenous Media Arts Festival (VIMAF), chosen for his outstanding work in film and animation within the Aboriginal community. He is the Lead Artist on the animated *Amy's Mythic Mornings*, and his animated shorts can be seen on APTN's *Nehiyawetan* series.

STEVE KEEWATIN SANDERSON

Steve is a seven-foot-tall Plains Cree illustrator and animator. He has worked as a storyboard artist for the Cartoon Network, on video games with Disney and Rockstar Games, and the Marvel television show *Avengers: Ultron Revolution*. His comic book work with the Healthy Aboriginal Network – creating stories around current issues in Indigenous communities – has earned Steve recognition in Canada and the US. Steve travels across North America for speaking engagements, and was part of the CBC four-part documentary *8th Fire*.

TANYA TAGAQ

Tanya is an internationally renowned throat singer, artist, and author from Iqaluktuutiaq, Nunavut Canada. Her work has earned a multitiude of awards, including Juno Awards, Canadian Folk Music Awards, WCMA Awards, Canadian Aboriginal Music Awards, East Coast Music Association Awards, and ImagineNative Film & Media Awards. She is passionate and poignant, with her work speaking out about the treatment of Indigenous peoples. In December 2016, she was named a Member of the Order of Canada, the highest civilian medal, awarded by the government for oustanding lifelong work and achievement.

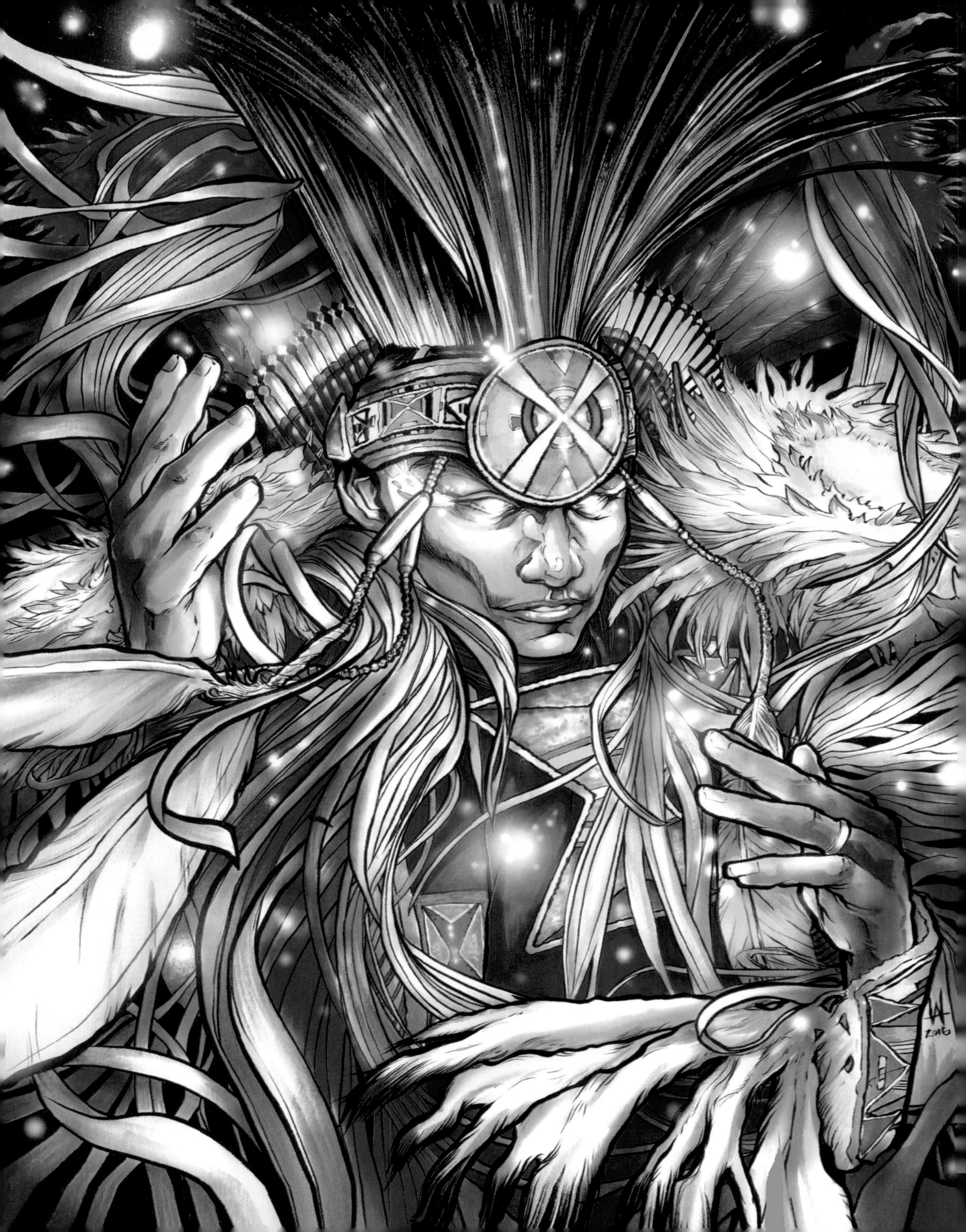

BIOGRAPHIES

TRUDI CASTLE

Born in London, England, Trudi is a comic book illustrator, concept designer, storyboard artist, and game artist living in Vancouver, Canada. Her artwork can be seen in some of the most popular titles in the gaming market, including *The Long Dark*, *The Hobbit*, *Halo Anniversary,* and the award-winning *Crysis I, II & III*. Trudi's work can also be seen on the *Lord of the Rings* card game, as well as various social games for smart phones and tablets.

WESHOYOT ALVITRE

Weshoyot is a Tongva/Scots-Gaelic artist who grew up at Satwiwa, a Tongva cultural centre founded and run by her father and located in the Santa Monica Mountains. She has produced a vast array of international work in design, albums, art, and comics. As a fifteen-year veteran in the world of comics, Alvitre's credits include titles by Dark Horse Comics, *Graphic Classics: Native American Classics,* and more. She is also one of the award-winning illustrators from *Little Nemo: Dream Another Dream*, a multiple Eisner- and Harvey Award–winning collection.

◀ *"Supaman" by Weshoyot Alvitre*

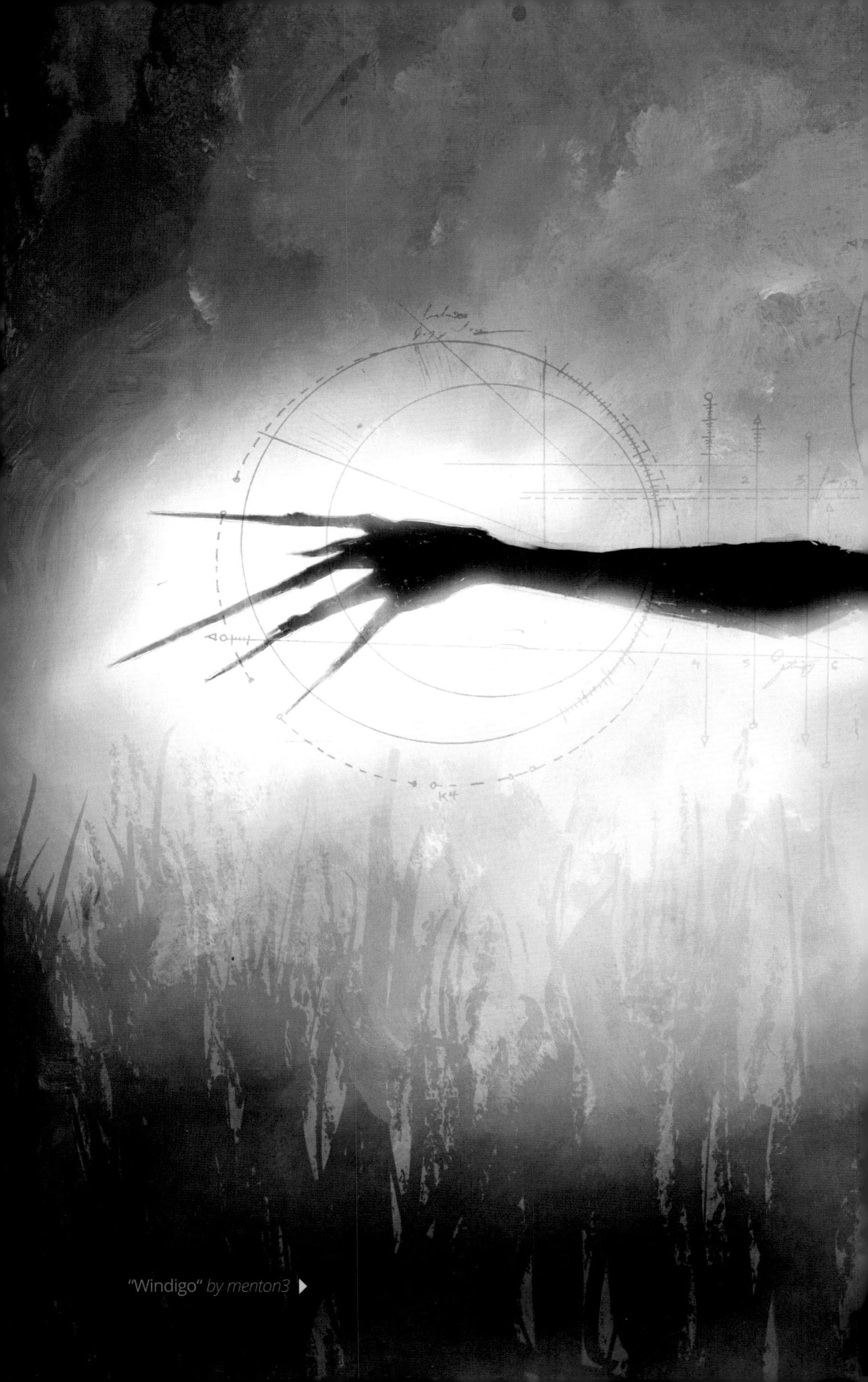

"Windigo" *by menton3*

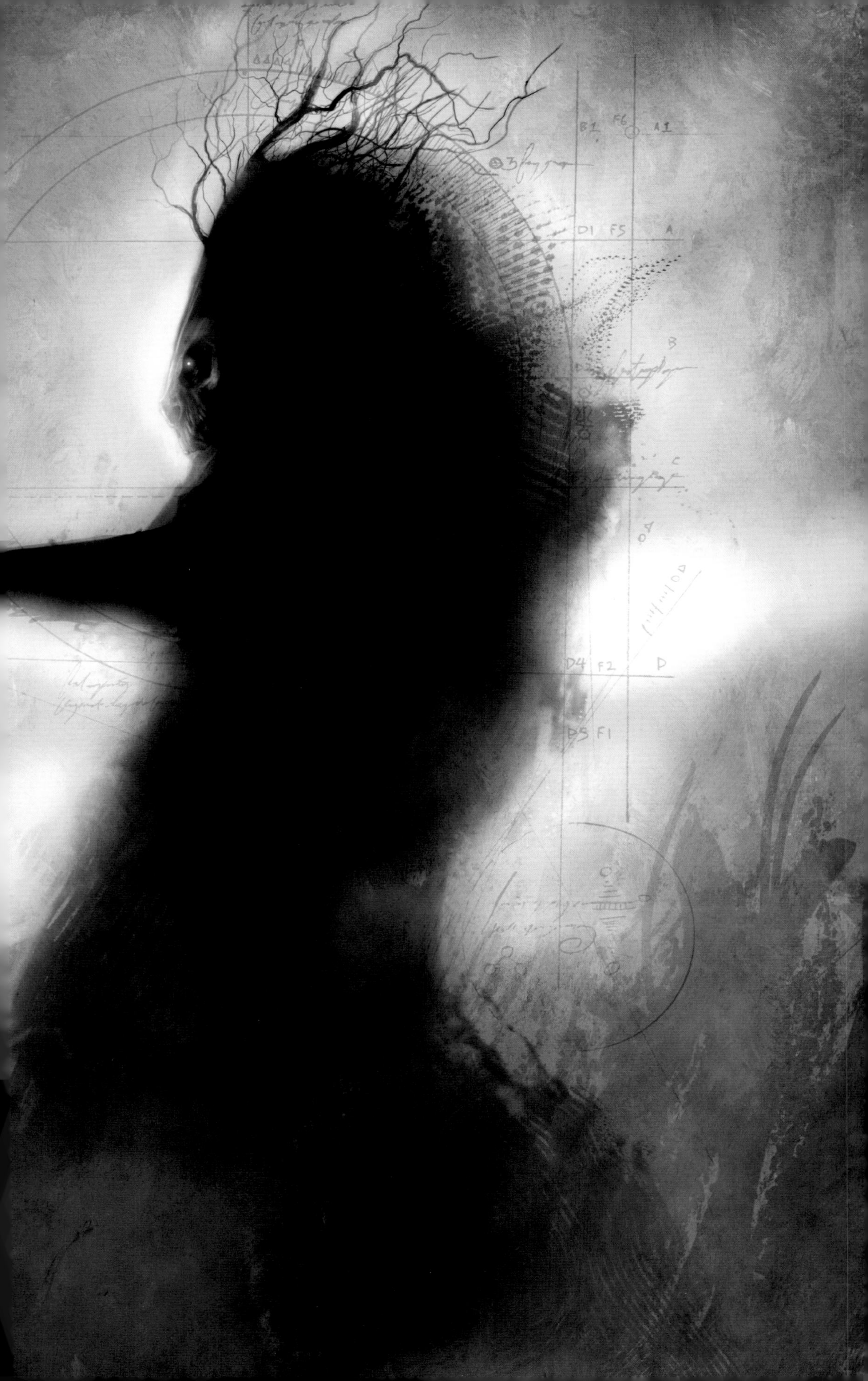
B1 F6 A1
D1 F5 A
B
C
D4 F2 D
D5 F1

MOONSHOT The Indigenous Comics Collection

SKETCHBOOK

Volume 2

BACKGROUND

From script to layout, lettering, pencils, inks, and colours, a lot goes into a single comic book story. A lot more goes into developing an entire collection of 14 stories, each one with different artists who bring their own personal style and body of work to the table. Arguably one of the more exciting stages of a publication like this is to see the artwork come to life during production. Even before an artist sets down to create the finished pages, a process of character designs, roughs layouts, thumbnails, and texture studies go into each piece. As we did with Volume 1 of the collection, here we've put together a few behind-the-scenes pieces to give you a glimpse into what goes into a collection like this.

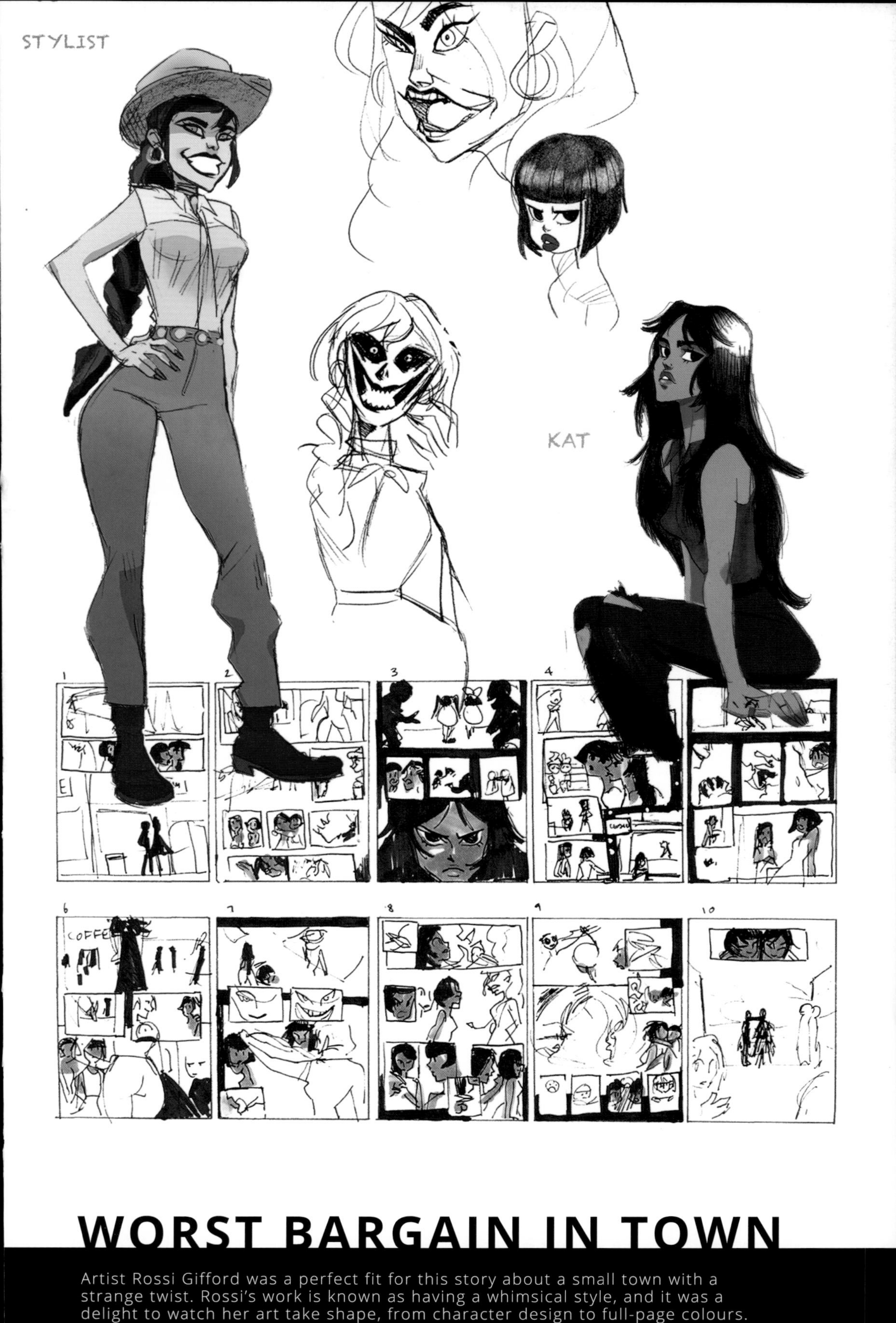
STYLIST
KAT
1
2
3
4
6
7
8
9
10
COFFE

WORST BARGAIN IN TOWN

Artist Rossi Gifford was a perfect fit for this story about a small town with a strange twist. Rossi's work is known as having a whimsical style, and it was a delight to watch her art take shape, from character design to full-page colours.

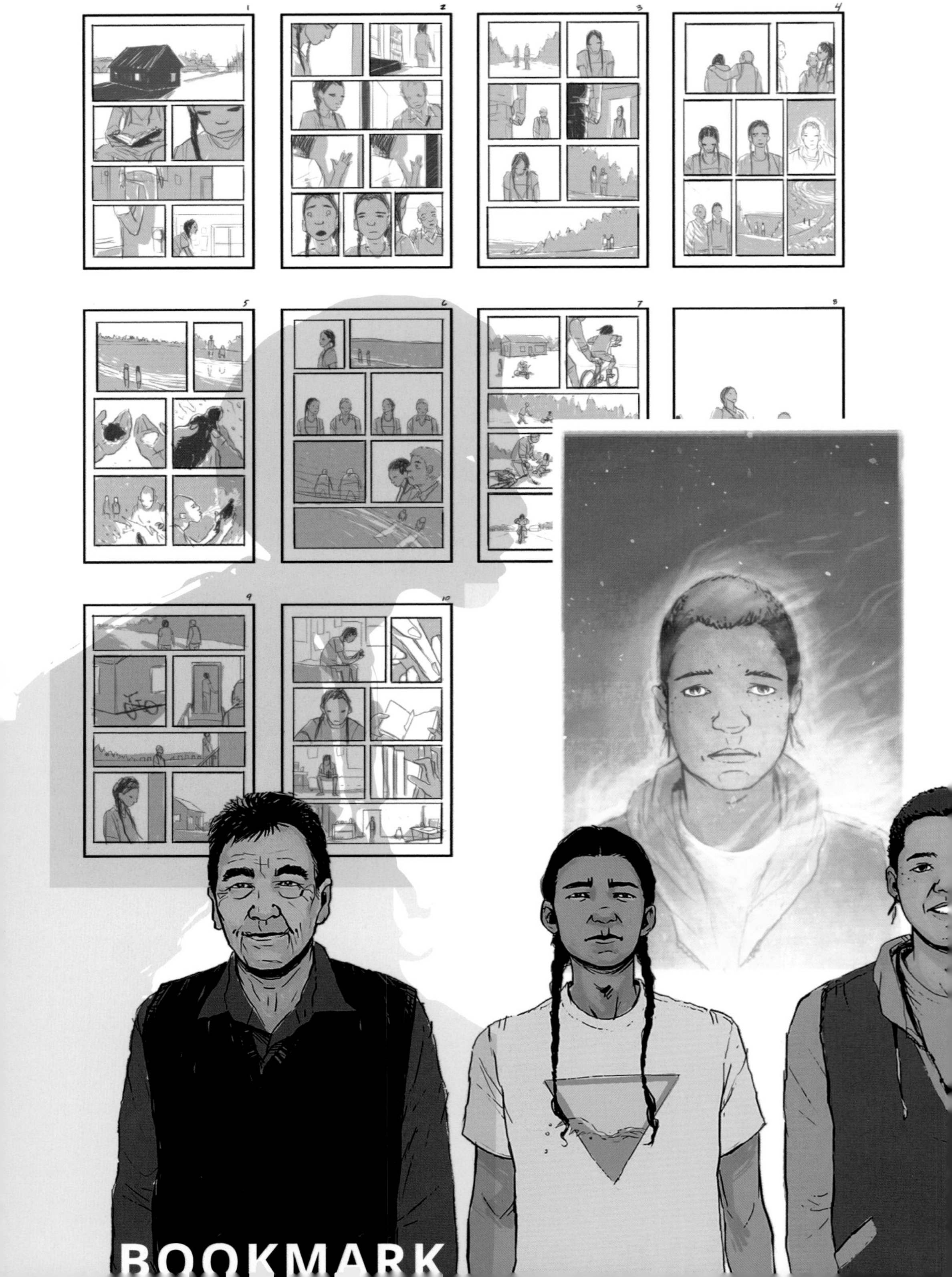
BOOKMARK

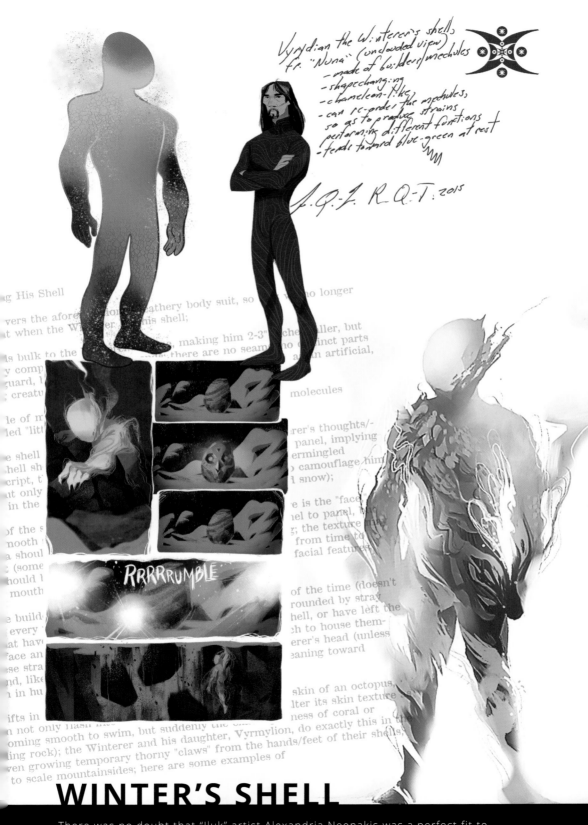

Vyrydian the Winterer's shell
fr. "Nuna" (unclouded view)
  – made of builder/imechules
  – shapechanging
  – chameleon-like
  – can re-order the imechules, so as to produce strains performing different functions
  – tends toward blue-green at rest

A.Q.Z. R.Q.T. 2015

g His Shell

vers the afore...ion ...eathery body suit, so ... ...o longer
t when the Wi...er ...is shell;

...s bulk to the ...ior ...w; there are no seam... ...chn...ller, but ...o ...inct parts

y comp...

guard, ...

creatu...

le of m...

led "litt...

e shell ...

hell sh...

cript, t...

it only ...

in the...

of the s...

nooth...

a shoul...

(some...

hould b...

mouth...

e build...

every...

at have...

ace an...

se stra...

nd, like...

n in hu...

ifts in ...

n not only flash the...

oming smooth to swim, but suddenly the onc...

ing rock); the Winterer and his daughter, Vyrmylion, do exactly this in t...

ven growing temporary thorny "claws" from the hands/feet of their shells;

to scale mountainsides; here are some examples of

molecules

...erer's thoughts/-
...panel, implying
...ermingled
... camouflage him
...l snow);

...e is the "face"...
...el to panel, the
...; the texture ma...
...from time to
...facial features...

RRRRRUMBLE

of the time (doesn't
rounded by stra...
hell, or have left the
...h to house them-
...erer's head (unless
...eaning toward

skin of an octopus,
...lter its skin texture
...ness of coral or

WINTER'S SHELL

There was no doubt that "Iluk" artist Alexandria Neonakis was a perfect fit to create the look of the Arctic fantasy world in "Winter's Shell." But the "shells" themselves were a challenge to construct. Developing their look was a long but collaborative process that resulted in the gorgeous creation you see here

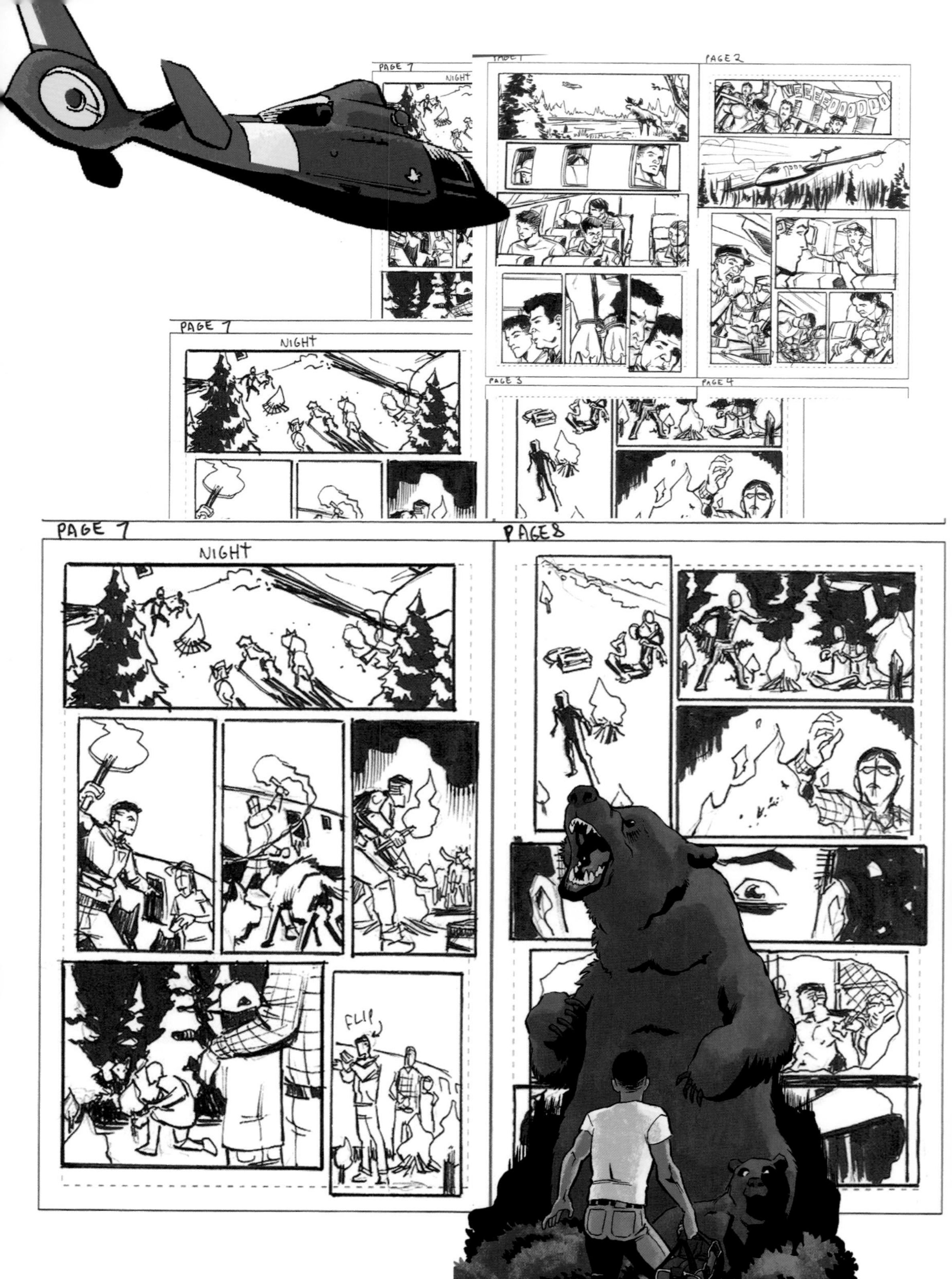
PAGE 7
NIGHT
PAGE 2
PAGE 3
PAGE 4
PAGE 7
NIGHT
PAGE 7
NIGHT
PAGE 8
FLIP

THE AWAKENING

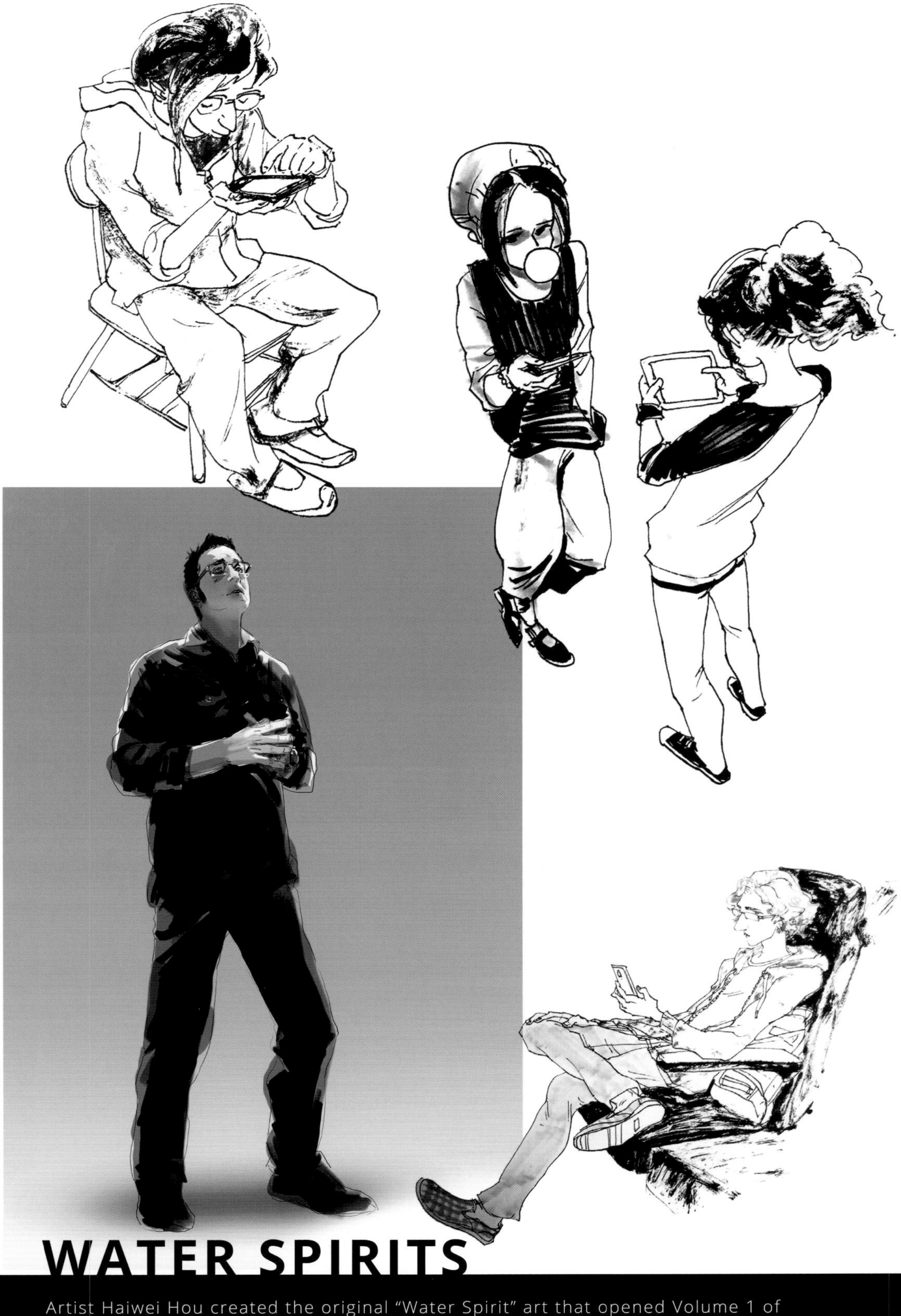

WATER SPIRITS

Artist Haiwei Hou created the original “Water Spirit” art that opened Volume 1 of the *MOONSHOT* collection. We were honoured to have her on board to illustrate the full story based on that single piece. An exciting surprise was also prepared for the author, Richard Van Camp, as the teacher in this story was modelled after him (Richard didn’t know until he saw the final art)!

MOONSHOT The Indigenous Comics Collection

END CREDITS

Volume 2

ACKNOWLEDGMENTS

The publisher would like to thank each and every one of the authors and artists involved in making this collection an absolutely masterful work, with special thanks to Beth and Richard Pace. From writers to illustrators to editor Hope Nicholson, all told over 30 individuals shaped this volume. While the whole is greater then the sum of its parts, it is truly not without the collective efforts of every single person involved. Speaking of the collective, the *MOONSHOT* series would not be possible without the incredible support from the Kickstarter community. Between Volume 1 and Volume 2 of the collection, 2,775 individuals from across the world helped this important series come to life.

And a special thank you to all of the Elders who put time and energy into consideration for which stories could be told for this collection. We are honoured at this trust and respect for the power of the stories within these pages.

THEY WHO WALK AS LIGHTNING

WINTER'S SHELL

WORST BARGAIN IN TOWN

KA'TEPWA: WHO CALLS?

BOOKMARK

THE AWAKENING

THE MAGIC OF WOLVERINES

9 MILE LAKE

THE BOYS WHO BECAME THE HUMMINGBIRDS

WATER SPIRITS

THE CREATOR TAMOSI

WHERE WE LEFT OFF

DO WILD TURKEYS DREAM OF ELECTRIC DRUMS

JOURNEYS

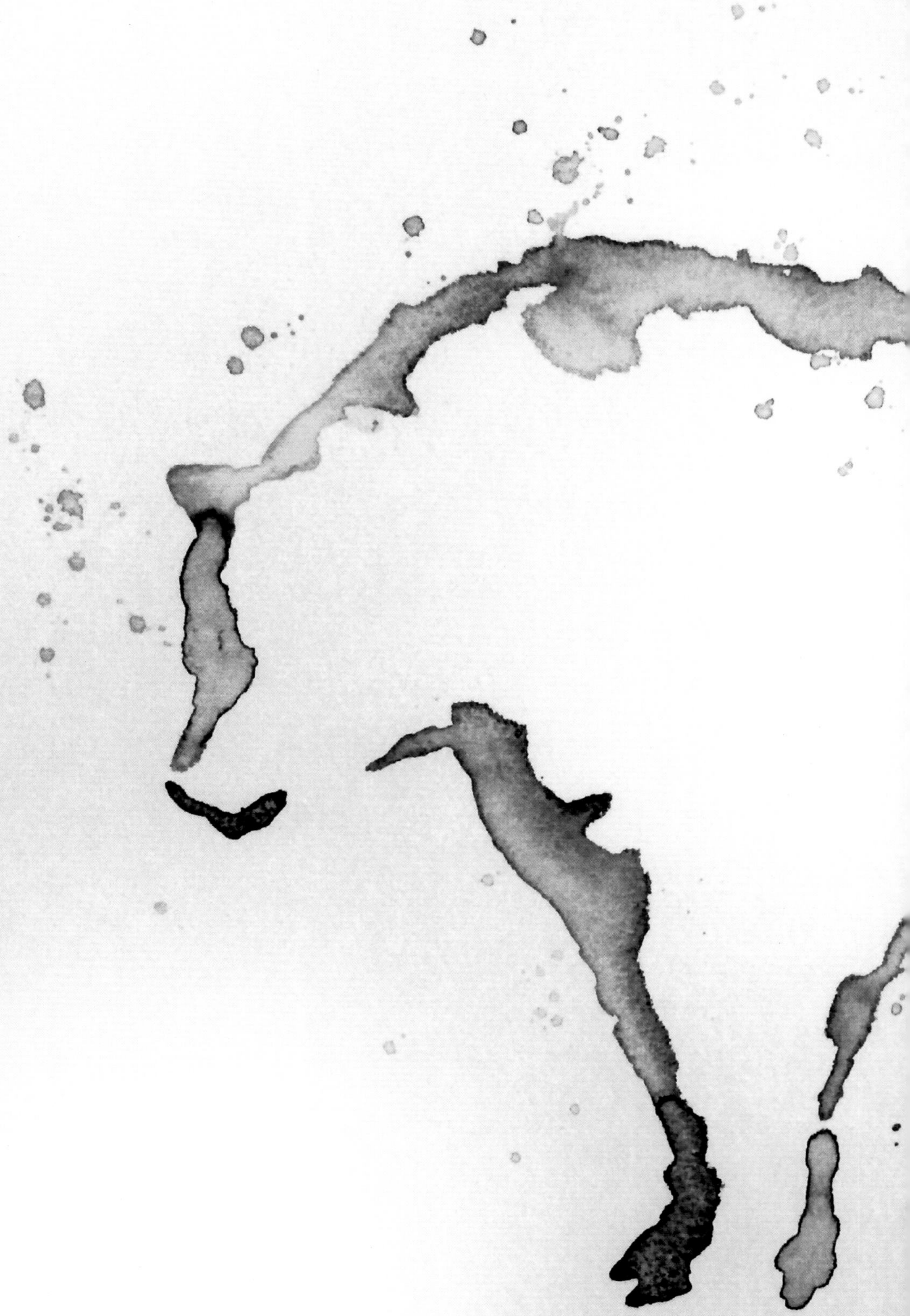

"Spirit Bear" *by David Mack* ▶

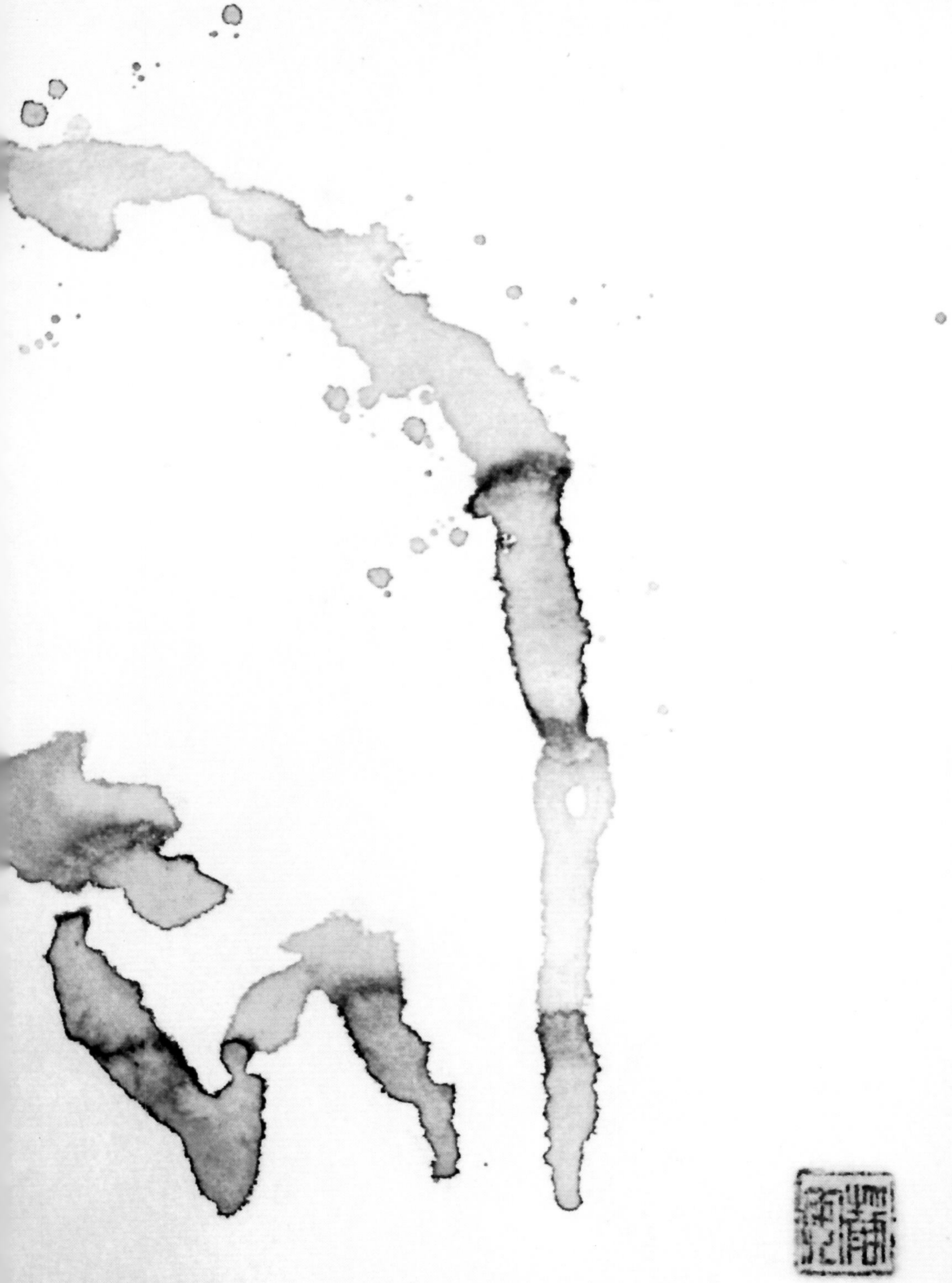

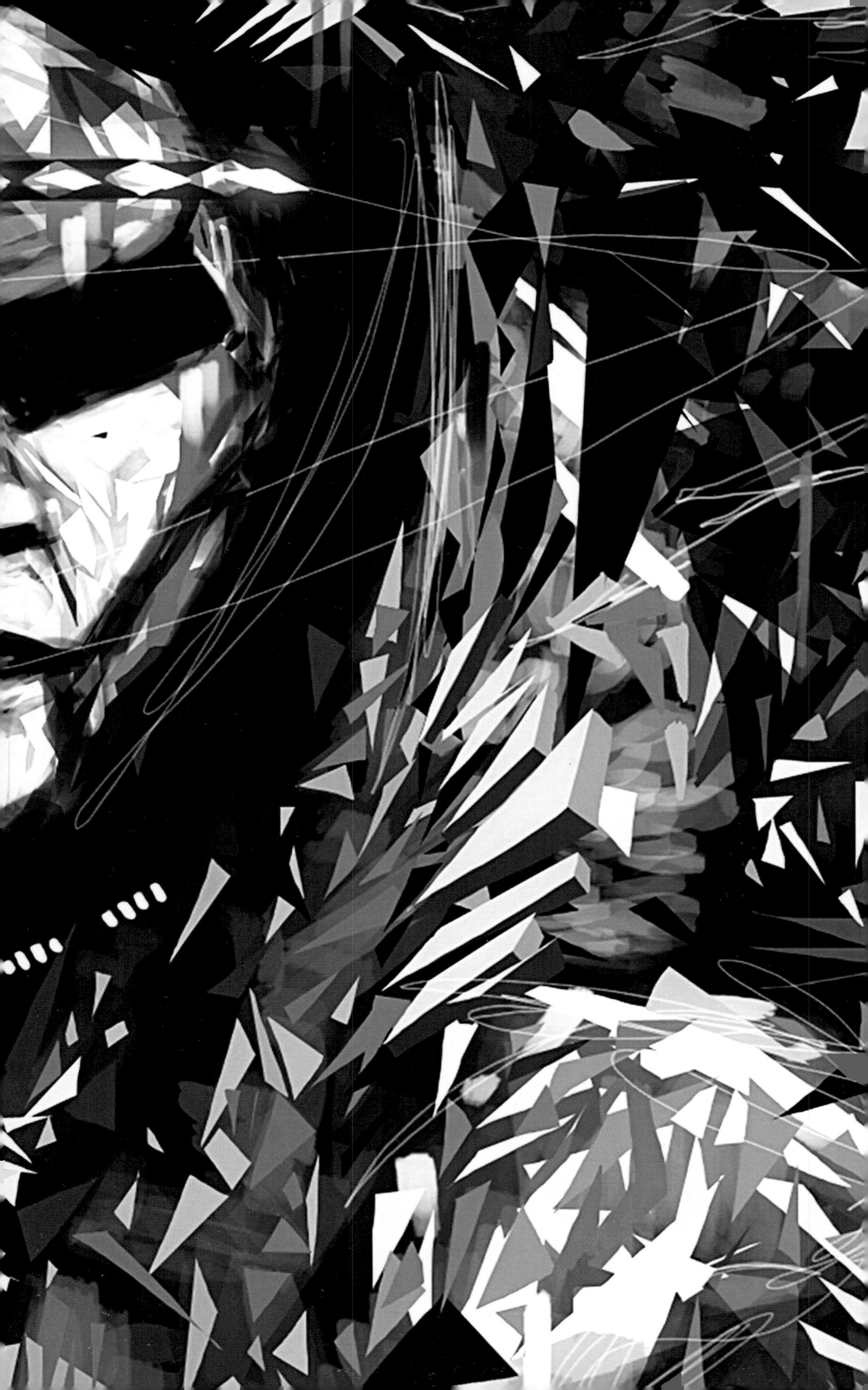